Behind The Moon

**First published in 2024
by Crackle + Hiss**

Cover design by Jamie Keenan.

All lyrics quoted are for review, study or critical purposes.

A CIP catalogue record for this book is available from the British Library.

ISBN 978-1-3999-9563-4

Behind The Moon

The Sundays,
The Fatima Mansions,
Prefab Sprout, The Apartments
and Trashcan Sinatras

TIM BLANCHARD

CRACKLE
+HISS

Foreword

*I*n June 2018, I was in the audience at the National Concert Hall in Dublin when Cathal Coughlan led Microdisney onto the stage for their first show in 30 years. It was a bigger room than any they'd headlined in back when they'd been an operational band with a major label record deal, and it was packed. And packed to a noticeable degree with people who'd clearly kept the T-shirts all these decades in the hope of having cause to wear them again one day. The show was a triumph.

A few nights later I saw Microdisney again, at the Barbican in London. This show was also a triumph. I went with Luke Haines, whose first band—The Auteurs—might also have filled a chapter of this book, having been under-appreciated at the time, and may, like the work of the artists examined in *Behind The Moon*, be said to have all at once missed, captured and transcended their moment.

A few years before Microdisney reformed, Luke, Cathal and myself had made a doggedly weird concept album together: *The North Sea Scrolls*. That record, and the accompanying tour, in which we lectured bewildered audiences about the hidden histories of the British Isles in song (while wearing pith helmets), endures in my own head, at least, as monuments to the marvels which can unfold when smart people (or so we liked to think) commit to absurdity with absolute determination.

I was struck by something Luke said after Microdisney's Barbican performance, as we proceeded to the after-show party. "He's got that now," said Luke, meaning Cathal at long-last had the memory of a deafening standing ovation from a sold-out theatre. "He should have had it a thousand times, but it's something."

That statement, like this book, poses a question: who really does speak (well, sing) for a particular era? Every one of the five groups considered—The Sundays, Trashcan Sinatras, Prefab Sprout, The Apartments, The Fatima Mansions—was outsold by any number of contemporaries. But each has, in their own way, outlasted their more fleetingly successful peers. If The Sundays, from whom nothing has been heard for nearly 30 years, could be tempted back onto stage, there would be queues around the block. Prefab Sprout, deigning to undertake their first tour in a quarter of a century, would be an arena-filling sensation. I did, more than once, ask/prompt/goad Cathal about reassembling The Fatima Mansions, convinced—and seeking to convince him—that, by golly, this time people would listen. With the wince of a man not wishing to push his luck, he demurred, citing logistical difficulties.

Of the groups addressed in *Behind The Moon*, these three were those I knew best. Cathal was a good friend, The Sundays I interviewed a few times, Paddy McAloon of Prefab Sprout a couple. I have a very dim recollection that as a very dim teenage Sydney street press writer I might have interviewed Peter Milton Walsh of The Apartments, but if I've forgotten most of the details of what was unlikely to have been a productive use of his time, I can only hope he has forgotten them as well. My path never crossed with that of Trashcan Sinatras—though this is no reflection of any seething personal animus, at least not on my part.

My point being that I am able to vouch for the accuracy of the characterisations of the artists depicted in this book. Cathal, for all that he commanded The Fatima Mansions on stage with the eye-bulging, temple-throbbing ferocity of a boxer informed seconds before the bell that his wife had left him for his opponent, really was as gentle, affable and courteous a fellow as you might meet. And every bit as smart and funny as advertised (I miss him). David Gavurin and Harriet Wheeler of The Sundays I recall regarding the fame they might have had for the asking with a combination of bemusement and indifference fit to infuriate any number of less talented, more avaricious peers. Paddy McAloon genuinely is pop's magnificent eccentric professor. The first time we met, circa 2001's *The Gunman & Other Stories*, I reported as instructed to a Newcastle restaurant, where I beheld at a table towards the back a lavishly bearded apparition, dressed entirely in white, studying a second-hand biography of some or other early-twentieth century classical composer through the lens of an immense and ornate magnifying glass. I was able to tell the waiter with some confidence that I believed my dining companion might have already arrived.

There is a case, maybe, that only the recordings of the proper hit-having superstars of a given epoch can evoke the time. The biggest-selling UK albums of 1992, a year in which The Fatima Mansions, The Sundays, The Apartments, Trashcan Sinatras and Prefab Sprout were all active, included Simply Red's *Stars*, Genesis's *We Can't Dance* and Right Said Fred's *Up*. Any of these works might serve as Pavlovian callbacks to the period. But none could be said to describe it, perhaps due to the artists involved being (respectively) too famous, too rich or too bad. But The Fatima Mansions, The Sundays, The Apartments, Trashcan Sinatras and Prefab Sprout, compelled by relatively modest circumstances to actually inhabit the time as most people did, had equally little choice but to react to it, whether by chronicling it, commenting upon it, revolting against it or attempting—and here I'm thinking of Professor McAloon particularly—the design and construction of the improbable, complicated and ornate apparatuses that might, with a favourable tailwind, enable an escape from it.

Andrew and Cathal, reporting for duty on *The North Sea Scrolls* tour.

Behind The Moon takes its title from a song, of course. It's by The Fatima Mansions, and may be found on their 1991 mini-album *Bertie's Brochures*. In the context of the Mansions' clamorous catalogue, it's an anomaly: a straightforward torch ballad, unpunctuated by squalling guitars or scabrous samples. It is a thing of exquisitely baleful beauty, and it's a shame Roy Orbison didn't live long enough to sing it, though Cathal's wracked baritone does it abundant justice. And though the song is not about—at least not directly—the struggles of the marginal to semi-successful artist, it does suggest something of the irresistible impulse which animates them: "What else would you have me do?"

Andrew Mueller, journalist, author and broadcaster.

Contents

Whirr and hiss

*T*here's witchery in the air tonight, rising from the river as a mist and uncoiling in the inky-black hollows around Parliament Square. Where leaves fall like rotten fruit, and the Victorian-Gothic spires and turrets are so many pins and thorns. There's a dreaming moon.

No one in the streets takes any notice of omens, because of the rain and din of traffic, and because of the march of feet that hurries the workers away to underground trains, their little carriages and lights and dingy human warmth. Like old magic carpets that deliver them, fitfully, to the comforts of teatime TV.

Inside the great medieval porch of the House of Commons there's still work to be done. Conspirators come and go through St Stephen's Hall with armfuls of folders and excited whispers; they watch and fidget and rub their hands, careful not to talk or laugh too loud. Blood is going to be spilt, but whose and when? The two adversaries themselves are elsewhere, gathering forces: Margaret Thatcher, the longest-serving British Prime Minister since 1827, and the miscreant, Michael Heseltine. He has the height and manner of a military man, but for some his floppy schoolboy fringe and plotting have given him the look of a sneaking knave.

As a result of the machinations that follow—Heseltine's attempt to end the reign of the PM and Thatcher's campaign to stop the ascent of Heseltine at any cost—both will take a heavy fall. The House is solemn and limp from witnessing such a historic betrayal. "If any of those who have used this device were to inherit the crown," warned Nicholas Ridley MP, "uneasy would lie their head." Heseltine knew his story had been written by the hand of fate. "He who wields the knife," he said, "never wears the crown."

Thatcher was taken from Downing Street like a dying queen, in a procession that moved through rooms filled with roses and the weeping faithful. Inside the funeral-black car that took her away, the cameras glimpsed a stricken face, the welling of a tear in the eye of a 65-year-old woman who'd lost her job and knew retirement was going to be purgatory. But there was still a final speech in the Commons to come, a chance to explain what 'Thatcherism' had meant for Britain. In this speech she didn't refer to the sorcery that had turned the population into a willing body of competing individuals; the need to obey the logic of markets was by now too obvious to bother mentioning. Instead, she chose to describe a more heroic aspect of this new reality: how Thatcherism had helped save the world from evil. Eastern Europe had been rescued from totalitarian rule, the Berlin Wall had been torn down. The world was coming together at last, through a global camaraderie of business and finance; but there could be no slackening in the holy war to protect the forces of economic growth that had made it possible. "When good has to be upheld and the devil has to be overcome," pronounced the Iron Lady, "Britain will take up arms."

The events of November 1990 were only sound and fury. Because the stagecraft of Westminster was small-time, a heritage show compared with the need for efficient management of the economy: the fairground of liberalism that offered wealth, freedom, happiness—maybe even goodness—to its paying customers.[1] The political ideologies of the past had obviously failed, had been only a distortion of unavoidable truths about human nature. People, after all, ain't no good. Financial institutions dealt in plain common sense, the irreducible truth of money, while beliefs and ideals of any other stripe were an irrelevance in the greater scheme of things. Best left as hobbies. The electricity of borrowing, spending and investment was what mattered now.

The changing of the guard could be seen happening on that same November evening, just five miles downriver from Parliament, where the final pyramids of steelwork were being lifted into place on the citadel of One Canada Square, the centrepiece to a £4 billion complex in Canary Wharf. This was London's 'Wall Street on the Water': 10 million square feet of offices for 50,000 finance professionals and an endless itch of round-the-clock, screen-based trading. The new financial capital of Europe had been made possible by abandoning traditional standards of regulation and controls and opening up the system to players from anywhere in the world. In the five years following the 'Big Bang' deregulation of 1987, a new universe had been created. The value of

---

[1] Bill Clinton's presidential campaign slogan in 1992 was "It's the economy, stupid". No subtlety required.

London's stock market had tripled, making it a bigger trading centre than New York or Tokyo; the financial services sector had grown to account for almost 20 per cent of England's entire Gross Domestic Product. The big money, the smart money, was now electronically charged and racing towards whatever would bring the highest returns. By 1992, Lloyds Bank had lent 165 per cent of the value of its entire equity to property and construction companies, Barclays 148 per cent. What the banks needed to do next was encourage the great mass of people on lower incomes to take out loans to buy homes—and for everyone to keep up the flow of spending, through cash or credit, in the new shopping centres and leisure parks; especially the younger demographic, the aspirational generations who still had their stock of future to play with.

The view from the heights of One Canada Square takes us out of London, past the miles of old High Streets and crowded red-brick suburbs, the streets stuffed with parked cars, the bright fascias of minicab offices and pizza takeaway outlets. From there we can see the signs of change across Britain. Close to motorway junctions and railway terminals are the new business parks, housing giant sheds of glass with triangular peaks and towers, many of them the headquarters of financial services, insurance, software and electronics companies. Here are the worker-ready office spaces rigged with cubicles and telephone systems, computer networks, fax machines and vending machines. There's a flimsy kind of wealth around. We can see more new cars (Fiestas and Mondeos for the many, Volvos and four-wheel-drives for the few). Sitting at a red light with its engine revving hard, a Golf GTi is ready to explode down the dual carriageway and screech gloriously into the car park at TGI Friday's. There are more chain restaurants around here now. Instantly-recognisable, reassuring neon brands that shine out of the darkness, like Deep Pan Pizza, Fatty Arbuckle's and the Berni Inn. The pubs and theme bars are overflowing at the weekends because a night out is taken for granted, it's a necessary release from the rules and pressures of the working week. Not everyone's dressing up in blazers and chinos or little black dresses any more, sometimes there are big jeans, hoodies, tracksuits. A baggier way. And if there are central locations around town that aren't so busy, the strategists at the Wetherspoon's and Slug and Lettuce pub co's will be the first to notice.

On the new estates, things are looking smarter and more comfortable. The number of new-build houses has reached record levels. Mortgage lending has gone from less than £15 billion in 1983 to closer to £50 billion (so the plan has been working). Meanwhile, the property boom means interest rates have reached a new high of more than 15 per cent. But there's no sign of panic or even concern around here. In rooms of serene magnolia walls and oatmeal car-pets, the central heating continues to hum, the new gas boil-er is just a whisper; the discreet uplighting and bowls of pot-pourri make for a soft mood of complacency.

We knew the bad times were over because so many evils had been dispatched, like Hollywood villains flicked from skyscrapers. Hunger, disease, the threat of nuclear con-flict, socialism. We'd found a formula that worked, that we didn't have to think about too much anymore; as reliable as the new annual cycle of seasons we'd become used to, not summer and winter anymore, but our sports events and blockbuster movies, the new models of consumer tech, the funny ads, chart hits and music tours. "Economics are the method," explained Thatcher. "The object is to change the soul." Maybe it had worked.

*

This is a sequel to *Like Magic in the Streets*—but readers of that book need to be ready for a different mood. The early Eighties was a one-off moment that couldn't last, a cool bright morning when anything seemed possible. There would always be a piece of blue in the sky somewhere. It was a time of beginnings that allowed an unlikely spirit of Romanticism in indie music to bloom, when even the most precious of outsiders could have their moment on *Top of the Pops*. Pop music didn't have to be stupid. You could dance to Orange Juice and The Smiths, fall in love to the sounds of The Blue Nile rather than Chris de Burgh, console yourself with the street poetry of Aztec Camera and The Go-Betweens. Little-known bands like Microdisney had better pop hooks than Bananarama. Prefab Sprout's manager Keith Armstrong believed the band's eccentric debut LP *Swoon* was going to be as big as anything by Dire Straits. "We thought we'd made a Chic record," said Keith.

By 1990 there was more a feeling of mid-afternoon. The light of common day. What happens after the Romance has gone and everyone knows there's no such thing as magic anyway? We had to grow up. The bands, the fans. There were exams to take, careers and property ladders to scale, unless you were willing to walk on blindly and drop off a

cliff. So we've reached the blue hours of the kinds of afternoons that are just part of the deal when it comes to accepting a routine of getting and spending.

The five bands we're going to live alongside in this
book were made from that early Eighties morning, either as
survivors from that scene or drawing on its source. Rather
than falling into a groove of cynicism, we'll see how the music of that time could be an even richer and darker thing.
With harsher truths. More violent colours. Wilful creativity.
How the age involved a search for origins and endings that
meant circling around different kinds of heaven and hell.
They're all bands that stayed separate from show business
and closer to ordinary human experience. The bright moon-
shine of the newly chosen ones, the Hollywood stars, the pop
celebrities and billionaire financiers and entrepreneurs, was a
blank glare. The early Nineties provided even more reasons
to build up separate habits of thought, to lay up stores of
your own way of thinking as a reminder that the world was
an older and better place than it often seemed.

*

Marcia arrives, the ideas lady. She's been a dynamo at Patter
Productions ever since she came over last summer from LA
and fell in love with London. Marcia can't get enough of the
grimy Victorian pubs, their tobacco-stained ceilings and
'pork scratchings'. She loves the quiet, amenable people of
England. Even more, the big geezers who hung around wine
bars shouting about soccer and the gilts market, then went
off for an all-night rave with their headbands and whistles.

She's going to marry one of them, her boyfriend who's a somebody in the City.

The sales and marketing team are already assembled in Meeting Room 1. There's Mike in the same old grey suit, always so serious, looking like a pencil with glasses. And Tony in his striped shirt and fat red tie, grinning his unstoppable grin.

"We're talking *Indie Baby*, right?" says Marcia, pint-sized in a peach-ensemble suit. Her smile drops like a stone. She sticks her head and its angular wedge of hair round the door to Patter's open-plan office: "*Someone answering that phone?* I'm-in-a straa-te-gy meeting. *Hey*."

She's back, giving the team both barrels of her sharp, heavily black-rimmed eyes and impossibly white teeth.

"We got pens for the board? Okay. So, fellers, we're re-inventing indie today. Feels like C86 was centuries ago. The energy's all gone, and isn't this meant to be the crazy stuff? If you have to wear jumpers with holes in and eat veggie burgers the music's really gotta have something going, huh?"

"Yeah yeah. So how about calling it *C90* and making it a cassette, like an actual C90?"

Marcia writes on the board.

"Thank you Tony, but aren't we doing CDs now? This —is—*Indie Baby*. We get today's hot independent bands together in one place. And here's the killer. They do covers of songs that got the whole indie thing started. We're making indie babies! Because there's a load of affection for those early jingle-jangle bands out there. They're like old brand names, like your HP Sauce and R. White's, and they're ready-made for pushing up sales in the fourth quarter. God knows we need it."

Mike's taking notes. Tony nods and nods and gives Mike a shove.

"And we make it a charity thing," continues Marcia, "get a kids charity involved maybe—is polio still a thing here? No? Sure? One that does poverty then. And then we've got another hook for getting a big label involved. So, let's update things—Mike?"

This is Mike's moment, and not one he's been looking forward to. He passes round publicity photos and makes a painstaking list on the whiteboard, using different-coloured marker pens to indicate the status of negotiations. Fluorescent lights flicker over the shiny laminate table while Marcia and Tony take turns pouring coffee from a cafetière. The silence starts to weigh heavily on the whole room.

So Marcia starts: "What happened to the Happy Mondays and where's The Beloved?"

"Yes, well, no—but we have got this year's big breakthrough act, The Sundays. The new Smiths," says Mike, swallowing hard. "So they say."

A photo of an unsmiling young couple in holey jumpers. Harriet Wheeler and Dave Gavurin, who somehow managed to turn the mess and insecurity of a bedsit existence into a gorgeous sound of indie melancholy. Like pink twilight framed in an upstairs window, a bowl of instant mash and beans on the table for tea.

"And who the hell's this?" asks Marcia.

"Fatima Mansions."

The unflinching stare of Cathal Coughlan. Like a bull that's broken out of its metal-barred pen and found there's nowhere else left to go. A wild and furious, gentle heart.

"The best live band around, it's said. Loud and angry."

"What are they angry about?"

"Well. Dictators, that sort of thing. If we take them we're more likely to get Prefab Sprout. Same label."

Paddy McAloon, songwriting angel.

"Always looked like a Christian rock band to me," says Tony. "They've got that long hair and coloured waistcoat thing going on."

"They're really not though," points out Mike to Marcia.

"The singer was a monk wasn't he?" adds Tony.

"No."

Why had he bothered spending so much time with Tony? Buying him pints of Stella and kebabs after work like they were friends. He took the piss in meetings anyway.

"Never heard of The Apartments," sighs Marcia. Her eyes have started to widen into a stare of disbelief. Not a good sign.

"Maybe because they're Australian? They had a song on a John Hughes film soundtrack like Simple Minds did. And it's okay, because they're here in London. I-I think."

Peter Milton Walsh looks back at them with a steady gaze, like a jock from Fifties America who should be sitting on the bonnet of a Corvette, a comb in his back pocket. But this is a Noir troubadour, like a siren going off in a dark corner of town that announces another wave of bitter emotions is coming.

"Then there's this Scottish band who are really big with American college radio at the moment."

A gang of lads straight off the number 11 bus to Kilmarnock, ready for the pub.

"Who isn't?" says Marcia. "My mom with a tambourine was big last year."

They all laugh.

"The Sinatras. So they're crooners?"

"Not really, they're part of the Scottish indie thing I'd say, but with their own take."

"What kind of music then?"

"Oh, you know, jingle-jangle," says Mike, giving up. He pushes his glasses back up his nose and returns to his chair. Done for another day. He's wishing he'd never taken an English degree if marketing was all it was bloody good for. He should have done computers and fiddled with disk drives, arrived late, gone home early.

"We need estimated sales figures per artist on this list. Then we can have another look and see whether any of it makes sense."

Tony spreads the photos out across the table and delivers the line he's been working on for a while.

"So we got The Sundays: this year's candidates for Student Union presidents. Some awkward bastards. The God botherers, Crocodile Dundee and a new edition of the Bay City Rollers."

Marcia walks to the door and makes a signal: "Can we get some more *coffee* in here? Call the store for sandwiches, and make sure there's *Kettle Chips*. We've having a late one."

Indie Baby has a difficult birth. The labels don't want it. There's too much happening around Madchester and the dance scene to look backwards, and it doesn't matter what bands get involved. *Select* magazine finally takes the CD as a cover promo and comes up with a feature on the survival of

seminal labels like Rough Trade, Kitchenware and Go!
Discs. But we, at least, still have a copy we can play. It's a
misty disc in a torn cardboard sleeve (Tony got his way with
the cover: it's Morrissey in a romper suit with a dinosaur pattern):

The Sundays, 'Cattle and Cane' (The Go-Betweens).
A young woman looks back to the days of walking home
from school with a leather satchel and a ladder in her tights,
ketchup on her homework book. There's no sugar cane
around but plenty of cows and trucks filled with dirty balls
of sugar beet. You can hear the birdsong and smell English
mud.

**The Fatima Mansions, 'Back on Board' (Aztec
Camera).** A murderer's on the run, heading for the top
floor. He's a desperate character looking for redemption. All
he wants is one sign of the possibility of salvation in the city
rooftops, in the sky, in the clouds. He finds pigeon crap and a
ventilator unit with a drawing of a cock and hairy balls. Anything that might have been wistful in that grey landscape
turns to agony, the beauty's too much.

Prefab Sprout, 'Automobile Noise' (The Blue Nile).
An early morning scene in the backstreets of Newcastle's city
centre, bathed in orange sodium. A background rhythm of
distant club music and the hum of the A167. The keyboard
music like is raindrops on the side of a parked Cortina; a
twitter of night birds. Paddy's voice is warmer than the original: a lighted window in the night.

The Apartments, 'I Don't Owe You Anything' (The Smiths). A teenage huff comes with a stream of petty pleasures, like self-pity, martyrdom and resentment. It gets more serious when you're older. Careless talk and uncontrolled emotions become dangerous, they change things between people, sometimes forever. You can hear all the danger here in a sweet and shaky tension.

Trashcan Sinatras, 'Tender Object' (Orange Juice). Exposes the original track, not only as a loose and hectic piece of work, but as the sound of a band not enjoying itself as much as it should have been. Edwyn and his pals mucked about down Sauchiehall Street, making fun of the squares and each other until they just preferred to go their separate ways. The Trashcans want to be there together, sharing the feel of the streets, the unpredictability, the longing, the let-downs.

*

The five bands of *Like Magic* were a useful bunch for understanding what was happening at a special moment in time, as the Romantic outsiders trying to re-make what pop music could be: a sunlit postcard of bands in shades and quiffs and bootlace ties. By comparison, this group of five looks muddled and rootless, easily taken for granted as strays on the Nineties' conveyor belt. That's what happens when strategic business thinking takes over, when sales targets and planned flows of products and promotions remove a sense of character. Too much diversification and differentiation, fusion, segmentation and line filling. By 1990, 'indie' itself had become a marketing label devoid of much meaning. No-one expected it to be more than a cliché signalling music for the pale and sensitive (songs with awkward DIY guitar lines by the Bicycle Clips). Or, as was increasingly the case, being used to add a stamp of cool otherness to conventional rock, pop and dance music. With 'Madchester' it was all three mashed together. The Madchester bands like the Stone Roses, Happy Mondays and the Inspiral Carpets (and others like the Farm and the Soup Dragons from outside Manchester) were "a surge of loose clobber, street swagger, wild drugs and great pop", according to John Robb in his book on the period. "The Nineties was a time when the barriers came down. It was a time when you could cross pollinate and grab the scene you wanted. After acid house and ecstasy created a mood where anything goes, anything certainly did go…" There were pockets of playful invention, new fusions of rhythms and sounds, much of it made possible by cheaper technology and the ability to digitise: to manipulate, twist and bump to a harder rhythm. But no trend was getting noticed without serious industry backing. Madchester was made thrilling by the marketing creatives, through hype and managed promotion; it was a scene built more from *NME* front covers, T-shirts and high-profile gigs than the listener's connection with the music. You could only feel baggy for so long. In other words, the market had made the zeitgeist, not so much the other way around.

Our new five—The Sundays, The Fatima Mansions, Prefab Sprout, The Apartments and Trashcan Sinatras— weren't part of any collective or scene. They were more realistic than the *Like Magic* artists had been about who they were and what they could achieve. The idea of spending nights in squats taking drugs and inventing a new universe of chords (with Nick Cave draped over a settee somewhere) had lost a lot of its charm. Compared with the early Eighties, this was also a time of incoherence when it came to ideas, political or otherwise. Introverted songwriting was just embarrassing when the coolest bands had persuaded the world that shambling around with a fag and a can of lager *was* the message.

Little connections between the five are worth mentioning before we start to think bigger. Cathal and Paddy were labelmates at Kitchenware and mutual fans of each other's songwriting, the lyrics especially. When Cathal left London, feeling lost and lonely, it was the Sprouts who helped him settle into life in Newcastle. So when Paddy was asked by the *NME* to choose his 'Dream *Blankety Blank* Line-up', he included Cathal alongside Wombles' composer Mike Batt, white supremacist Eugene Terre'Blanche, TV magician Paul Daniels and Jane Seymour. The Sprouts' Wendy Smith and Cathal shared a love of filthy jokes. Because of her floaty, ethereal image Cathal once gave her a custom-printed t-shirt with 'FUCK FUCK FUCK' on the front (Wendy wore it to a Björk concert). They enjoyed making plans for their version of the Elton John and Kiki Dee classic 'Don't Go Breaking My Heart' with alternative lyrics ('Don't Go Stretching My Arse'… "I couldn't if I tried" etc). It was Sprouts drummer Neil Conti who recommended a friend of a friend, Hugh Bunker, as bass player for The Fatima Mansions. Nick Allum, the Mansions' drummer, still plays with Peter's Apartments. Coincidentally, Paddy's favourite film director was Billy Wilder, co-writer/director of *The Apartment* (1960), the inspiration for the band name. Cathal, Paddy and Peter were all devotees of Scott Walker and Frank Sinatra (and it shows), while the Trashcans' songwriter/guitarist John Douglas was often to be found in a *Scott 1* T-shirt. The Trashcans were the support band when the Sprouts toured the *Jordan* LP, and would go for drinks with Martin McAloon and Neil; "star-struck" John got to say hello to one of his heroes, Cathal, in a rowdy bar at the end of tour do. When John ended up busking for cash in London, one of his regulars was 'We Let the Stars Go'. Douglas's wife Eddi Reader has collaborated on songs with the *Jordan* producer Thomas Dolby. The Trashcans (with 'I Hate Music') and the Mansions ('Keep Music Evil') had a similar attitude when it came to T-shirt slogans. The Sundays used Frank Sinatra's 'Come Fly with Me' as their walk-on tune.

*

The five are together in this book because they express something important about living through what could be a poisonously bland age—as well as a spirit of resistance against it. They had grown up but not given up.

Each chapter is going to unpick how these classic albums were made, using a combination of cultural and personal histories as a way of revealing what was under the mask that the music was made to wear. While *Like Magic* was the story of youthful Romanticism, this book follows what happened next: the tightrope years of leaving home, trying to make a living, finding somewhere to settle and someone to share it with—what could be the best and worst of times. So it's not a blow-by-blow account of the products, the hits or the tours, that official, press release version of things that treats the music as meaningless (part of the built-in obsolescence that makes sure we move on to the next purchase).

We're used to the idea that pop music makes the world feel better, by lending it some glamour and dusting our most dour and empty moments with plastic glitter. But it mostly happens the other way around. It's the stupid beauty of ordinary life, its unexpected poetry, that makes the best music resonate. Our five albums are good examples of this: the songs haven't been manufactured for glittery pop effect, but come from what's been found, seen and felt. They are unofficial histories made from evenings in bedsits with just *Cheers* and a four-pack for company; dispatches from cheap hotel rooms; waiting in the studio for the takeaway to arrive; lonely walks by the canal.

Because that's what 'culture' is. Nothing to do with going to the opera or expensive restaurants —the kind of pretension that annoyed Paddy, seeing all those smart people dressed up for dinner dances[2]—but what's left when the memes of education, media and advertising have been taken away: our direct relationship with the world and what we make of it.

Which is why *Behind the Moon* begins with a scene from Nineties life. A very ordinary moment that could have happened to anyone. And why these scenes continue to appear, as a reminder and a recreation of the everyday look

---

[2] 'Elegance', *Swoon* (1984): "If you confuse this dinner dance with elegance... Please be ashamed that you're afraid, equating elegance and real estate. When all the bullion in the world cannot transform what's simply second rate."

and feel of that time and place. The particular world that made the songs, and the world that made us need them.

1.

"I can't be sure what I want any more, it will come to me later."
The Sundays, *Reading, Writing and Arithmetic* (January 1990)

*H*is toothbrush didn't belong there, not on that sink. It belonged at home next to Dad's grey torpedo of *Imperial Leather.*

Adrian arranges his cassettes for the third time and tries to forget the stains he's seen on the sink in the bedroom corner. Technique *goes to the top of the stack,* Bossanova *underneath. He listens to the footsteps in the corridor that go back and forth, the slamming doors. The echo of a storage facility.*

Craig's supposed to be coming back. Then they're going for a pint at the Union. Craig had come into the room with his long face and round nostrils like a dragon, dumped a couple of bags and a Sony CD Walkman on his bed and gone straight out because Craig said he knew lots of people already.

Adrian puts Bossanova *back where it was and looks out of the room's window, to where the last of the blue autumn light is leaving the campus that only an hour before had been filled with the mellow browns and golds of afternoon. So this was him. A new world for the next year, and the two years after that. The ring road and its bubbles of passing traffic, the distant hum and wail of city operations. Dad and his moustache wouldn't be back home for another hour. Out there somewhere on the M1, his hairy hands would be gripping the steering wheel at "ten to three" and tapping along to Gloria Hunniford on Radio 2. 'Unchained Melody' again. Mum and Terry had a BMW 8 Series, but Dad had wanted to do the trip, so Adrian had turned up on the first day of uni in a Mini Metro with an old leather suitcase and Safeway carrier bags filled with clothes. He'd sat through those long stories of Dad's about being a student at the Tech; when he had lodgings with Mrs Parker and ate her jam sponge puddings; the Friday afternoons round the pubs, and the time they'd dumped the Tech's caretaker in the fountain.*

Didn't Dad know it was nothing like that now? Adrian could call and tell him, in about an hour or so, tell him it wasn't like the Sixties anymore, with the £5 Phonecard Dad had put into an envelope for him.

Another face comes into the room and looks around. Has he seen Craig? A staring face above a cut-off denim jacket and AC/DC t-shirt. Yeah—well, I mean, no. Adrian could follow the denim jacket out and see where the Union was. He could go down the corridor and introduce himself to whoever was about; he could go down to the phone booth and speak to Dad.

Adrian rearranges his stuff, looks at the letters to read and forms to fill out, then gets undressed and gets into bed to wait for tomorrow. He watches the square of light where the curtains are. Listens to the traffic.

When Craig comes back he's been asleep. Bags get unzipped, things are dropped, and Adrian can sense that strange dragon face blinking in the darkness. Sniffing. Craig takes a piss in the sink.

*

Before the Sunday Trading Act of 1994 changed everything, a British Sunday was made from a special kind of misery. A Sunday couldn't be mistaken for any other day, it had its own look and atmosphere. It was pensive, like a well-kept cemetery. A phantom day when the shopping streets were empty, the pubs were closed for the afternoon and their curtains were shut; a day for glum roast dinners and visits to grandparents who'd be watching *Bullseye* and looking forward to *Highway* and Harry Secombe's sorrowful baritone, so reminiscent of birds flying over the English fields and a horizon of oaks and elms and the stone of church spires.

Morrissey was tapping into an ancient repository of feelings with his long sigh of a song, 'Everyday Is Like Sunday' (1988). As a journalist visiting London from Paris in the 1850s, Théophile Gautier described Sunday in the capital as "peopled by inhabitants who have turned to stone... the thought of suicide is born in the most resolute heart; it is not prudent to fiddle with your pistols or to lean over the balustrades of bridges". The music of church bells, said Louis MacNeice in his poem 'Sunday Morning' (1915), "deadens and endures". Sunday wasn't a holiday, it came with an unspoken obligation to do nothing much, to spend time on quietly redundant hobbies (like sorting through your fossil collection) and brooding. Even for the fiercest of rebels, rebellion didn't seem possible on a Sunday: "The Sunday's sticky, home with rain / Sedition never entertained," sang Cathal on the *Viva Dead Ponies* LP.

Bands like to play down the importance of their names, and The Sundays have been no different. They'd been booked for a support slot and had to come up with something, they said. No big deal. But they'd been thinking about it ever since they started writing songs in student digs, years before, when they'd been dreaming about how John Peel was going to introduce them. They might have been 'The Joy Strings' or 'The Neighbours'. Why then lumber yourself, especially during the Eighties' celebration of quick and noisy modernity, with such doleful associations? They chose to be The Sundays because it wasn't any old Sunday they were talking about. It wasn't the Sunday of Nineties Man Alan Partridge, with the car to wash, newspaper supplements to read, the kids under his feet. It was the Sunday of students and recent graduates, the twenty-somethings whose Sundays were made for hangovers and regrets. Harriet Wheeler and Dave Gavurin managed to turn those experiences of crappy housing—living with two-bar fires and dead people's furniture—into an essence, a mood that's almost physical. Wistful and plangent rather than miserable in itself. And an example of what might well be a singularly British genius, the ability to find charm and humour, even a perverse kind of happiness, in the saddest of hinterlands.

*

Studentland in the Eighties was another kind of reality. You didn't have to get up, you didn't have to go to bed. There was nothing that couldn't be eaten straight out of a tin and milk had no expiry date; no toilet could be expected to contain toilet paper or be free from that one, ubiquitous pubic hair. Outside of halls, accommodation was a comical squalor. There'd be holes in the carpet, holes in walls and even holes between the upstairs and downstairs floors. Old mouse droppings, best ignored. Kitchens radiated every flavour of decomposition. You might spend whole days leafing through the minor works of Dostoevsky; sitting round the kitchen table smoking and talking about the existence of God or the topology of Felicity Kendal's bum; or just stay wrapped up in a duvet taking the piss out of daytime TV. You made sure you turned up to seminars and college dinners as another person, wearing the look of an almost-articulate adult. But the nights out drinking, the drinking in the Union bar, in the pubs, at the crappiest of crap gigs, all of it to the accompaniment of a thudding parade of music, those nights were both the true purpose of existence and its strangest mystery. Because of the thousands of lost hours softened and distorted by booze and animated by so many different faces: the cool, the manic, the woozy, damp faces. Because there was an unlikely chemistry that kept happening between assorted personalities—the knowing, the artless and the lost—that resulted in so much comedy, attachment, pain and despair. It was an education in itself to live among such a hotchpotch of accents, ideas and quirks. More than anything else, you learnt there was no 'normal'. There were going to be alternatives (even if it was a lesson that might later be forgotten in the mist of conventions, the commute, the satellite TV deals, the dinner dances).

Meanwhile though, Higher Education wasn't working for Britain the way it was meant to. Not because of its fanciful traditions and oddness, but because there were too few students joining in, a bottleneck of access that meant a lack of human capital for the economy to work with. In 1987 only 35 per cent of 16- to 18-year-olds were in education and training, compared with 80 per cent in the US and 77 per cent in Japan—the lowest rate of among major economies globally. There had been only 216,000 full-time students in 1962, more than a million by 1990, but it wasn't enough, especially as most of the new students coming through were from middle-class backgrounds and were female. The Government needed to steer the traditional working classes, so unsuited to the needs of the 'knowledge economy', out of the factories and dole queues and into university study. Work on 'widening participation' was happening long before it became a stock New Labour term from 1997. Like the abolition of the divide between polytechnics and universities in 1992, when Britain tried to imitate the big European 'degree factories' and put more emphasis on technical qualifications and work-related skills. Universities were rewarded for taking more students, while having 'new' universities helped remove some of the snobbery around students who went to a poly. It was a sudden step up in status for institutions in old industrial towns like Bolton, Huddersfield, Luton and Sunderland. But the change in image also encouraged confusion about what HE was really for. Was it to cultivate understanding and wisdom, or to provide equipment for a career? The debate still goes on (slipping further and further onto the side of expediency) but it was around this period that the soul of universities changed forever. They became business-like, revenue-focused and willing to begin competing for funding by offering the lowest price per student.

Universities were a kind of changing room. Young people from different backgrounds tried on different looks and outfits. Kids from council house estates wore Oxford shirts and tweed jackets from charity shops, read Samuel Beckett and drank wine; the private school crowd wore jeans and sweatshirts and shared kebabs. Not really social mobility, just a little stir of the identity pot. Wherever you came from, whatever persona you adopted, you were likely to end up in the least pretentious parts of town. There was never enough university accommodation to house everyone, and the expansion of student numbers meant increased reliance on a town's cheapest housing stock, the seedy Edwardian flats on ribbon-roads and the suburbs of Victorian terraces; , the houses with old bikes outside and a tie-dye throw for a curtain. Even if they were only slumming for a while, students got to see pieces of real life: what it was like to be stuck in rented accommodation alongside neighbours trapped in low-paid jobs or stuck on benefits, with a coin-operated electricity meter, using the local launderette down the street, the phone boxes and dirty old buses, the shop on the corner for its overpriced, processed food and little shelf of wilted vegetables. They had to rely on dirty old buses to get around and lived.

The years in Studentland included an introduction to some big and complicated emotions. Like loneliness. Not the mildly romantic loneliness of walking back alone from a night out—still a singleton, whistling sad songs—but a bleak, destructive loneliness. Away from home, some students would be searching for people they could depend on, while others couldn't care less: the party was never going to stop. The combination made for a hothouse of relationships. A mess of love and sex, fatalism and resentment. Weren't student days meant to be the best time of your life? Even with lectures to attend and essays to submit and hangovers to get over, there was a lot of time to think, and wonder whether making your own future was going to be as easy as it had looked. Feeling the sadness at the heart of things—contrary, unreliable, disappointing. Anthony Powell in *A Dance to the Music of Time* called it "the crushing melancholy of the undergraduate condition".

*

Reading, Writing and Arithmetic was made by Bristol and its university. Harriet and Dave met as students in the city, and an affection for that (sometimes) magical time stayed with them. It's no coincidence that both their children studied at the University of Bristol; or that both Billie[1] and Frank[2] ended up taking jobs at the University, staying on to live in that place of stories and glad association.

---

[1] Dr Billie Gavurin is a Lecturer in English. She took an English degree (like Mum), and her research area has been animal-human hybrids in late-nineteenth-century literature and visual art (think HG Wells' *The Island of Dr Moreau* (1896)). Billie is also a talented illustrator and an active feminist, a Liverpool FC fan who liked to pretend she was Robbie Fowler in back garden kickabouts. She's not named after Billie Holiday; her parents just liked the name.

[2] Frank Gavurin is a Policy Researcher. He studied for a Politics and Spanish degree (similar to Dad) and was a contributor to the *Epigram* student magazine. Frank volunteered at the Action on Empty Homes charity and taught English in a school in Spain before returning to the University. He's also a Liverpool FC fan.

Universities played their part in forming each of the five bands. Cathal studied at University College Cork for a Bachelor of Science degree in Microbiology; "until I discovered drugs," he explained, "which had a severe impact on my dedication". Before he dropped out, Cathal met Sean O'Hagan at a student party. They began meeting up regularly to put together the guitar accompaniments to pieces of student poetry that were the beginning of Microdisney. Paddy took an English Literature degree at Newcastle Polytechnic (before it became Northumbria University in 1992). He was the first in his family to enter HE, and sometimes it showed. "I wore dungarees and I had a little black cap, and I used to carry a little tin of cigars in my front pocket," said Paddy. "I went into this lecture room and the history lecturer looked at me and said 'All right, you've come to do the windows.' I looked at him and he realised I was a student. He was mortified." It was another local university, Durham, that was the source of early gigs and Sprout fans. It was a Durham student who arranged for Paddy to have free access to the University's Electronic Music School, its studios, multi-track recorders and synthesisers, and the chance to be part of an intellectual community excited about experimental music.

Peter was on the edges of the University of Queensland gang as someone who'd exchange Blaise Cendrars books with Grant McLennan and Robert Forster of the Go-Betweens and get involved with their late-night chats about New Wave cinema and politics—but he kept to his own scene, a foil to the student fun and its stripy sunshine. His favourite reading included Albert Camus, the dark, alcoholic reverie of Malcolm Lowry's *Under the Volcano*, and Hungarian poet Miklós Radnóti, who'd been imprisoned and murdered in a work camp in 1944 ("Bloody drool hangs on the mouth of the oxen. The men all piss red. The company stands around in stinking wild knots. Death blows overhead, disgusting.")

I've Seen Everything was a different record from the Trashcans' debut *Cake* (1990), partly because of the departure of the original bass player, George McDaid, to the University of Aberdeen. "Davy [Hughes] joining really galvanised us," according to lead singer Frank Reader. The band was well-read without the motivation of formal academic study. John Douglas has mentioned the influence of poets like Robert Burns, Dylan Thomas and WB Yeats, along with Lewis Carroll, Mary Shelley (*Frankenstein* (1818)), Raymond Chandler (the Philip Marlowe detective novels) and Flann O'Brien (best known for modernist novel *At Swim-Two-Birds* (1939)), and their interest in playing with language to convey emotion in unusual ways.

Cathal talked about escaping Microbiology by entering the counter-cultural worlds of William Burroughs and Philip K Dick. By 1987 he was into other, similarly thoughtful and uncomfortable books, like Milan Kundera's *The Unbearable Lightness of Being* (1984), Charles Bukowski's *Post Office* (1971) and Iain Banks' *The Wasp Factory* (1984).

Paddy's shelves were heaving, but not because of his degree. There was a *Complete Works* of James Joyce, a lot of Vladimir Nabokov and Knut Hamsun (the Norwegian who pioneered the psychological novel); as well as the trashy, lyrical books of Thomas Pynchon. There was more straightforward reading in the form of F Scott Fitzgerald's *The Great*

Gatsby (1925); Jane Austen's *Emma* (1815); work by the Angry Young Men of the Fifties, Alan Sillitoe and John Braine; Georges Simenon's Maigret stories; some Graham Greene novels, of course;[3] and Martin Amis's tale of glorious adolescent pretension, *The Rachel Papers* (1973). Paddy was a student of English literature in a more purposeful and potent sense.

The Sundays didn't talk in interviews about their bookish interests, even though Harriet was an English lit student and Dave would have been reading many French and Spanish writers like Arthur Rimbaud and Federico García Lorca. This kind of reticence is a signal of how more people were becoming self-conscious about their class and image. Unlike the incoming generation from homes with a few Agatha Christies and a Haynes car manual on the shelves— who got a thrill from (being seen) reading Kafka—they didn't necessarily want to be considered as arty types. Being Brideshead-posh wasn't cool anymore. "Poetry is not for me," sang Harriet on 'My Finest Hour'.

What mattered most of all for indie music was the way universities worked as little motors of fanaticism. Students read the music press and fanzines and shared copies around, stuck up flyers and posters in their rooms and were happy to get on board the latest obscure ride to nowhere fast. The Pop Guns. Curly's Watts. They all sounded like the future of rock when they first started pogoing around to a fat bass rhythm in the SU. The Sundays' first appearances, supporting Throwing Muses in February 1989, as well as their first headlining tour in 1990, were constructed around uni-

---

[3] The lyrics of 'Don't Sing' on Swoon are based around Greene's novel *The Power and the Glory* (1940).

versities: Leicester University, Liverpool Poly, Manchester University, Nottingham Trent Poly, Portsmouth Poly and Queen Margaret University Glasgow. One of the first outings for The Fatima Mansions was the University of London Union (February 1989). And in earlier times, the Sprouts played Dunelm House, Durham's SU in 1980, and kept on picking up admirers for their gawky delights all around the uni circuit.

*

Harriet Wheeler grew up in Sonning Common, a village in the Chiltern Hills near Henley-on-Thames, the daughter of an architect and a teacher. They were the hairbrush years. Harriet would keep finding herself called up to replace Michael in the line-up for the Jackson 5 at the last minute. The first actual gigs came in Bristol, when she would help out friend Kevin Jamieson by singing backing vocals for Cruel Shoes. "I first met Harriet in 1983 I think," said Kevin, the band's lead singer. "It was in a shared student house off the Gloucester Road, adjacent to the Montpelier area of town, a Bohemian and slightly gentrified kind of place even then, which appealed to some students. I recall Harriet's black Dr Martens boots and dungarees. It was a relatively new thing for girls to wear DMs at the time, so she seemed very cool." She already had that trademark hair, once described as a "cottage-loaf kind of tonsorial affair, a bouffant, large granary swell topped by a smaller follicular croissant"[4]. Harriet was distinctly Harriet. "She was bright, witty and good fun to be with," added Kevin. "A big fan of Joni Mitchell I remember, and she was the one who introduced me to the Cocteau Twins."

They met in that phase of student life that took place outside of the halls of residence, the years when groups of friends moved outside of the uni bubble and into actual Bristol—a city made from hundreds of years of an often unscrupulous overseas trade. In his poem 'Bristol', written in 1768 when he was 16, Thomas Chatterton explained why he had needed to leave the port city that had been his home for London.

> The Muses have no credit here, and Fame
> Confines itself to the Mercantile name;
> Then clip Imagination's wings, be wise,
> And great in Wealth, to real Greatness rise…
> Damn'd narrow Notions which to disgrace
> The boasted Reason of the Human Race.
> Bristol may keep her prudent Maxims still,
> But know, my saying Friends, I never will.
> The Composition of my Soul is made

---

[4] Joe Cassidy of the rock band Butterfly Child used to live opposite Dave and Harriet in London. When he had guests over they used to play a game of trying to catch sight of Harriet with her hair down through binoculars. No-one ever managed it. Speaking to assistant Randee Dawn during the video shoot for 'Here's Where' in 1990, Harriet said her hair had never been cut, and left loose would reach down to her legs.

Too great for servile avaricious Trade —[5]

In the early Eighties the harbours and wharves were rundown and sea-stained, not yet the premium waterside location for leisure and retail outlets they would become. Alongside the familiar Bristol landmarks of the wooded gorge, the
Clifton Suspension Bridge and high banks of coloured cottages, there were signs of de-industrialisation everywhere, in
the derelict warehouses, abandoned factories, rusty black gas
holders and stretches of waste ground. Even the streets of
fine Georgian mansions—many of them built with slave
trade money—were looking dowdy. New forms of wealth
were moving into Bristol via defence and electronics industry
companies such as British Aerospace, Westland and Hewlett-
Packard, but unemployment was still high and the city had
slums and estates known for a particular West Country
squalor, soaked in cheap cider. "Many students moved down
from the smarter halls in Stoke Bishop and Clifton to the
rougher areas around St. Paul's in their second and third
years," said Kevin.

> Mainly to save money but also because of the
> vibeyness of the area. There were plenty of
> down-to-earth cafés and pubs with scruffy old
> men sat in the corner. There was an old feller
> in the caff at the top of Whiteladies Road in
> Clifton who used to smoke Woodbines, the

---

[5] Chatterton was famous for the 'Thomas Rowley' fraud, for passing off his poems as
being from lost 15th-century manuscripts and creating a publishing sensation. A hero
of the Romantics, he was found dead in his room in London, aged 17. It was assumed
to have been a case of suicide, but Chatterton's death may have been the result of the
arsenic he was taking for venereal disease.

classic Bristol cigarette with no filter, with a
pin stuck in so he could smoke it down to the
very end. Cigarettes were important to us
back then. Almost everyone smoked and the
brand you chose was very much part of the
image you wanted to put across. The serious
hardcore would smoke the non-filtered
Woodbines or Park Royals. I smoked the
reasonably heavyweight, but at least filtered,
Embassy Regals in packets of ten, as a nod to
my mostly Northern mates—or occasionally
JPS Black which were also quite heavy. The
girls—including Harriet—went for the more
sophisticated Silk Cut or Benson and Hedges
Gold.

The Suspension Bridge was known for suicides, especially among younger men.[6] "Once I saw something odd that
looked a bit like a body floating out to sea. The next day we
found out that Shirley Bassey's daughter drowned in the river
there."[7] One of the places Kevin lived in was known as 'H
block', a "near squat" in the mostly grand district of Clifton.

The rent was cheap and nothing was ever
fixed. The lintel above the front door was
cracked and dangerous, there were big holes
in the walls and the backyard would fill up

---

[6] Until barriers were put in place in 1998.

[7] The body of Bassey's daughter, Samantha Novak (aged 21), was found at the foot of
the Bridge in the River Avon in 1984.

with effluent. It became a kind of doss house for some unfortunates, people like 'Frequency Dave', a homeless ex-student who got too involved with drugs, and who later sadly died at a young age. I lasted about six months there and then moved down to City Road in St Paul's.

This was the area where much of Bristol's Afro-Caribbean community lived, and the centre of an underground music scene. There were late-night sound system parties; houses with windows open wide, pumping out mixtapes; slow-moving cars circling the streets with their stereo volume turned up full. Together they were like the community's own radio station, a collage of looping, bass-heavy broadcast of reggae, ska, funk and hip-hop over the airwaves of the city. For most white middle-class students this would have been their first exposure to a living black culture, the street slang, the rapping, the body-popping, the graffiti art. The strength of identity in the area was demonstrated in the organisation of protests against police racism in the summer of 1980.

"St Paul's was home to the so-called 'blues clubs' that were often in basements of rundown Victorian houses," Kevin has recalled. "There'd be big black men on the doors who'd charge you whatever they felt like, or let you in free if you were lucky. Inside it was dark and there would be a sound system in one of the rooms booming reggae or dub music. There was also a great club called the Tropic Club that played soul and funk music, and a pub called The Inkerman that charged 'white man's prices', meaning an extra 20p on your pint. We'd go to a fantastic dingy basement club in Park Street Avenue in Clifton called the Dug Out with sticky tables and crusty carpets that sold the Courage Best we liked. It was a great place for black and white kids to mix and dance together 'til three in the morning."

Lindsay, who'd go on to play a part in the making of The Sundays' first LP, was Kevin's younger brother.[8] He would visit when he was back home from Lancaster: "The University there had this terrible campus that was miles from anywhere. It was like they'd said to themselves 'Right, how will students get on if we base our architecture on Swedish prisons, on a big hill with the wind and the rain. Let's see how many of them jump off the roof.'" Bristol was more fun. "I was the young impressionable one going out with his big brother. I remember one night seeing an early version of the Thompson Twins before they went pop, playing Trinity Hall [a converted old church building near St Paul's]. Then a band like Animal Magic.[9] The singer came on and took all his clothes off, got his penis out and start screaming 'ANIM-AL MAGIC!!' There was a real scene in Bristol, a positive kind of tension." The local bands to see in the early Eighties were the Brilliant Corners, Pigbag and the Blue Aeroplanes, or reggae bands like Black Roots and Talisman. The most famous music venue in Bristol was the Granary Club in the basement of a giant Victorian factory next to the harbour, where Iron Maiden, Genesis, Thin Lizzy, Yes and Lindis-

---

[8] Lindsay Jamieson is a branding consultant based in Nashville, US. He still plays drums for a number of bands, including Astronaut Pushers with Matt Slocum (of Sundays soundalikes Sixpence None the Richer).

[9] Animal Magic were a local dance-vs-punk band; the lead singer was Howard Purse. John Peel played tracks from their 1982 debut session three times—more than many bands who'd actually got a record deal.

farne had all played. But for students with limited cash there were small venues like the Stonehouse and the Green Room for local bands: Essential Bop, Vitus Dance, Sneak Preview, Out of Order. Anywhere but Busby's, the townies' nightclub with its Sixties mega-mixes and 'erection section'.

*

Evening comes, and the last member of the household shuts the front door with a bang and a rattle and heads into town. He's bored of *Les Liaisons Dangereuses,* and can't be bothered anymore with figuring out how to play the fussy guitar line to 'Follow You Follow Me'. No-one else had been in for tea, and the kitchen had an even more depressing look when he was alone in the half-light with that Fifties tub of a cooker, its missing dials and beige puddle of scum. The smell of Fray Bentos and damp carpet wouldn't budge. Thankfully his parents had never come down from their gracious London home to see the place he'd ended up in. They knew it wasn't great; he'd told them some things, but the grubby details— like the atmosphere of unwashed sheets, fags and joss sticks —were probably more than they'd be able to stomach. The Schiele and Monet postcards brought a reassuring touch of culture, but then they'd also see the table made from old Perfect Pizza boxes and the copies of *Bristles* rag mag with the tits and fanny graffiti. His accountant father would look away and be working out the number of rooms versus bathroom facilities, irritated by the landlord's net returns.

Outside, Bristol's streetlights are burning orange, the office blocks have emptied out and the workers have turned into traffic. The fryers are simmering lustily in the fish and chip shop. Dave sees his reflection in the hairdresser's window: an overcoat collar turned up on some serious Roman-helmet features. Handsome brown eyes that were made for Mediterranean places and for all those smooth, luxurious sentences with silky Latin rhythms that never seemed to belong in Bristol. He'd soon be in Spain for his year abroad with the guitars and bougainvillea and a warm starry moonlight. Then again nothing was ever that simple. Did he want to go and leave Bristol now? Not when everywhere, every grey scene, had started to look like home. The hillsides and their rows of lights, the tower of St Paul's on the skyline, the Saturday crowds shuffling along Broadmead, the Revolver record shop. Not when he might—maybe—have met someone he wanted to stay in Bristol with, and be spared the walks into town with nowhere much to go. Not that Harriet had called, and maybe wouldn't call again. He'd see her in the Arts & Humanities building sometime, there was no need to hang round the lobby anymore, pretending to read the notices about departmental socials. How did it happen that you could see someone a hundred times without thinking much about it; then one day they detach themselves from the meaningless faces and bags and books around them and they start to sting. Stinging in a way you don't want to stop. He had to stop the jokes about the hair though or he'd get that look in return—that deliberate look, like she's trying to figure him out. And not in a good way. Where did he sit in the list of candidates? Next to the limber athletes, the guys in leather jackets reading Kerouac, the smooth and capable prospects already talking to Arthur Andersen?

Dave's feet keep walking him into town. The city centre was now the HQ of a different kind of empire.[10] By the late twentieth century only a state-supported institution like a University could afford to spread itself so comfortably over such grandiose and elaborate premises as the Wills Memorial Building, the Victoria Rooms and the Royal Fort House. Great places for costume drama. Like the University kind of was, thought Dave, at least it was for the private school crowd who couldn't get into Oxbridge because they were thick. The Rahs[11] always loved the first year in halls—especially if they made it into Wills, where you got to live in your own Gothic quad and there was proper three-course catering like luncheon at home: the tomato soup and bread roll to start; fish on a Friday, a fillet of plaice with buttered potatoes and garden peas; lemon sponge and syrup as a dessert. Lots of formals and garden parties to dress up for, meaning plenty of classic Varsity photos for their parents to bring out at dinner parties.

He doesn't want a drink tonight, but he ends up at the Ents building anyway. A concrete block that would be perfect for the office drones of a big insurance company to work in. High up in the grey-blue air was a long deck of golden light. It was too early for anything to have started in the Anson

---

[10] The University of Bristol had been in the Premiership of British universities since the 1960s. It formally became a member of the Russell Group of elite institutions in 1994.

[11] British private school students were sometimes known as 'hoorah' Henries and Henriettas.

Rooms,[12] but the bar would be full of students getting into groups, seeing who was there, making choices about who to flirt with next. He wasn't going up there just to see who was with who. Harriet knew where he was, she'd got his phone number. He was better off outside with the evening, with his beat suede shoes and a fag. After all the months of nights out, the murky pubs and clubs and the dirty throb of his head from all the booze, an evening like this, just walking through the streets of town was like medicine. You could turn any corner and the rush of air was as clean and simple as a hymn. Dave looks back to the lights of the Richmond and thinks about a tiny figure in a smoky hot crowd. An imp of a girl with big blue eyes and a shiny buckle belt.

*

As a boy living in Seventies' Wembley, Dave Gavurin would go every week to Habonim or 'Habo' in his uniform of shorts and a blue shirt with red strings. The kids would line up for a parade before the real business of the evening started: learning a mix of new pop songs and old folk dances. "For the lower-middle-class, arty, boho end of the Jewish religion, its appeal was as a kind of hippy Jewish scouts," said comedian David Baddiel of Habo. He'd met his lifelong friend Dave there. At Habo there would be food, the chance to meet girls, and the prospect of summer camps. Officially, it was a youth movement based around a mixture of social-

---

[12] The Student Union or 'Ents' was based in the Richmond Building, a piece of brutalist Sixties architecture that included the Anson Rooms for gigs. Orange Juice played the Anson in February 1982, as did The Smiths in February 1984 (tickets: £3). Gary Glitter also played there for a rag ball in the Eighties as part of his comeback tour.

ism and Zionism, but it was always far more about art than politics, and the Habonim were known for their chilled-out encouragement of creativity. Besides Baddiel and his scriptwriter brother Ivor, Dave was at Habo with Howie B (producer of U2's *Pop* and Björk's *Post*) and documentary filmmaker Jes Benstock.[13] A young Sacha Baron Cohen joined the same Habo at just about the same time when Dave was leaving. So chances to play music were always around in Dave's young life, but none of them felt serious. He'd played guitar in school for a while, tried being a punk. But university was never meant to be about starting a band.

For students, the second year was different from the first. The nights out had started to feel like business as usual, the encounters they led to were kind of routine and could come with as many feelings of emptiness as excitement. The *News of the World* image might have been of careless sex romps but it wasn't true. There would be a small proportion of 'shaggers', more well known and less respected as each year passed; another small group with steady boyfriends or girlfriends, or who didn't want to bother with relationships; and a very small number who were openly homosexual (and in the Eighties and Nineties that meant trouble). Most students were in the middle. They'd learnt how cold things could be out there, and without looking too serious, were hoping for something real.

Dave and Harriet met through mutual friends and finally became an official couple during their second year as

---

[13] Dave (with Harriet) wrote a song for the soundtrack of *The Infidel* (2010) about a Muslim man who discovers he was adopted and is actually Jewish. The film was a Habo reunion: David Baddiel wrote the script, and The Sundays' track was produced by Howie B.

undergraduates in 1983. They were together so often that it stopped making sense for them to be apart: "sitting on garden walls talking about all the absurd things you talk about when you're 20 and drinking too much and smoking an inordinate amount of rollups." Harriet would go round to Dave's and they'd play his songs. There was his acoustic guitar, but as the songwriting became more serious he collected the ingredients needed to create the sound of The Sundays: a drum machine, a bass guitar and a four-track recorder. Over the months of coupledom, the *Reading, Writing and Arithmetic* songs were pieced together, not from rehearsal room jams, but bedrooms and shabby front rooms, with leftover mugs of tea and plates of biscuits, for the fun and frisson of writing songs. And that approach alone made those songs different. It meant an unusual patience and concentration. They could go about the whole thing as ordinary people doing something for themselves, a Sunday hobby, without the freakishness and sometimes plastic charm of pop stars bargaining their way to attention. "We didn't have a clue what we wanted to do with it all, but the actual writing of the songs we took incredibly seriously," said Dave. "We'd be sitting there for days on these things, getting really into it. In a bad as well as a good way. They were happy times—interesting times, anyway." Maybe Harriet had raised an eyebrow at "happy times"; that was oversimple, interview puff.

> The way we write is I'll put down a lyric, and
> then Harriet will write the next line. I admit,
> it's kind of weird since I don't know how
> many other writers work that way, but it

works for us. We like that a person can be
writing a song one way and then the other
person can take it on a completely different
tangent. Actually, it's the only way we know
how to write.

Unlike other songwriting partnerships, which could become
more like duels than anything else (Lennon/McCartney, For-
ster/McLennan), Gavurin/Wheeler were a fusion over a
number of levels. It's all there in the TV and press interviews
where they would check with each other for a look of
agreement, even finish each other's sentences. Harriet would
monitor Dave for his jokes, because she knew they were
sometimes better off kept at home. Playing live, Harriet
would hold her hands behind her back and look over to
Dave for reassurance. But they were also a typical long-term
couple, unsentimental and unshowy, at least in public. Asked
about Harriet's role in an interview with MTV in 1990,
Dave said: "People just think you want to have a female vocalist, to have someone pretty at the front—which unfortu-
nately we didn't get." Oh Dave. And where are the love
songs? The dynamic of a settled and secure couple sharing
the writing duties changed the content, making the lyrics fall
out in less personal or confessional ways.

There was music they both liked, but that didn't mean
it was influential. Dave always insisted they were nothing like
the Cocteau Twins even though the group were favourites
along with the Smiths, New Order, folksters like John
Martyn and jazz and dance music. Instead they brought
their own individual, personal qualities. "I find it very odd to
talk about my voice," said Harriet after the first Sundays gigs

led to press attention. "I don't think my voice is extraordinary. I don't sing like a lot of women in the charts but then
that's because they don't sing in a natural way, that's all."
Like Suzanne Vega, said the reviewers. A bit Elizabeth
Fraser of the Cocteaus or Mary Margaret O'Hara with
Morrissey's phrasing. A "coy, romantic voice. Slurred, petu-
lant, desiring… like Lolita without her candy." "A delirious
elastic carolling sound," said Caitlin Moran in *The Times*,
"not unlike a tipsy lark spiralling westward after a very good
evening". It didn't work for everyone ("Little-girl inflections
and a deliberate-sounding flatness which is intriguing for one
track… irritating for a whole album"). Criticisms like these
could be reassuring for someone who didn't want to sound
like a singer from the pop factory, just as long as you didn't
tell Harriet she reminded you of Clare Grogan. "I'm really
glad I can't hear it, because if I could, I'd probably give up,
I'd be very depressed." Most importantly for The Sundays
individual sound, Harriet's singing wasn't just sweet and
loose and drifting but able to rough it up with whoops and
growls when it needed to.

Dave's guitar, meanwhile, feels under-appreciated by
comparison, treated as if it's only the backing track—maybe
because he was drawing on the classic spangle shapes of
Johnny Marr and James Honeyman-Scott of the Pretenders.
He provided far more than that: a palette of guitar elements,
from sounds that were like the ripples of light on water, the
spotting of rain on a windowpane, or far-off church bells,
along with some skewed, woozy guitar coils. There's also a
rolling runaway strum and a more grubby blues, flavoured
by the grit and carbon monoxide of Bristol's A-roads. Dave

worked by layering simple parts together, electric and acoustic, using the sounds of his growing guitar collection, a black-edged and orange Gibson ES335 (kind of jazzy, good for distortion) and a Fender Telecaster (bright and clean for the angular sounds); and to add acoustic warmth, depth and shimmer, a Martin D-41 Dreadnought and a Lowden 12-string. Dave was able to use his guitar lines to turn the songs into duets. "I don't just like to use the guitar to fill in space when Harriet isn't singing. That's why you'll often hear me playing a detailed melody while Harriet is singing a detailed melody." The guitar parts came first, followed by the tunes second, giving them a honed quality (and maybe that's another reason for the Smiths comparisons, Marr had done the same for Morrissey). The sound of The Sundays comes from their careful constructions of interplay: how the guitar parts work both with and against pieces of melody, making for exquisite tensions and shifts in counterpoint.

Harriet and Dave started using the rehearsal rooms at the top of the Ents building and brought in first-year student Paul Brindley to play bass.[14] Next door, Kevin would be on the uni's piano, working on his own material. There was a creative buzz around the place—and the potential that came from making your own music—especially after when Marr and Morrissey arrived in February 1984 to play the Anson.

Then Dave went away for his year in Spain for his course. Harriet would hang out at the flat Kevin shared with friend Nick Hannan, a shabby-genteel Georgian place in Hotwells on the A4 overlooking the Avon. "We would sit out on a wooden pontoon on summer evenings drinking the loc-

---

[14] Paul was three years younger and didn't start at Bristol until 1985.

al scrumpy, watching the ships coming in on the high tide. Harriet used to come and visit us there, and quite often sat reading in a big old beaten-up armchair looking out onto the river." Nick's brother Patrick had finished a course in electrical and electronic engineering at Farnborough College of Technology and would drive over to Bristol in his Mini, getting to know the gang that included Harriet. She was in the middle of helping out with recording demos for Kevin's new band, a busy Mod-skiffle-ska combo mixing up influences from all those nights dancing at the Tropic and the Dug Out. Nick was on board to play bass. Lindsay, who'd just finished his degree in Marketing and French at Lancaster, was the drummer; and as far as the other band members were concerned, Harriet would be joining them as backing singer. Harriet was the one who'd thought up the band name Jim Jiminee, a play on Kevin's full name: James Kevin Jamieson (and how both his Dad's name and his Grandpa's name was James—so Jim Jamieson, Jim Jimmy, Jim Jiminee). But before the band could get anywhere, Dave came back and took Harriet with him to London. Lindsay, for one, hadn't seen it coming. "By the time I'd got down south I'd found out that Harriet had left and formed a group with Dave. I remember Harriet had always been talking about Dave when he was away, and I'd be thinking who is this Dave guy? When I met him I found out he was a brilliant bloke, very funny. But when Harriet went she also left us with that name. It was a quirky name, and I don't think people took the music seriously. It ended up being our downfall!"[15]

*

To the outside world they would look like the lost years. While most students at an institution like Bristol would be cruising the 'milk round', meeting the best employers and applying for traditional graduate trainee programmes with the BBC, the Civil Service and Marks & Spencer, Harriet and Dave shrugged and stayed in Bristol on the dole. The merry-go-round of critical reasoning assessments and psychometric questionnaires wasn't for them. The only notable step towards making a career was taken by Dave: a training course in filmmaking where he learnt to use a movie camera and cut-and-splice celluloid. (To watch the film he'd made as homework, they invested in a projector they'd seen in a jumble sale, but the ancient machine's bulb set fire to the reel.) Why did Harriet and Dave drop out? It wouldn't have been easy to turn up at family gatherings and face the same, crisply polite, questions again: what are you doing now? "Oh yes, but which profession will you choose?" "Oh." Those pauses and patient, concerned expressions. "The dole? Really—oh. But have you thought about teaching?"

It's likely they stayed jobless because they were happy. They met up with friends, read books, worked on their songs. Attitudes had been changing towards work and career any-

---

[15] By contrast, brand consultant Lindsay sees 'The Sundays' as ideal. "It's future compatible with anything, it's so noncommittal. And a British Sunday also comes with powerful emotions of those old Sundays. Whenever it rains here [in Nashville], I'm straightaway thinking, is it Sunday?"

way. While their parents' generation had seen sacrificing their lives to a career as the highway to wealth and security, a means of being part of the history of material progress, the Eighties' graduates weren't so sure. It wasn't as if they would be able to impress family with anything they did anyway— after taking a university degree, career success was just something taken for granted. Proof of wealth would be needed. There were all kinds of signals coming from The Sundays that they wanted to look and sound like the most ordinary of red-brick ordinaries, to be divested of their conservative English milieu and its bourgeois accoutrements, the violin lessons, hostess trolleys, conservatory furniture and investment planning. They were making a bid to be classless. There's Dave and his earring; Harriet and her fags, attractively toofy; the twang of Estuary English in their voices. And there's the talk of links to the downmarket town of Reading—the 'Reading' of the album title. Sonning Common wasn't as posh it might sound (a large village with mixed housing, not all of it chocolate box), but still, someone would only choose to say they were from Reading to avoid being associated with boring middle-class England. Because if it was a case of referencing somewhere more familiar than a village, they could have said Henley-on-Thames, a better-known place than Reading (but with much worse upper-middle-class connotations than Sonning).

They wanted to do something. For all the bravado, it was a period of uncertainty about the future that made them want to look back, wistfully, to a simpler past, to the kinds of themes and feelings that filtered through into *Reading, Writing and Arithmetic*. Harriet and Dave moved to North London in

1987 knowing they (probably) had at least documented what had been special about the Bristol years in their demo tapes. The Jiminees would come up and stay, and they'd have dinner parties and go round the pubs in Camden and Kentish Town. They'd try the Goth rock gigs organised by Mick Mercer of *Melody Maker*. Sometimes they'd meet up with David Baddiel and his girlfriend Janine when he first started doing stand-up comedy in pubs.[16]

Paul Brindley was just back from his own year away in Spain, teaching English, when he got the call about rehearsing for live gigs. For Paul it was like a fan being asked to join one of his favourite bands. Meanwhile The Sundays drummer was meant to be Lindsay Jamieson. But he turned the job down. "I thought I'd sworn a blood oath to my brother to be in Jim Jiminee, you know, the kind of bullshit you think when you're young, that if you were loyal to one band, you couldn't be loyal to another. A real shame." Lindsay recommended Nick's brother Patrick instead, someone he'd grown up with in Fleet.[17] "I started teaching Patch how to drum when he was 11 and I was about 14, just the basics I'd learnt from my drum teacher."

The band's first booking was at an old-style pub rock venue, The Cricketers in Kennington next to the Oval cricket ground, where they were on the bill with Jim Jiminee and comedy singer John Shuttleworth. They hadn't yet decided on a band name that could be used for the flyers and posters. 'The Joy Strings' was the first choice. But the name had

---

[16] David Baddiel went on to use The Sundays' track 'Another Flavour' from *Static and Silence* for his walk-on music.

[17] 'Patch' Hannan was the youngest band member, born in 1969.

already been used by a pop group set up by the Salvation Army as a way of reaching out to younger people in the Sixties ("If we need to," said band founder Joy Webb, "we'll take up guitars and go into coffee bars"). They had two top 40 hits with singles recorded at Abbey Road. Harriet did the polite thing and approached Joy about sharing the name, but it was a "no". The other idea they had in mind was 'The Neighbours', until they realised they wouldn't be able to shake associations with the Australian soap opera. "We didn't know about the show at the time," admitted Harriet. The promoter crossed it out and wrote the other option instead, The Sundays. "We liked the sound and feel of it," said Dave, "and because it wasn't a name that was bigger than the music."

Rehearsals started in earnest at the Premises studios in Hackney in June 1988 and demo cassette tapes were posted off to London venues by what was just another fledgling band in the queue of wannabes. Dave and Harriet swallowed hard at leaving the legacy of their student years in the hands of commerce—such intimate, haunted creations—and went off on holiday. They came back to a bunch of telephone messages and bookings, one of them for a Vertigo Club gig at The Falcon in Camden on 20th August supporting the Caretaker Race.[18] The Falcon was classic Eighties

---

[18] Sounding like an English Go-Betweens (but with mostly b-side songs), the Caretaker Race were signed up by producer Stephen Street for his label, but recorded just one album, *Hangover Square* (named after the brilliant Patrick Hamilton novel of 1941).

Camden.[19] A squat and sturdy Victorian pub that was like a comfortable living room for the punks, Goths and head-bangers drinking snakebite who enjoyed nothing more than a hard-faced and threatening atmosphere. In summer, the Falcon's back room was like a homemade sauna of body heat and booze; you'd be breathing in sweat just for the oxygen. That night in August the sound levels were set ready for the usual; heavy drums and guitar, so when Harriet started singing she struggled to be heard and got shouty. But the melodies would always stand up for themselves and even in that hard rock setting the effect wasn't obscure or ethereal but propulsive. The unusual virtuosity of the songs broke the shell of expectations. Chris Roberts of the *Melody Maker*, sent to the Falcon to write a review of the Caretaker Race, almost passed out with excitement. "The Sundays are the most beautiful thing I've heard since I was one year old… I was hanging from the chandeliers and squealing. Then after that I got *really* into it… Harriet has a voice which is precisely like nothing else on earth. When she cries of souvenirs on 'Here's Where the Story Ends', your life doesn't just flash before you, it sits down and lights a cigarette and starts apologising."

After The Falcon everyone wanted a bit of The Sundays. The next gig, at The Boston Arms in Tufnell Park, suddenly came with a lot more pressure. "Everything has gone like a clockwork dream for The Sundays," wrote their Number One Fan, Chris Roberts. "They have the magic…

---

[19] Later, when Camden had moved towards gentrification, the Falcon was where Blur, Oasis, Franz Ferdinand and Coldplay also got themselves noticed. The pub closed down in 2002. In January 2023 the building was re-opened as a luxury, split-level three-bed/four-bathroom apartment available to book on Airbnb yours for around £500 a night.

They just sound wonderful. They sound lovely. I could try a million words but that's what would transpire." Everything was happening so quickly, and there was so much to think about. The requests for interviews, the questions about who they were, what made them different, what the songs meant. What did they want to do with all the fuss they'd already created? Consequently, Harriet wasn't sleeping well—before they'd even recorded anything for public release. They didn't want to waste the opportunities that were going their way, but they wanted to do things the right way; and not be five-minute wonders, all hype and trousers. "We weren't looking for it. We think that's embarrassing… There's no reason why we should be treated like that, but I don't think we are [the next Sex Pistols or Rolling Stones]." There was even a sense of guilt at how easily the attention had come to them—knowing how their mates in Jim Jiminee had been doing it the hard way: gigging round the 'toilet circuit' and getting some interest from record labels, but nothing like this. Every step of the way, Dave and Harriet kept trying to hold things back. They turned down interviews. In spite of all the free promotion he'd provided, it took Chris Roberts four months to get to sit down with them. They also said no to the offers of front cover features. They purposely didn't rush into recording the album, and when the first single was released they refused to hire a plugger to get them onto Radio 1. As far as they were concerned they hadn't "burst onto the scene" anyway, they'd "apologetically shuffled". The Sundays wanted to stay indie: take the smaller sales that went with being played by cooler, alternative radio stations, and avoid the noise of playlisting and record deals that could swamp the music itself. Paul and Patch were brought on-board as band members who wouldn't insist on becoming celebrities. The band was wary of being tied into business contracts but still didn't have a manager either, not until after 1990. "They closed in when the success came," said Lindsay. "They wanted to manage everything very cautiously, because they'd got to that stage of credibility and respect and they didn't want to fuck it up."

It was billed as the race to sign the next indie super-stars. The majors tried taking the couple out for posh din-ners. "Mostly, the people we met were surprisingly free of bullshit and nobody suggested Harriet should get her tits out. They all tried to convince us they had their own ideas for us and we kept on hearing the phrase 'sympathetic engineer' mentioned."[20] But it was always going to come down to a choice between the two top indie labels of the time, 4AD and Rough Trade. With their ultra-stylish, hazy velveteen designs, and a roster that included the Cocteau Twins, 4AD looked like the frontrunners. That was until owner Ivo Watts-Russell made the tactical error of asking a closed question: when you thought about making records, which label did you dream you'd be on? Yeah, now you ask, they told him— that would be Rough Trade.[21] Dave liked to say they only signed with Geoff Travis because the offices were just down the road from their flat, and he was only half-joking. There was something easy and normal about the fit between them. Geoff had met the couple them for a chat in a little café

---

[20] An interview with Andy Strickland—the same Andy Strickland who was singer/guitarist with the Caretaker Race.

[21] This was reputedly the first time that an offer from 4AD had ever been turned down.

round the corner and they had split the bill. He'd explained upfront that they wouldn't have to do interviews if they didn't want to. Jeanette Lee, Geoff's assistant, could see immediately that The Sundays weren't like the usual bands. "First impressions of this incongruous duo were that he was very tall and introverted, and she was very small and extroverted. What appealed to us about the two of them was that they seemed incredibly straightforward… For us Rough Trade was this immensely cool and significant label, yet there was no arrogance about them. They basically came across as a couple of unassuming music fans."

A working day for Dave and Harriet meant leaving their flat in Holloway and taking a twenty-minute stroll down the Caledonian Road to their "home-from-home" at Rough Trade. A long, tree-lined arterial road that eventually went all the way south past HMP Pentonville and King's Cross into central London. First they would have passed by the Georgian houses and Edwardian villas, as tall and upright as soldiers, one or two of them with bright recent paintwork and newly tiled mosaics of footpaths, but the rest had been left untouched. Sallow and mouldering places with their curtains always closed, a naked lightbulb burning upstairs, looking uncared for in ways that hinted at some tragedy or loss (or that they were occupied by students). They would walk over the railway bridge with its open vista of trackways stretching out towards the east, and head past the Caledonian Road train station, another edifice of Victorian wealth, clad assertively in a coat of glossy purple-red bricks. Without a manager, Dave and Harriet needed to work directly with staff inside Rough Trade HQ, "the white open-plan offices above, with records, tapes, artwork crammed into every available corner". They planned their own bookings and touring schedule, and worked with designer Jo Slee (responsible for many of the Smiths' covers) on their artwork. "The only problem was they took a long time to make decisions," said Jeanette, "so it always took forever to get things going." They missed meeting Cathal Coughlan by a few years. Not in the offices, but downstairs in what Dave described as the "netherworld of the ground floor warehouse with its anarchy-staff stuffing boxes while blasting out German industrial music", where he and Microdisney had been working to make some extra money by packing boxes of Smiths records.

The Sundays still tried to keep the brakes on. They wanted to limit the marketing of 'Can't Be Sure' and its chances of making the Top 40 and avoid the calls from bookers at *Top of the Pops* until the album was ready. Even so, the single made number 45 in the main charts and was top of the indie charts for two months from January 1989. The *NME* made the "rainy-grey madrigal" of 'Can't Be Sure' one of its Singles of the Year, and it was the number one choice of John Peel for his Festive 50, chosen above strong competition that year from The Stone Roses, Happy Mondays, Morrissey and Pixies. A John Peel Session was recorded in February. But, if anything, that only encouraged their caution. Session producer Dale Griffin had been adamant they had to play four songs; Dave only wanted to do three and there was a falling out. The big studio setting hadn't suited them either. They liked playing live some of the time, but they would have preferred to be just writing songs for the pleasure of it; kettle on; friends due round at the flat for tea. "If we hadn't been so bloody lucky with getting all those reviews right at

Harriet and Dave at a record signing in the Kemp Mill Records store,
Washington DC, in June 1990. Courtesy of Will Fulgueras.

the start, I could imagine a situation where we wouldn't have
stuck at this for bloody ages."

*

The songs never seemed to belong in a studio. Dave and
Harriet would have released the demos recorded on their
four-track at home if they could have done. The studio
sound was "just too dry and clean", they said, it took away
the spirit of murk and dampness in their little flat: the
frowzy, peeling wallpaper feel that the original songs had
been written with, starting in student days, along with the

"industrial noise of the hot-water system and the frequent burglaries".[22] It was the same batch of songs after all. Lindsay has remembered listening to tapes at Dave and Harriet's flat in Bristol in what would have been 1985, and says they were the same songs he was later asked to develop drum tracks for, in 1989 in a rehearsal studio.[23]

> I worked very hard to get the drum parts down. I was in an experimental mind set in those days, trying to do what had never been done before. It wasn't a pre-meditated drum track. I played it through two or three times for them and they recorded everything like precision engineers. Harriet and Dave took my weird drum beats and programmed them obsessively, paying attention to absolute detail—they were obsessive almost to the point of fear. They might say, "listen, the drums sound too human in places, they're late on this bar or another". But what Patch managed to do so well was to be a brilliant crossover between drum machine perfection and a true human sound. When you saw him play with The Sundays live you could see his hands cross over and do all kinds of unnatur-

---

[22] The roof of their Holloway flat eventually collapsed just the day before The Sundays left for their US tour in 1990.

[23] "I remember thinking the demos were bloody brilliant," said Lindsay. "For me I heard a mix of The Smiths and the Cocteau Twins and I thought: that's it, you've done it."

al things, because the process had been so experimental.

Recording began with Ray Shulman as producer. He'd been the man behind The Sugarcubes' breakthrough indie hit 'Birthday' and the LP, *Life's Too Good* (1988), and had already worked on 'Can't Be Sure'. So it was a similar situation for Ray, trying to deliver something special in response to press excitement, with another wonky sound and girlish vocals. The Sundays took a functional view of Ray, seeing him as an easy-going co-producer who knew more about the technical side than they did. "[Ray] said what he thought, but we didn't really want a producer saying 'here, use these keyboards', or 'why don't you try this'. It was more that going from four to 24 track involves using equipment that we hadn't used before. Consequently, we felt we should have someone with us that would know how to use the equipment. So that is largely the sort of role he played… It's really easy to feel completely relaxed with four-track recordings. In the studio we try to recapture that relaxed feeling. That's our sole intention."

Ray took them back to Orinoco Studios, where he'd worked with the Sugarcubes. He used the same engineer, Gail Lambourne, alongside Alan Moulder—the sound engineer who went on to become the king of the mixing desk for Nineties alt-rock.[24] Orinoco was a recently opened studio in a converted warehouse off Tower Bridge Road in Ele-

---

[24] Including work with Ride (*Nowhere*), My Bloody Valentine (*Loveless*), Smashing Pumpkins (*Siamese Dreams*) and Nine Inch Nails (*Downward Spiral*).

phant and Castle.[25] It was an anonymous-looking depot in a side street surrounded by council flats and tower blocks. But there must have been something to the feel of the place. Irish singer-songwriter Enya named her song 'Orinoco Flow' (1988) in its honour. But it was all much of a muchness to Dave. They weren't looking for ideas from Ray, and, arguably, Alan learnt more from his work with The Sundays than they did from him, helping to colour his trademark sound of shimmering reverb. "The studio is a very sterile place... We ended up using a tape delay for the vocals which is a kind of old-fashioned effect," Dave said. Of all the songs they recorded, it was the closing number 'Joy' which Harriet felt sounded most like what they'd hoped for.

The sessions in Elephant and Castle with Paul and Patch took three months, including many exhausting days that ran over into the night, because The Sundays didn't want to blow their one chance with the songs they had. "They were particular, they were slow," said Rough Trade's Jeanette. "But only because they wanted to be very certain about what they put out... They're both the funniest people, and we had such a laugh making that record. Obviously, they are a couple but they're a very good working couple as well. A very solid double act." They also had the chance to get Lindsay involved by playing the tambourine (just back from holiday in Portugal and still disappointed he'd said no to a band that was already looking famous). "It wasn't as simple

---

[25] Oasis recorded some of *What's the Story Morning Glory* (1995) at Orinoco; the Chemical Brothers recorded *Dig Your Own Hole* (1997) there.

as bashing it out—if you're so precise over the snare then the tambourine has to be perfect too."[26]

There was no time left for finessing the album cover. In the end they ad-libbed and took some photos of fossils they'd kept from a long-ago school trip to Lyme Regis. An image that's redolent of Sunday hobbies, the dusty smell of old cardboard boxes and the drawer where unremembered things have been put away, the sadness of coming across neglected, unappreciated things; unwanted gifts and half-read letters. The final look of the LP was an obvious rejection of Eighties gloss: an anti-product made with fanzine lettering and a black and white photo. No band pics and no added marketing.

*

Sarah feels old, watching the new girl go through exactly the same office induction that she had. About the phones, the fax machine, the kitchen, and to "watch out for the man who comes with the sandwiches". Like a foal just learning to walk in her heels and pencil skirt. Was that how she had seemed six months ago? wonders Sarah. Not so dressed up, she'd have been in flats and trousers, but that same keen look. Trying so hard her eyes bulged.

James and fat Nigel are sniffing round the new girl's cubicle, fiddling with their ties and trying to think of reasons to get talking. Her name's Janine and she's pretty, in a skeletal kind of way. With the straightest fringe she's ever seen. James and Nigel were going to be wanking over her for months. Janine has started to take on the job of

---

[26] Lindsay also played percussion on *Blind*. Kevin took on the role on *Static and Silence*.

answering the phones and she's as red as a London bus. They'd make fun of her stuttering over S-s-stanton's for a while, but she'd have her turn to get them back someday. That's just how it worked.

It was ten to four, the time in the afternoon when the hands on the clock stopped moving. An office smog had descended. Strip lights and heating. Coffee breath. Perfume. The smell of second-hand fags on clothes. Printer ink. Sarah only has a dog end of attention left for the pile in her in-tray, so she collects up the mugs and takes them into the kitchen. She stops by James's cubicle, writes 'J ♥ J' on a Post-it note and sticks it on his monitor, next to his postcard of a Ferrari and his Leeds United rosette. Along the way she sees Fraser, his head in a phone book, chewing a biro. Were they really going to move in together? Sometimes she'd ping an elastic band at his head to get his attention, but not today. It felt like they had serious stuff to talk about, and even eye contact would be awkward, too loaded.

Nowhere to go but back to her desk. Phones are ringing everywhere because Janine's retreated to the loo. It's still ten to four and her desk can't get any tidier. Two heads appear: Alison and Smell.

"You doing the office outing?"

"Maybe. Got stuff to do though," says Sarah.

"Dump him, whoever it is."

"Fraser? Face like a ball-sack," adds Smell.

"Tonight, ladies, we've got a date with Patrick and a pottery wheel."

*

Reading, Writing and Arithmetic lives and breathes an older England. It's there in the title: "A nice polite title… We wanted something that sounded quite nice and quite like things that sounded old, not as in Elizabethan with wobbly writing, but slightly retro," said Harriet. "We're very Victorian," explained Dave; then he went further. "You see, we're a reactionary band. It's something we haven't talked about enough." The lyrics are certainly part of an English tradition: reserved, eccentric, flippant—and most of all, they're empirical: opposed to anything that might seem like an abstract idea. There's no story or manifesto, but that doesn't mean the words are meaningless. Dave and Harriet laboured over every line, waiting for just the right words to appear, because they wanted the lyrics to sound 'natural', and natural is always the hardest thing to manufacture. So they relied on a collage of plain, seemingly unimportant memories (like "What's so wrong with reading my stars / When I'll be in the lavatory / And what is so wrong with counting the cars / When I'm all alone"). "Our lyrics are more of a jumble of personal impressions. In the confusion, important feelings get mixed up completely with meaningless garbage." Much like ordinary consciousness then. "They're all about something, about being a person who's alive and around now," explained Harriet in 1990. "They're not about being rock stars, which we aren't, or being lovestruck teenagers, which we aren't. They're just little bits of what feels true." Dave: "going out and coming home, wandering about"; Harriet: "feeling mildly pissed off".

The Sundays wanted to avoid vacuous pop escapism and stay in the day-to-day. To begin with they'd planned to call the album *The Town and its Washing*. It was their taste, their belief in the secret qualities of the ordinary. One of their favourite films from the Bristol days, for example, was Jim Jarmusch's *Stranger than Paradise* (1984), an undramatic, beatnik movie where the camera takes pleasure from lingering over the most mundane pieces of black-and-white scenery. In a similar way, their songs were meant to express the contradictions and ambivalence of everyday life, something beautifully morose: "going out, full of hopes and excitement, and things not turning out that way, but not meaning in the depressing sense, of coming home all sad, but just the idea of the excitement never quite being what you think it might be. The lyrics do revolve around that." In other words, they're describing the passing of innocence. What it feels like to grow up. The sweet sadness of disenchantment. "Most people's lives are static. Hopefully our lyrics reflect that. You've got your ups and downs, but there's this large flaw where nothing in particular is happening. That's the most realistic way of expressing how we experience life."

Both the lyrics and the music are secondary. The mood is everything. "People have this desire to have conclusion, a meaning, and I wonder what the point of that is? The meaning for me is a prevailing mood—what you get off it or what you don't," said Dave, ahead of the album's release in 1989. "If you can get a mood off a record rather than 'I mustn't do this because I've been told by a band not to', I think that's a more lasting sentiment than a statement." Creating a mood is a way of saying unsayable things. So trying to define the mood of the album feels both essential to understanding *Reading, Writing and Arithmetic* and an impossible task. The mood sinks deep inside, fetching up feelings that seem too personal to mean anything to anyone else; that relate to a time and place that only we could know—even though that's obviously not the case. A mood, then, that's rooted in a common dream we've all had. One that feels strangely significant, because of something happy and something important in it that's become blurred and obscure; where the past moves further away and nostalgia comes closer. A memory that's been lost in the past that shouldn't have been, we need it back, if only one more time. And it's not just 'youth' itself, it's not anything that easy. Other cultures have more words for describing melancholy pleasures. In Japanese there's *aware*, what Alan Watts described as "the sense of echoes in the courtyards of the mind after the sun has left and the people have gone their ways forever." Maybe it's something like that. Trying to work it out gets exhausting, it's confusing, dealing with such a delicious and strange kind of sadness. Again, it's a foggy English mood in its lack of definite emotion, in the way its not specifically blue or angry or lovelorn or even simply a case of playing it cool. The mood is made from an English landscape of whites and greys, sombre browns and greens. A thin afternoon light on the roofs of terraced houses, filtered through net curtains. Autumn rain on pavements.

"The mood I feel when I listen to The Sundays," wrote Everett True in a *Melody Maker* feature, "is decidedly Wednesday afternoon at a loose end, wondering where it all went wrong, shuffling back through lightly dusty old photograph albums and hearing that bitter-sweet laughter echoing through the halls again." The feeling includes a nostalgia for that special early Eighties period and for student days. The university life and setting is there in the details, from the cardigan Harriet has been sick on after a student night out, to the typically lazy days ("It's perfectly fine to sleep in a chair / From Monday 'til Saturday"); the little arguments that come with shared houses ("it's hard to get to sleep in my house… I have to pull the blankets up to cover my head", "I won the war in the sitting room"[27]); never having much money ("My finest hour that I've ever known / Was finding a pound on the underground"); and the wicked student humour: "I never should have said, that the books that you read, were all I loved you for."

Early reviewers were distracted by what sounded like a straightforward elegy for the end of innocence. "The Sundays picture a time before sex, before money, before worry… when life could be idyllic, could be pure, naive, and beautiful… The Sundays are that moment just before the knowing, the wisdom, the cynicism of adulthood bursts upon us… That first naive love, that ridiculous, wonderful, ideal-ism." With hindsight, that's not true; the bus has left the sta-tion as far as idealism is concerned, and the lyrics are resol-utely realistic: because their "hopeless youth is really very young / Just really very young." References to young love come with a gently mocking tone: "I keep hoping you are the one for me / I'll send you letters and come to your house for tea." Because there were the tea and cakes, but also those moments in the shed which made them turn red. The alley-ways of memory keep leading to the same conclusion, straight to an acceptance of how things actually are in a grown-up world: maybe desire's a terrible thing, sings Har-riet, "but I rely on mine"; she might have kicked a boy and made him cry, but she knows she was right, "he's such a child"; sometime we have to face up to how "we're just flesh

---

[27] The line is also a reference to the Vietnam War. Media theorist Marshall McLuhan had famously said that TV had taken some brutal truths about the war into people's living rooms, turning public opinion against military action.

and blood"; and "England's as happy as England can be / Why cry?". And when it comes to those episodes of love? "I can't say I really care at the end of it all."

The music press—especially the men—wanted to find something vulnerable there. It was the Harriet factor, that sweet girlish voice combined with something more knowing and indie, someone who'd throw up after a skinful and do it in the shed. The little downmouthed figure of Harriet was both unobtainable and also maybe sort of available—making for the worst kind of torment for a music hack.

That's not to say The Sundays had already made the transition to a more certain or comfortable adulthood. Nothing was easy about leaving home. The world was big and alien and you could get lost: "I went to the circus, Piccadilly Circus / It was very strange"; "Hideous towns make me throw up"; "Never one to roam, I took the first bus home". Those rented places weren't homely ("We lived in a house, in a cold room"), or even menacing ("I would be careful living in a block of flats / And I'd never take the lift to the top").

They're wondering, constantly, what the hell they're going to do with their life. The modern image of success had its allure: "Love, luck and money, they go to my head like wildfire / It's good to have something to live for, you'll find / Live for tomorrow / Live for a job and a perfect behind, high time." But giving yourself to the graduate fast-track and worrying about having a nice bum? Maybe that was a bit shallow. They tried jobs with the Civil Service and even the Salvation Army "but it didn't help". In the end, the Eighties culture of yuppy careerism was an ugly thing, oddly brainless, made for a breed of people who were "beautiful and young, and critical of nothing", who had a "supercilious smile". And a trap. "It's not difficult to see that you're / Young and selfish, but liberty and money don't go": "It's not quite my style / Work and vanity". If a conventional job wasn't right, then there was the option of dropping out of the system entirely. The 'Lone Ranger' of the closing track decides to sell his stuff and become a true Bohemian. "On some days he's more than humble / On some days he's cold and mad, mad as hell", because you can't live on dreams. The charm of having a poetic vision to cling to will dissipate: "Those lakes of golden water / Those lakes of gold are all running out". Maybe it might be okay though, if you have each other to depend on? But that doesn't work in the difficult world of The Sundays either: "So they rode out west to the seaside / And they gladly decided to stay / After two hours wandering outside/ The sea air drove them away… I've been wondering lately / Just who's gonna save me". The lyrics are full of doubts and insecurities like these, but also a youthful petulance, some little outbreaks of arrogance and self-obsession. Streaky with Morrissey-like traits. The 'I' is centre stage, in all the "I know's" and I don't mind's" and "I don't care's"; and the knowing flick of the hair that goes with lines like: "If I could have anything in the world for free / I wouldn't share it with anyone else but me"; "I'm too proud to talk to you anyway"; and "I'd marry you, but I'm so un-well".

It wouldn't be right to focus on the negativity, because the mood, in itself, is saying much more. Harriet said: "I don't know what it does for anyone when they hear it, but I know that every time when I finish the song, it's really made me feel something high." Truth might be severe and disappointing, and ordinary life uninspiring, but wasn't it better to see and feel that reality than become caught up in the striving for a 'showbiz' kind of life? The fake, plastic-coated, MSG-flavoured life. Our ordinary moments, just in themselves, keep on being a kind of poetry, with their flow of bittersweet felicity and consolation. Chris Roberts heard it that very first night The Sundays played the Falcon: "Their grasp of emotion recollected in tranquillity is vital, precious, and, I can only reiterate, believably beautiful." The album was going to be called *Joy* (but the title had been used too often before). Not in recognition of the sports-car-driving, champagne-drinking, promotion-winning joy, but the com-mon, old-fashioned walking-down-the-street joy.

The album was meant to be a swansong for the Eighties, out on the shelves for Christmas shoppers in 1989. The need to co-ordinate with European and worldwide distributors led to a delay until the next year. The *Melody Maker* couldn't wait to shout about it. "Now the band have released their stunning album, *Reading, Writing and Arithmetic* and are ready to set the world on fire… You were jealous, annoyed, *too aware* of a music press's desperate search for a New Big Thing, a group to justify their continued existence. You didn't *believe*. Stupid, stupid you." Maybe because of this enthusiasm from a com-petitor, the *NME* was always ready to be nonplussed about such "trendy buggers".

Harriet and the chaps have aroused an irrational degree of attention by virtue of releasing a refreshing 45, hopping through a handful of gigs and vanishing for the majority of the past year. Easy, eh? So *Reading, Writing and Arithmetic* creeps into the spotlight, blinking nervously with expectations running higher than a quizzical giraffe's eyebrow…. they go back to basics, using simple tools and rudimentary methods with economical, if not Scrooge-like intuition.

"Safe", concluded the *NME*, "a paddle in Morrissey's era of slipper-and-cardigan sorrow (8 out of 10)". With its "middle-class maturity", the most suitable place for The Sundays CD, it added, would be right next to Fleetwood Mac. It wasn't 'indie' enough.

In the US, the album was ready-made for college radio and the soundtrack to the pre-snogging hour of desultory conversation and drinks in student dorm rooms. "*Reading, Writing and Arithmetic* is an alluring slice of lighter-than-air guitar pop," said *Rolling Stone*, "a collection of uncommonly good songs graced by Harriet Wheeler's wondrous singing. While her band mates play with shimmering economy, Wheeler brings an exceptionally expressive voice to bear on the rich melodies and homely lyrics that offer offbeat thoughts about life, love and the English climate." According to the *Chicago Sun-Times* "the insidiously seductive songcraft" of the album "practically re-invents the ABC's of rock", having found a way to make something new out of the interplay of bass, drums, guitar and voice. But an early period of hype can poison attitudes towards bands for ever more (which is why The Sundays had worked so hard to avoid it). The reviewer in *The Times* just knew he wouldn't like it: "The Sundays is one of those insufferably hip groups that pop up from time to time, whose prime function seems to be to provide music journalists with a raison d'être… Their cool, arty poise and predictably jangly guitar sound betrays a host of impeccable (independent) influences, most glaringly the Smiths… and the Cocteau Twins… The songs are self-conscious, soulless artifices."

Dave and Harriet were pleased that Rough Trade (and Geffen in the US) didn't push the album through mainstream channels and sell more copies. "I have a real fear of what that kind of success does to the music," said Dave. "Fame would be more of a hassle than anything else." *Reading, Writing and Arithmetic* still made number four in the UK album charts, 39 in the US (in the wake of lots of MTV and radio airplay for 'Here's Where the Story Ends'), selling around 500,000 copies. To compare, Madonna's (much hated) *Dick Tracy* soundtrack sold seven million that year, George Michael's *Listen Without Prejudice*, eight million. And as an example of what happens when alternative music hits the right spot, Depeche Mode's *Violator* sold 23 million.

*

Nothing about this story suggests The Sundays would allow themselves to become a public commodity on the stock exchange of musical celebrity, with never-ending rounds of writing, recording and tours; turning up on kids' TV, charity specials and *Strictly Come Dancing*. The years of uncertainty about what to do with their life ended in a stronger certainty. The answer had been there all the time: they'd be an ordinary family, with plenty of time at the weekends to sit on the loo and read the paper.

The fears they'd always had about going public with their back-bedroom material were quickly realised: they lost control of the songs, the image and what it all was about. As the lead singer and focus of the photos, the weight of attention was on Harriet, often singled out by the press as the magic ingredient. The strain of touring meant her voice didn't hold up and the big finale of the album tour in London had to be postponed. They were just another Smiths, said the critics. Harriet was a bit Björk, a bit Edie Brickell. Even the *Melody Maker* was now willing to take pot shots.

> On their first-ever US gig, supporting only
> one release, The Sundays are greeted with a
> full house of howling fans… Their subtleties
> are perhaps too subtle, their arrangements
> too similar to fully appreciate one right after
> the other… the cat's meow from a band
> which purrs and mopes far too much…
> mostly it's just accurate—and flat.

The marketing could make them cringe, like the campaign promoting a performance in Dallas, Texas: "See The Sundays on Sunday with ice-cream sundaes!" The business side had always felt shaky and Dave and Harriet had seen things go very wrong at Rough Trade. In 1989 the Christmas party had to be cancelled because of money worries. Rough

Trade had tried to bring in more experienced businesspeople from major labels, adopted more ambitious strategies and expansion schemes—meaning more risks, power games and expensive layers of management—and moved further away from the home-made indie spirit that had been holding operations together under the surface. The distribution arm of Rough Trade went into administration in May 1991 (meaning the 'Here's Where the Story Ends' single wasn't ever released in the UK and *Reading, Writing and Arithmetic* went out of print until 1996). Geoff Travis lost everything: his label, the team of people he'd worked with for a decade, the back catalogue, and even the right to use the Rough Trade name. Geoff and his partner had two small children at the time, and went through a nightmare of worry and insecurity that wouldn't have been lost on Dave and Harriet.[28]

The problems led to delays in The Sundays' plans—they weren't just another product on Rough Trade, they were friends with Geoff and the gang, and they didn't want to rush into anything. Which is why the follow-up, *Blind*, didn't happen until late 1992, after their signing to EMI/Parlophone. Meanwhile the pull towards a more secure and domesticated life was stronger than ever. Billie was born in March 1995 and Frank in June 1999. In-between time they spent some royalties on a 24-track home studio in their spare bedroom, using mattresses to soundproof the room to make

---

[28] Geoff went straight back out to the gig circuit, looking to start again with more unsigned bands.

In Hoxton Hall, Islington, recording the video for 'Here's Where the Story Ends'.
Courtesy of crew member Randee Dawn.[29]

sure the children stayed asleep at night. Arguably, the two
final Sundays albums included more variety and 'better',
more sophisticated songs; they'd been getting into other
kinds of music in those in-between years, like Miles Davis'
Kind of Blue (the pinnacle of mood music), Van Morrison, Al
Green, Frank Sinatra and French film scores; but the songs
didn't have the same deep well of immediate experience,

---

[29] Randee was an intern working with the video makers, standing guard against passers-
by at what was a local community centre. "I was the gopher on the set, getting candy
for the band, generally lifting and carrying and being inconspicuous. The band were
generally shy but over the course of the day let me take a few snaps (and I also may
have taken some surreptitiously)." "I initially introduced myself to David thinking he
was with the production company (called State). My notes say Harriet was sweet and
nice and we were all fascinated with her hair, which was a 'deep shade of burgundy'
and coiled up on the back of her head."

those Bristol feelings, to draw from, and the mood started to lose its melancholy nuance. By the last album there was more of a feel of IKEA furniture and spot lighting involved. And finally, having Billie on the bus with her Winnie-the-Pooh cassette tapes for the *Static and Silence* tour, put everything into perspective.

The history books of indie haven't been that fair or considered: The Sundays "felt like a band that had been focus-grouped to try to fill the vacuum left and prove that Rough Trade could still break bands into the Top Forty," claimed Richard King in *How Soon is Now: The Madmen and Mavericks who made Independent Music 1975–2005*. Having such a short-lived career can look like a verdict on the quality and contribution of a band. At the same time, disappearing into the thin air of normality has made The Sundays legendary.[30] Fans love them even more for their absence, and for the mystery of what could have been.

We shouldn't forget the rest of the band in this. Paul was philosophical about his role—he'd played great songs with a great band, been part of something big, and moved on to make a career sharing knowledge and thinking with the music industry.[31] Patch had wanted to stay on the road.

---

[30] Dave and Harriet have declined interviews since the *Static and Silence* period and kept away from social media. The exception is one, unremarkable email exchange with the American Airlines magazine *American Way* in April 2014. That same year, David Baddiel told BBC Radio 6Music the couple had never stopped making music, but "they're the most paranoid people about actually putting stuff out there." In a 2020 interview, Patch revealed that he'd been asked to play drums on a number of Sundays recordings that probably wouldn't be released. A WhatsApp group was set up between the band members to mark the 30th anniversary of the first album.

[31] Paul Brindley is the co-founder and CEO of Music Ally, a company providing insight reports, events and training to music labels of all sizes on how to make best commercial use of digital platforms and marketing.

As a drummer he'd relied on the income from touring and the decision to take an indefinite break was "terrifying, sad". He was only 28 and had a young family at home to support.[32]

The most surprising moment of The Sundays' story came at the very beginning, in the way student songs arrived in such a fully formed, mature and pristine state; songs that seem less attached to a particular period of time than a shared memory. A reviewer who attended the early gig at The Boston Arms in September 1988 put it like this: "Creation survives in fragments under the ruins of a world for which we can no longer find expression. The Sundays have quarried these fragments and fashioned them into something larger than life: a shape that fills the void with warm, spiked silhouettes." One explanation would be that The Sundays were a smart distillation of British indie, made from a seasoned tradition of songwriting and guitar music: a late flowering of the early Eighties' genius. The unhurried pace of the writing meant the alchemy could happen in an unself-conscious and unforced way. As Dave has said, in straightforward Sundays fashion: "Everything sort of went into the pot with us."

*

The Sundays came and went for the best of reasons. They had always been on a separate course from modern pop cul-

---

[32] Patch had been part of the band Star 69 while he was waiting for the next Sundays work, then went on to do sessions and gigs with Robyn Hitchcock, Arnold and then Kimberley Rew of Katrina and the Waves, before becoming part of theaudience with Sophie Ellis-Bextor.

ture and its obsession with image-making, its dream of people living their best lives. They skirted pop and disappeared back into the ordinary, where actual joy lives; in this moment and that moment, anywhere and everywhere, when you least expect it. Far less often in what has to be bought and manufactured.

Trouble is, you can't change anything by fading away. Sometimes the sense of injustice, the hatred inside, gets too much.

2.

"Got a trampoline: your fucking head."

The Fatima Mansions, *Viva Dead Ponies* (April 1990)

*T*hink of all the indie singer/songwriters who didn't survive the Eighties, who ended up in a bonfire of hope and invention and remaindered stock. Some kept going by limping round the local venues; some embraced pop so they could live up to record label expectations.[1] Only one turned Evil.

It shouldn't have been that way. With Microdisney, Virgin Records had gorgeous melodies and a special crooner loved by John Peel. Microdisney should have been subverting the whole rotten business with their combination of listenability and waspish lyrics. But this was Cathal Coughlan. And

---

[1] Like Scritti Politti, who ditched the bedsit Communism of 'Skank Bloc Bologna' for ultra-pop; Roddy Frame went looking for a glossy coat of American production and session musicianship; Primal Scream changed identity to fit into the dance scene etc.

in Cathal's Microdisney performances there were phosphor flickers of a gathering storm, in that careless meatball figure, his draggled quiff and hair-trigger eyes, hunched over the mic like he was being screwed deeper and deeper into a clenched intensity, his legs jumping and jerking. By the time he formed The Fatima Mansions, Cathal was a different man. Like someone who'd been through Hell and reached a place of eerie calm. A vigilante in a black T-shirt staring directly back into the TV cameras, his eyes growing small, round as pennies, receding into a darkening brow. A case of possession by fury. And what could be more counter-cultural in 1989 than a demonstration of real anger? The Second Summer of Love was a time for blissing out. All-night raves and cheap Ecstasy, holding hands with strangers and wearing smiley-face badges and bandannas. Because we were all daft capitalists by then.

Instead, Cathal's Mansions vowed they would 'Keep Music Evil'. There'd been a prominent campaign across music venues to 'Keep Music Live'. Stickers were being given out in strips and left dotted everywhere, in foyers, up stairways, on seating and all round the toilets. The Mansions' Grimmo[2] had one on his guitar and it was devilishly easy work to reverse the letters for a T-shirt slogan—one of a series that helped express what the new band was really about: like 'Fuck Your Show Business' (devised by their manager, Keith Armstrong of Kitchenware); 'Raggle Taggle? Nein Danke' (a dig at the Irish folk-revival);[3] and one that

---

[2] Lead guitarist Aindrías Ó'Grúama was originally part of Irish band Zerra One (think epic, melodic rock, they were compared with U2 and Simple Minds).

[3] When city folk flirted with a romanticised version of Irish gypsy life, a phenomenon that was later epitomised by Mumford & Sons at 'Glasto'.

could only have been Cathal's work: 'Portillo and Lilley's Fisting and Pissing Parlour PLC (formerly known as Britain)', with a helpful infographic.[4]

It wasn't just T-shirt talk or Gordon Ramsay-style branding, the Evil—such as it was—was going to be put into practice. Like when Cathal and Grimmo visited Ireland's holy shrine of Knock[5] (cheekily kissing the runway tarmac as they stepped off their Ryanair flight from Luton), handed out condoms and swung on statues of the Virgin Mary. "Don't shag!" called out Cathal to the dark spaces of the Basilica (quietly, there were nuns around). Then the unauthorised performance that blocked the entrance to HMV in Henry Street in Dublin. When the police arrived, Cathal launched into his cop-killing anthem 'Angel's Delight' (*"Got a word for you: dead…"*). And the greatest Evil of them all, the U2 concert of 22 May 1992, when the Mansions used their appearance at the rock event of the year to scandalise the world's population of one billion Catholics. The Zoo TV tour was big business. In the US alone it sold 5.3 million tickets and made $151 million. It was stadium rock up-cycled to justify the premium ticket prices needed for A-list artists and Brian Eno's art installation look and feel, for the banks of flickering TV screens and Communist-era Trabant cars used as spotlights; the live satellite link-ups with Sarajevo; the

---

[4] Rumours were circulating at the time that Michael Portillo (the minister put in charge of implementing the Poll Tax) and Peter Lilley (Secretary of State for Trade and Industry) were having an affair.

[5] Knock became a major shrine in 1879 after the apparition of Mary, St Joseph, St John and Christ as the 'Lamb of God'. Knock's reputation as a holy site was confirmed by a series of 'miracle cures', including blindness, Multiple Sclerosis and deafness (when an ear made contact with a piece of cement from the shrine's gable wall). In 2018, 45,000 people booked tickets to be present at Pope Francis's visit to Knock.

fireworks, belly dancing and theatrical costume changes. The support acts were chosen for their alt-rock cred, like the Sugarcubes, Pixies and PJ Harvey—and it was the Edge who thought the lads from the Mansions would be a good addition. But things didn't start well. "The tour manager and sound engineer for The Fatima Mansions was the same person," explained Keith Armstrong. "He had a heart attack when we were in Paris, so the first thing we needed to do was ask the U2 people whether we could use their sound guy. It's the cardinal sin of touring—but they were brilliant, they gave us everything." On the first night at the Forum di Assago, a sports arena in the suburbs of Milan, the Mansions faced the usual support band abuse, some booing and heckling from 12,000 U2 fans. Cathal lost a crown from one of his teeth and had to combine his usual roaring and gnashing performance with keeping an eye on where it had dropped and been kicked around. The signs of a herd mentality—in the football shirts, the pop-Catholicism and the submission to sing-a-long jingles—was a red rag to Cathal, especially given his state of mind: "I was abusing every substance I could find, whatever was available, mainly alcohol. They nearly had a hospitalisation on their hands a few times during the Zoo TV tour. It was all self-inflicted but I just didn't care." On the second night, the Mansions were ready. Grimmo wore a Barcelona FC shirt—the team that had beaten Sampdoria (and Italy's beloved Gianluca Vialli) in a niggardly European Cup Final two days earlier. Cathal came on and made an announcement: "I'd like to thank the Vatican for destroying my home country." Then he pretended to stick a Virgin Mary-shaped shampoo bottle up his arse, shouting: "FUCK your traitor Pope." Now that's blasphemy.

The arena exploded in rage and confusion and the Mansions were pelted with cigarette lighters and lira coins. "We thought we'd get kicked off the tour," said Keith, "but Bono said it was the most exciting thing he'd ever seen." "If U2 represent God's country," said *Rolling Stone,* "then The Fatima Mansions must surely dwell in that country's Hell."

Cathal backstage after the 'Battle of Milan' (with the shampoo bottle).
Courtesy of Hugh Bunker.

And yet, everyone who knew Cathal would say the same thing about him. He was the kindest of men. Polite, thoughtful, genuine. When he was writing the liner notes to *Viva Dead Ponies*, he didn't conclude with 'Keep Music Evil' but 'Keep Music Evil, please'. Much more him. "A very quiet guy 'off the pitch'. Really quiet," Keith said. "He liked a beer in the pub, where he'd talk to you forever about politics, poetry, writers, music. He'd be passing on info about who to listen to—like American Music Club, say, who we both liked." A collaborator, the producer Jacknife Lee had been expecting a "ball of rage".

> Fatima Mansions was just fucking intense. I saw them a few times, loved them, but it was so intense. He was the complete opposite— very gentle, very, very funny, generous and caring. I would be cavalier about upsetting people, not asking people for permission to use video, and Cathal would always say 'we have to ask them, make sure no one is upset'. He was so sensitive to other people's feelings, which I wasn't expecting.

The people who lived their days and nights with him felt the same. "Cathal was just a nice person to be around," according to bass player and Milan survivor Hugh Bunker. "On stage he seemed to transform into someone else, this demon character." But it wasn't performance art, or the consequence of some kind of divided personality, it was all the same Cathal. "You could always see the performer in the man," confirmed Victor Van Vugt, producer for the Mansions (best known for his work with Nick Cave, PJ Harvey and Beth Orton).[6] "He was a gentleman and a scholar of course, but he definitely had an edge. Cathal had those

---

[6] Victor worked on *Bertie's Brochures* (1991), *Valhalla Avenue* (1992) and *Lost in the Former West* (1994). His production credits include Nick Cave's *Murder Ballads* (1996), PJ Harvey's *Stories from the City, Stories from the Sea* (2001), Beth Orton's *Central Reservation* (1999) and Athlete's *Vehicles and Animals* (2003). More recently he produced *Inferno* (2019) for Robert Forster.

strong political opinions, so he'd let rip on stage and wouldn't mince his words off it." Anyway, maybe it's the consistency in public personas we should be wary of—the easy smile and blameless demeanour—and not the seemingly contrary jumble of Good and Evil. "You'd never meet a more intense person than Cathal. It was always a genuine performance with him, it came from the gut," added Keith.

There was something boyish and vulnerable about him, even in the demonic Fatima Mansions days. It was there in his slow and deliberate way of speaking, flavoured by a south-country Irish accent. A sea-green brogue made for speaking Gaelic rather than the foreigners' English. And the way he answered questions, fetching up thoughtful observations on the state of the world like they were heavy, heavy stones; knowing truth was a difficult thing, and he might not be understood, not the way he wanted to be. The demon Cathal was spawned from the clashes between an unusual sensitivity and an unusual intelligence that made him unruly and restless. The tension was a burden he carried, and, for mysterious reasons, he seemed to want to carry. Whatever the consequences.

*

Graduation was traditionally meant to be the end of an education. The beginning of a life-long vocation. The Eighties broke up every fusty assumption about careers and what was appropriate for the 'educated'. An economy didn't want the slow and considered application of knowledge and experience; goods and services just needed to be kept moving as fast as possible. There needed to be a mobile workforce, supplies of finance, a spark of entrepreneurship, and management that would muster skills and motivation. By 1990, the idea of a career had been overtaken by a much larger and vaguer belief in the search for 'opportunity'. There was an open jobs market, not single ladders meant for particular types of people. The reality was that a privileged background and networks were still what mattered most in making a successful career, but the image, the myth, was of Britain's new meritocracy.

Enter John Major. A Prime Minister perfectly suited to the time, careful to avoid any of the unnecessary noise of the Thatcher era and quietly manoeuvring the party around meaningless phrases like 'compassionate Conservatism'. A manager in a grey suit: "his greyness is part of his skill in reaching the top," wrote commentator Anthony Sampson in 1992, "offending no-one, keeping options open." Tory MP Edwina Currie acknowledged how the role of Government had changed in a diary entry in 1991: "We are not slaying dragons anymore, just cleaning up the shit they left behind." Labour's Shadow Chancellor John Smith, meanwhile, had been sent out on his 'prawn cocktail offensive' to persuade senior figures in the financial services sector that Labour could be trusted to look after their interests. The party had made sure the word 'socialism' wasn't mentioned in its latest manifesto, and Major didn't like the way Labour were muscling onto his patch. Blandness was his territory, and he could see the danger of a New Labour party that didn't need to stick to any of its old principles of tax-and-spend and supporting the working-classes.

The decline in political debate went unnoticed. The left-leaning *Guardian* had been publishing an average of 300-700 lines on politics before 1988; by 1992 it was below 100 a day. In an effort to generate more public interest in political debates, the House of Commons was opened up to TV cameras, but viewing figures were minuscule (except in the US and Europe, where the transmissions had gained a following as a kind of sitcom). The recession of the early Nineties was met with feelings of resignation rather than a sense of wrong and the protests and resistance to redundancies that would have happened in the past. Well. What could you do? A downturn in the economy was like a spell of cold weather.

An unlikely political consensus was formed inside Parliament around the idea of a classless nation. Class conflict, like political ideology and union activism, was so much dust and gunk in the economic machine. Believing in a classless society was an essential part of the new national psyche—an evolution of the Thatcherist concept that there is no such thing as society—meaning that everyone needed to take personal responsibility for their success or otherwise. Your situation had nothing to do with social background, because you'd played the same game as everyone else. So the Minister for Housing could appear on Radio 4's *Today* programme in 1991 and say, without any cloud of conscience, that the homeless were "the people you step over when you come out of the opera". Because he didn't see himself as denigrating a lower class or admitting the existence of a social problem, he was talking about those who had simply failed at the game of life. There was a full-blown campaign to lodge the notion into British consciousness. John Major used his first speech as PM to set out a vision for a classless society and the "changes necessary to provide a better quality of life for all our citizens." Like the slogan of 'Education, Education, Education', it was a wonderfully sly principle for politicians to attach themselves to. No-one would argue against it; and it didn't matter if it was based on lies. By 1996, Tony Blair was able to be bolder and more explicit: "our task is to allow more people to become middle class." Even Prince Edward was getting involved. "We are forever being told we have a rigid class structure. That's a load of codswallop," he said. "In many cases there are more opportunities to do just about anything you want." In 1998, the New Labour government declared the UK was officially middle class, and they were going to scrap the use of outdated social classifications.[7]

In fact, income inequality had reached record highs in 1990—the result of a decade of policies designed to avoid re-distribution of wealth—and now that situation was going to be shored up with the story that class war had ended. There was no need to make a fuss about inequalities anymore, everyone had a washing machine and a TV and a whole skinful of opportunity.[8] But the classless society was just a convenient phrase, said Andrew Adonis, an education

---

[7] *Financial Times*' education correspondent Chris Cook regularly published articles that upset New Labour and Alistair Campbell. They showed how New Labour's 'Education, Education, Education' mantra—and the relentless initiatives, the super-teachers, the super-heads—were wrongheaded. His data (and much other research) all led to the same conclusion, that social background kept on determining exam results, nothing much else. Governments have known this for decades: if you really want to create a cycle of improved education standards and a better society, close the income inequality gap and pay people on low incomes a lot more. Chris Cook, by the way, lost his job on education.

[8] Cathal saw the deceit involved, as per: "A holiday in a box. Opportunity knocks."

and public policy journalist, in his book *A Class Act—the Myth of Classless Britain* (1997): "a clever ruse to discredit the notion of class divisions without actually denying their existence".[9] Rather than a levelling of society, Adonis argued, the Nineties had seen a new élite pull away. A 'Super Class' had been formed from the money generated by financial services and its related professions, made up of professional couples who were then breeding 'super families' by making the most of a selective education system.

The 'best' graduates weren't interested in careers in the public sector anymore, the top choices were law, banking, accountancy and management consultancy. Because of the super-sized salaries. In 1985, Sir John of Barings Bank earned £293,920. By 1993, his son Peter was earning £1.3 million doing the same job. The Super Class was also looking for power in Parliament. In 1999 only 13 per cent of Labour MPs were from skilled labour backgrounds. They were businesspeople and barristers instead. The reality of the Nineties was a small group getting richer at one end, a great bulge of 'classless' workers sweating in the middle, and an under-class who'd given up. In his book, Adonis pointed to the "ghettoisation of council estates". Around 1.6 million council houses had become privately-owned properties between 1980 and 1995, and of the remaining occupants of council houses and social housing schemes, 80 per cent were relying on welfare benefits. They were the long-term unemployed, single parents, long-term sick, disabled, and over 60s.

---

[9] After the publication of his book, Adonis was recruited to join the Number 10 Policy Unit (so they could make sure he was inside the tent pissing out), and he later became a New Labour cabinet minister.

Unwanted people (unreliable consumers), left behind in towns and estates only ever remembered for being shit. Few family roots and ties anymore, no community, and no shops or businesses that actually wanted to be there. Parents struggling to control children. Youth Training Scheme jobs that paid less than dole money. Crime and drugs for entertainment.

*

The extinction of political ideas was one void among many. The war over hearts and minds had been won in the Eighties and now there was an inevitable sense of a slump: the End of History wasn't going to be exciting, when there wasn't much sense of any conflict, a bigger purpose or meaning anymore. The saviour for many people was business and work, and the potential for joining the Super Class. Doing business became more than an occupation or just a science, it was a lifestyle, a look, an obsession. Even a religion. In Bill Forsyth's film *Local Hero* (1983), oil company man Mac gets called in to see the boss. He climbs to the top floor like it's a stairway to heaven, holding his breath as he rises to a place where the lighting and carpets are softer, there's art on the walls and soothing celestial music.

It was an unlikely turnaround. For the whole of human history until then, commerce had been considered small-time at best, an occupation suited to the low-minded, the devious and money-grubbing. In the medieval cultures of the West, the merchants were put into a class beneath that of peasants; and as recently as the Seventies, the stereotype of a businessman was a pompous gent with a military background or an untrustworthy weasel. But then management theory moved on from dull rational models to centre around the idea of the heroic leader, someone with charisma and flair, flushed with animal instincts. Like Sir James Goldsmith, the entrepreneur who relished his image as a predator in the business jungle, pouncing on vulnerable businesses he could shake up and strip out. Suddenly, business was feeling kind of sexy. By 1987, *Wall Street*'s Gordon Gecko was acceptable as a brazen anti-hero with his motto "greed is good". The American management gurus were evangelists whipping up a fire of enthusiasm for giving 1000%. Your soul wouldn't be saved, but instead you'd have a three-storey Edwardian place in a good part of town, private schooling for the kids and a pad in Cornwall for the weekends. Tom Peters' *In Search Of Excellence* (1982) was the Old Testament for this new era of business, with its focus on the role of people and passion and organisational culture in achieving business success. Stephen Covey's advice on how to maximise your personal perform-ance in *The Seven Habits of Highly Effective People* (1989) sold more than 20 million copies—the New Testament. The management gurus were sought after celebrity performers, touring the globe as the High Priests of personal transforma-tion. By the early Nineties, Peters was charging $80,000 per seminar.

Creaky British institutions—the universities, the NHS, the civil service, local government—wanted to act more like businesses and were familiar with the language of manage-ment: the need for re-engineering, performance targets and attention to the bottom line. An old working-class sport like football, plagued by hooliganism, was reinvented as (classless) family fun by satellite TV and a £250 million deal to create the Premier League. Public ownership of anything was looking tediously inflexible and inefficient. In the years between 1987 and 1997, Britain sold off British Steel, British Petroleum, Rolls Royce, British Airways, British Rail, British Coal, Powergen, National Power and the regional water boards— leading to some monumental pay increases for the new business leaders: a 250 per cent rise for the CEO of Powergen in the first two years; 75 per cent for the boss of British Gas (who then laid off 5,000 workers). British Telecom's Iain Vallance sacked 100,000 staff when he was first appointed and awarded himself an extra £50,000 a year. Untouched by the revolution of the early Eighties, even the Royal Family had to start thinking like a big business, turning to market research and a new PR strategy to counter a collapse in the Firm's image. A plan which could be summarised as a focus on the Queen and her long service; making a conciliatory gesture by finally offering to pay some tax; and, only letting the Duke of Edinburgh speak in public when there was a script (for Christ's sake). No longer would Prince Charles be ringing up his old pal Jimmy Saville for advice on what to say to the media to sound appropriately sympathetic, as he had after the Lockerbie plane crash in 1988.

Work had become very different for twenty-somethings. It was now an environment of taut management thinking, performance-driven, fraught and tenuous. Employees were 'empowered' to take on more duties and responsibility (shifted off the desks of senior management), while the highest ranking executives became remote and untouchable. As Cathal put it: "you command me from the depths of gin, to walk the tightrope in a gale force wind." But why would you not do as you were told? Organisations were relentlessly impressive. Their offices were places of modernity, even luxury, with their great boxes of technology you wouldn't have at home, their blinking walls of servers, rooms of photocopiers and fax machines, their air conditioning and professional letterheads and business cards. The clean, natureless magic of revolving doors and marble pillars. It was the place you dressed up for. Work didn't only mean a nine-to-five routine and wages at the end of the week, it provided identity and status, a high stakes psychological contract. Unlike a politician who could never be believed, you didn't argue with the boss—because this was business, nothing to do with anything other than the irrefutable truths of profit and loss. Computerisation was meant to reduce working hours, but many employees wanted those long hours, they wanted their fix of pressure and recognition and rewards. It was cool to be in back-to-back meetings, working late and only thinking business. In 1993, in spite of the introduction of so much labour-saving technology, the Harvard economist Juliet Schor estimated the average American was working 163 hours a year longer than they had twenty years' earlier.

This was the world of meritocracy and opportunity. New recruits saw the glamour of the employer brands and were drawn inside, soon to feel the hard edges that came with it. The cold, pressing weight of a relentless machinery.

*

Our five knew the places behind the moon, where all hope was gone. Knew them well. The dole money and dog-end jobs. Each of the bands was named after out-of-the-way corners of life that would be more familiar to the underclass than Nineties whizz-kids. Empty days, blighted housing estates, building fungus, corporate exploitation and rubbish bins. While the *Like Magic* era was about making use of major record labels for their own ends, trying to keep hold of indie credibility when they could, now there was disgust for anything that treated music as just another commodity. "There has to be something better than just being regarded as a crap version of Ronan Keating," argued Cathal, "the idea that everybody who's making music must be judged solely on his or her commercial success, which has become very prevalent." Asked to list reasons for suicide in an *NME* Q&A, Cathal included "Stock Aitken Waterman (the Leni Riefenstahls of Britain's Era of Enterprise)".[10] The Mansions, he explained, "had a philosophy of: if that looks like the right thing to do, let's do the opposite." They had been fortunate to fall under the enlightened management of Kitchenware, the problems started when Cathal signed to US label Radioactive. "The whole philosophy of the way they do business is completely different. Everyone has to seem enthusiastic all the time," said Cathal in 1994. "It's not enough to be personable with someone and let them know, in whatever way, that this isn't necessarily what you'd like to be doing. Nobody ever does that in America, so you never know where the fuck you stand. It's just bullshit, bullshit, bullshit." For Peter Milton Walsh, "the record industry had become a soulless monster, only driven by money, profit, not

---

[10] Leni Riefenstahl was the Nazi propaganda film-maker who wooed the German masses with the stirring, soft focus romanticism of works like *The Triumph of the Will* (1935).

by music, incapable of loving," he said. "Whereas the world, for its part, has a soul." Trashcan Sinatras turned down a Duran Duran support slot in the US when 'Ordinary World' was number one in the Billboard charts; plans to give 'Send for Henny' a radio-friendly baggy beat were rejected: "Kate Bush had '50 Words for Snow'. We had 50 words for 'no'."; "we said no to a lot of things that could have really helped our career; like doing television shows," said guitarist Paul Livingston. "It would've been nice to be really successful, but in retrospect I think that if we'd done them and had reasonable success in the Nineties we probably wouldn't be together now." Paddy McAloon was protected to an extent, by Kitchenware, and the awe of industry suits who knew they had someone special on their hands. "Paddy is in touch with the aspect that's been largely missing from pop music in the last 10 or 15 years," Thomas Dolby told *Rolling Stone* in 1991. "It's that part that doesn't have to do with moving product and selling your image, the part that has to do with real risk and adventure." The Sundays made the ultimate protest against the music industry by losing interest in it. They'd only ever wanted to avoid proper jobs anyway. They'd written the songs "largely through a fear of not wanting to sit down in the same room all day," suggested Harriet. "I never wanted to be in a band when I was younger, like many kids do," added Dave. "It just dawned on me gradually; 'Well fuck, I want to do something I like doing. What do I like doing? I might as well write songs'."

*

In a weary, mistrustful world where Americans were brash, the Russians were sinister, the French were pretentious and English yobs had bad teeth, everyone loved the Irish. It was a sea-washed island of fiddle music, folk dancing and plenty of places to drink. To the big nations of jaded consumers the people of Ireland were appealingly simple-hearted and happy with their lot, and if the towns in those wet emerald fields had a neglected look to them, that was all part of their charm. By the mid-Eighties, the financiers and speculators saw something even better about Ireland: a broken economy with cheap, under-developed land and industries. It was old-style Britain with a young population. Cathal himself, speaking in 1988, could see what was coming. Ireland was stuck in the past, he agreed, "but you do have these bastards there who are trying to create the same atmosphere as you have over here [in London]—you get these stockbrokers appearing on TV talking about share-ownership at a time when you have vast unemployment in the rest of the country. It's even more of a nonsense than in England. And they're talking about privatising the buses as well—I mean, nobody would get two bob for the Irish bus service. It's practically non-existent already!"

The Irish government started to follow the British model of putting business first. There was a new preferential tax rate of 10 per cent on corporate profits on exports (slashed from 50 per cent), along with cuts in public spending and a push on wage restraint to keep inflation (and labour costs) down. Investment went into Higher Education to build a skills base for the knowledge economy, and by 1995, 27 per cent of Ireland's 25 to 24 year-olds had a degree qualification (above the 23 per cent average among the 38 countries of the Organisation for Economic Co-operation and Development). The State also set up the International Financial Services Centre (IFSC). This offered banks and insurance and accounting firms a bundle of tax breaks and a base to run tax avoidance schemes,[11] in return for re-locating into Dublin's docklands. Ireland was suddenly attractive to global firms as a cheap, English-speaking base. US pharmaceutical firms and other high-tech multinationals piled in, and an additional 513,000 jobs were created between 1986 and 1999. Travelling through the land of the Celtic Tiger in 2000, Anne Marie Hourihane saw how the country had changed over the preceding decade. "Out of eight houses that are occupied on the left-hand side of the cul-de-sac we count four jeeps, one Jaguar and one Porsche… As you look around the development, the Japanese-style pond, at the yellow apartments with palms, at the top balconies, you wonder where you are. It could be a holiday village in Southern Spain or perhaps Florida, rather than a housing estate in South Dublin."

There was more wealth—but as other countries around the world would testify, unhappiness doesn't come from being poor, but feeling poor by comparison with the other people around you. In 1997, United Nations data suggested Ireland's population had become the most unequal of Western countries: the richest 10 per cent were 11 times wealthier than the poorest, and had the second largest proportion of people living in poverty in the West after the US. Water trickles down, money doesn't. Public spending in Ire-

---

[11] A University of Amsterdam study in 2017 claimed the Irish financial centre was one of the world's biggest 'conduits' for helping big business avoid paying taxes.

land was in decline and the infrastructure of housing and transport was being left to rot; racism towards migrants and alcoholism was on the rise—along with the suicide rate (between the Seventies and 2000, the rate of suicide among older Irish men doubled).

Communities of people were being left behind and forgotten. People in places like the Fatima Mansions, a housing estate in Dublin. Built in 1949 as a modern development to replace inner-city slums, the Mansions became the city's circle of Hell, used by the Irish press for head-shaking stories about all that was wrong with the city. In 1987, 75 per cent of its working-age residents were unemployed (and 100 per cent of 18 to 21-year-olds). The complex of concrete stairways, rat runs and balconies—designed with all the flair of a multi-storey car park—had been turned into a heroin supermarket. A malevolent adventure playground for criminal gangs that was ideal for secret meetings, hiding gear, dumping stolen cars, violent attacks and a quick exit. The Mansions were also a warren of rotten doors and window latches that meant easy access into anywhere, anytime. Burglaries, especially in the homes of older residents, were commonplace, and even old clothes hanging from the washing lines strung across the public spaces were stolen and sold for cash. Children would often be found playing with heroin needles left in stairwells.

Fatima Mansions was also a home to people who'd been there for decades. They loved the place—families were known to move away because of the drug gangs but then want to move back. Some members of the Garda might be well-known and liked among the locals, but they'd keep away from the Mansions and its 'herd' of pushers and addicts with their guns and knives. In the late Eighties there was a campaign among residents to bring about change themselves—if the council wasn't going to do anything—and they set up cooperative enterprises, sports and social clubs and created new play areas for children. But they couldn't hold back the tide, especially not in the later Nineties when a crackdown on drugs in central Dublin forced the dealers back into Fatima. The residents of Fatima Mansions gave their support to the demolition of the estate in 2003, but only in return for a promise that the site would be used for affordable housing, a community centre, sports facilities and a social regeneration plan. The developer built 150 public housing 'units', 70 homes for first-time buyers (initially priced at between €170,000 and €200,000, around £250,000 in today's money); and 360 homes (each costing more than €400,000, £540,000 now). The new area of 'Herberton'—bearing the obvious signs of cheap and boxy utility development—was opened by the Irish President in 2009. The poverty and drug use around the area remains.

Cathal was in a hurry when he chose the Mansions name, and there were regrets later. He didn't want anyone to think he was taking the mick out of the place or the people who lived there. But the name works as a wormhole into thinking about the state of Ireland. Just in the way the city authorities had used the aggrandising (and silly) word 'Mansions', and how they wanted to impose an edifying connection to Catholic legend. Fátima is a village in central Portugal, named after a 12th century princess, a Moor. Famously, three children were visited by the Virgin Mary while they were out in the fields watching over the sheep during the years of the Great War. Mary appeared as a figure made of light, hovering above an oak tree, and told them there would be peace on earth if they spread the message of the importance of prayer, instructing them to return to the same place at the same time on the 13th day for the next five months. The Virgin kept her appointments in the village field—along with a growing number of bystanders, who couldn't see anything but reported there had been a humming tension in the air—to share what became known as the 'three secrets of Fátima'. Lúcia, one of the three children, saved the secrets for her memoirs, published in the 1940s. Mary's first secret was that Hell was a real place where souls were burning in a sea of fire at the centre of the earth (in other words, for all your modern ideas, you're not getting away with it sinners!); the second, more prosaically, was that there would be another world war. The third secret was held back until 2000 when her two cousins were beatified (their entrance to Heaven confirmed). This was that Christians would be persecuted, there would be an attempt on the life of 'a Bishop dressed in white'—which was taken as a premonition of the shooting of Pope John Paul II in 1981 (on the 13th of May).

The Fatima Mansions estate was a place of violent contradictions, an estate of nightmares that had a statue of Mary, 'Our Lady of Fatima', as its centrepiece. As an image it fits perfectly into Cathal's blackened vision of an absurd modern world, where people were excluded, kept low and kidded by myths, old and new. He wasn't just born into a musical land, made for words and song, the rage came first.

*

We've come to another estuary, another harbourside city. Cork at the end of the Seventies. Take in a good sniff of the air and you'll get a nostril full of harbour smells, the diesel oil and rank fishing boats. Ocean country. A city breathing river and sea, facing the winds and the rolling weather, the sudden bursts of sun, reams of purple clouds and their squalls of showers. Looking inland, you'll see the lime-green hills and a horizon of smoky chimneys burning 'slack', the coal dust that would keep the fires going longer. More smells, sour and sooty mixed with the sweetish aromas come from the Beamish stout brewery.

The city, Ireland's second largest, still had the character of an old port then, with its warehouse-fronted harbour and nests of streets, some of them seedy. But walking down the main avenue of St Patrick's Street you'll see what a grand old place it was. There's a boulevard of fine buildings, including the plush emporium of the Roches department store. Roches was the best place to meet—especially for first dates, because no-one would ever miss its palatial frontage and copper-coloured dome, turned green with the sea air. A magically-pale verdigris green. The tourists would come to Cork for Blarney Castle and its kissing stone, like it was just a place for history, but it was clear Cork was catching up. There were modern jobs now that would do you for life: at the Dunlop factory where they made shoes, tennis balls and golf balls, or over at the Verolme dockyard. You worked hard and they looked after you. With proper money in your pocket you could take the family to the new fast food place, Burgerland. There were three cinemas, the Cameo, the Ritz, the

Capitol; and like the most cultured cities in Europe it had its own jazz festival. The Ford car factory was better than any of them. Because once you were taken on by Ford you were one of the family, you had your hot meals in the canteen and spent evenings at the company's social club where the drinks were cheap. Ford belonged to Cork, that's what folk always said, with maybe just one little branch over the waves in America.

We do the usual. Wander round the English Market and then go to the Green Door café in Academy Street for a cup of sugary tea and a Connie Dodger, a giant biscuit covered in chocolate that comes with the added satisfaction of getting one over the priests.[12] The dry shites. There's a copy of the paper, the *Cork Examiner*, left on a table for us to read. Something cosy about the look of its old Gothic masthead and raw inky smell. Lots of news about hurling as well as the two teams the city had in the football league: Cork United and Cork Celtic. Then the stuff about income taxes being too high again, another referendum on divorce coming up, and those doings of government. The man at the top, the Taoiseach himself, was a Cork man, which meant he could be a pig-headed bastard if the occasion warranted, if the necessity arose. We get to daydreaming rather than read-ing, thinking about wet and windy Cork; such a fine place to be living now it was on the move and getting its share of the world's wealth and progress. And wouldn't it be the berries to find a new place for ourselves and the family, not in the

---

[12] Named after the local Bishop Cornelius Lucey and his efforts to enforce the rules of Lent—no sweets, no cakes, no parties, no dancing. You were allowed a biscuit with your cup of tea though, leading to the creation of the Connie Dodger, a fat biscuit about the same size as the plate you put it on.

dirty old city, but one of those new bungalows in a village facing the sea?

There had been plenty of development at Glounthaune, the home of the Coughlans on the shore of one of Cork harbour's many inlets. The village was a scattered thing. Really only a slope of fields leading down to the railway line and the water, a sparse kind of place made up of lanes with low stone walls and tunnels through the trees, weedy corners and scattered houses; many of them with views out over the estuary, all grey river and sky. In those days, Glounthaune was a rural outpost, where the locals themselves weren't especially wealthy, only the in-comers who'd bought property further up the hill could be called that. There weren't many career options outside of the docks and the factories, but the Coughlans had a foothold in the professions. Eleanor was a primary schoolteacher and Paddy a modestly-ranked civil servant. Paddy was also a fixture at 'the Field', the Highfield Rugby Football club in Cork where he'd watch the first team play and coach the junior teams. They had three boys at home, Cathal, Pat and Denis. The village the boys grew up in was more sombre and lonely than idyllic, a place where "seagulls shriek 'til hoarse through the empty ferry port."[13] The mood of Glounthaune seeped over Cathal like he was a sheet of photographic paper: "the place where you first see the light of day leaves its imprint on the way you see daylight for the rest of your days. It's not like I left [Ireland] when I was really young: a lot of things were pretty well developed… But place for me is very important.

---

[13] From the Telefís song 'Ballytransnational', which Cathal said was "about home in a way".

It just never really stops." A stained imagination: "There are landscapes in the part of east Cork I grew up in, and Cork city, that come into my head unbidden, and form that kind of inspiration." The aura and immanence of moving tides of water became important to Cathal as a symbol of both a simple, earth-bound peace and the potential for change and renewal. "I just need to be by a body of water. Being by it I can hear its imprint on the sky, and see maybe a bit of black and blue. I have also always had this sense of peripeteia [a sudden reversal in fortunes]—it's always been with me, travelled with me, that sense of possibility." His mental landscape was also formed by a boyhood of watching television, and especially the creepy, low-budget Teilifís Éireann (RTÉ) programming for children. Schedules filled with cheap cartoons from Eastern Europe (many of them featuring the adventures of an intrepid mole), the flying dog of *Wanderly Wagon* and Eugene Lambert's creepy witch puppets in *Murphy and his Friends*. "Seeing the Lambert puppets on the telly at age three or four, that defines a whole lot of things for me," said Cathal in 2022, "what it is to be scared, to be looking into the unknown, ideas of death. None which were deliberately put there by the Lamberts. But there's no walking that back, it's always just there."

Secondary school was one long education in elitism and the techniques of superiority. Cathal went to the fee-paying Presentation Brothers College in Cork, a Catholic school for the city's wealthier families where religion and rugby were priorities, where he was one of the few relying on a scholarship. Being the scholarship boy made him an instant outsider, and it didn't help that there were money worries at home. Paddy had been involved in a car accident that left

him partially paralysed and unable to work. Cathal wore his
regulation blue blazer and stripy black tie like a curse, and
lived each school day with the sneers and condescension that
were given an extra sting by the self-consciously holy and
condescending way they were delivered.

There were two sides to religion in Ireland. The *Father Ted* side made up of afternoon visits for cups of tea from
priests with misty views and motivations; the street corner
gossip about unlikely happenings and unseemly behaviours;
the pantheon of patron saints like Top Trumps cards, with
saints for everything in life, from marketing and ice-skating
to truss-makers and facial hair; and all the routine visits to
holy sites and their souvenir shops selling pink plastic rosaries
and Jesus snowstorms. Talking about his record collection in
1987, Cathal pulled out one of his comedy favourites, *The
Songs Of Pope John Paul II.*

> There are some great song titles. Here's one.
> 'Do Not Be Afraid Mary, You Lily'. I mean,
> he's really such a bastard. Listen to the sleeve
> notes: 'These songs should be sung by miners
> on their way to work, and young people on
> the train, or hiking, or while sitting around
> the camp fire'. Jesus, if anyone started singing
> this shit when I was on the train I'd pull the
> communication cord and risk the fine. He's
> the CIA pope, really he is.

And that was the other side to religion. A powerful, alien regime led by a distant ruler. The sinister luxury of Catholic houses of faith and their dark wood carvings, their rich velvets and metals, their costumes and instruments of belief. A system for living that was drilled into the psyche of a vulnerable and conflicted nation, reinforced by webs of control within the Irish state, education and social welfare, limiting its ability to question tradition. "It was the new colonial authority, that's all it was," Cathal has said. "We weren't trusted to look after ourselves, so a babysitter had to be sent in, in good time for 1921 [the year of partition, when Northern Ireland was created], and it was the fucking Romans, basically."[14]

Cork might have been parochial and conservative in some ways, but it had a cosmopolitan strain because of its life as a harbour. There were currents and connections to a wider world, especially since Ireland had become part of the European Communities. "I don't feel I've ever given Cork enough credit for being the place I come from... Cork was still the place with the second-hand bookshops where you could always get William Burroughs and Philip K Dick books, and exceptionally good second-hand record shops that you could treat as a library." All kinds of music would wash up in Cork's bargain bins: "anything from The Seeds and the Stooges to Miles Davis and Carla Bley". If the weather was clear and you played around with the aerial you could maybe pick up signals from Radio Caroline and John Peel on BBC Radio One, and sometimes Raidió na Gaeltachta would play the art-lab rock of Henry Cow. But

---

[14] Cathal's hatred of religion was ingrained prior to the public scandals involving Catholic priests in the Nineties in Ireland and around the world: the hypocrisy of hidden relationships (both heterosexual and homosexual), the mistreatment of unmarried mothers, and the horrific scale of child abuse.

the music scene of Cathal's teenage years was dominated by the 'show bands' who toured the ballrooms playing Eurovision pop and 'bastardised' folk-cabaret music. Bands like Thin Lizzy and the Boomtown Rats who broke into the rock mainstream were big news because they were so unusual. The Coughlan family itself didn't think of itself as being musical, but as was typical for many households there was an upright piano at home and the boys were given piano lessons. Eleanor's brother and sister were both known as singers. But it didn't take much to distract Cathal from his piano practice. "I got lazy when I heard Slade… Noddy Holder stopped my Shostakovich!"

*

Cathal was someone to avoid at student parties. He was the gloomily pissed medical student from University College Cork who no-one knew that well. He'd come from a posh school and could act like it. He'd take the piss if you talked about the post-punk stuff you were into, and could poke holes in any argument you made about anything. The sort of character who'd go to a party and stand stone-faced next to the bloke playing expert folk guitar, look nonplussed by the artistry on show and say: "Yeah. Okay—but don't you know anything by the Fall?"

This had been the scene on New Year's Eve 1979, when Sean O'Hagan met Cathal. He wasn't put off by Cathal's sullen drunk routine. And he liked The Fall too. Sean wasn't one of the students there but a factory worker. He'd grown up in Dunstable in Bedfordshire and had eventually followed his parents back to their home in Cork, taking jobs in the industrial area of Little Island, including work at a spaghetti factory. Sean and Cathal ended up sitting in the corner of the party with their cans of beer talking about the kinds of music they liked, everything from Suicide, Magazine and The Only Ones to Erik Satie; then the crap music and taste of Ireland. Why couldn't they come up with something that sounded nothing like Cork's favourite singer-songwriter Jackson Browne? "We met up next day in his kitchen, me with a guitar and him with his keyboard," said Sean. "I'd made a conscious decision to forget everything I'd learnt from listening to folk music, Steely Dan, stuff like that. So we came up with this tuneless, rhythmic thrash over which Cathal would rant his reams and reams of... whatever it was."

Cathal had turned out to be "really fucking useless" when it came to Microbiology. "It was just the wrong, wrong thing to do, and nobody forced me to do it except myself." Leaving after two years in 1980 wasn't popular at home ("My father hated the music I played. When I dropped out of college he knew I'd never get a proper job")—which is probably why he started making music so determinedly, as a proposition and not just a hobby. "We rented this tiny, damp flat in the centre of Cork," recalled Sean, who provided the practical know-how for making the music, "we'd meet there every day with a guitar and keyboard and just write thousands and thousands of tunes. We'd do that eight hours a day, five days a week, a really weird, intense way of working that showed up in the songs." Sometimes they'd stay over at the bedsit in Daunt Square, too tired (and too drunk) to go home, sleeping on settees underneath a less-than-restful print of Picasso's 'Guernica'. A nightmare of sunshine and ob-scene violence.[15] Rather than the coming together of a con-ventional band this was a full-blooded creative experiment with 'mutant funk', with discordant poetry and guitars in-spired by the agit-prop of the Gang of Four and early Scritti Politti. "I think I probably saw popular music as an easy route to cultural mobility, wherein a person with my then-fitful attention span and limited tolerance for the 'wider pic-ture' of learning could live a creative life," Cathal explained. The product of the experiment was mostly noise—because it wasn't cool in the Cork scene of makeshift bedroom and kit-chen jams to sound like anything from a recognisable genre. The two-piece of the 'Constant Reminders'[16] turned into the five-piece of 'Micro Disney', named after one of their early songs, but they were still writing 'module-music' made up of "a continuous screaming sound from start to finish". "We were terribly into playing funk riffs as fast as we possibly could and telling everyone we were not a punk rock group," said Sean. "We were of course." Not that the clientele of the wild bars of west Ireland were worried about the fine distinc-tions to musical categories.

> We'd set up these little shows [remembered
> Sean], and it would be literally just locals
> drinking, and we'd set up the drum machine

---

[15] Andrew Mueller, in the sleeve notes for *Daunt Square to Elsewhere* (2007), wrote: "The room was decorated with a large print of Pablo Picasso's surreal apocalypse 'Guernica', which seems retrospectively appropriate in that it is easy enough to imagine the painting as a reasonably accurate portrait of the contents of Coughlan's head."

[16] Along with Mick Lynch as a second vocalist. He went on to join Mean Features in the April of 1980.

and play these songs in these bizarre little places. One show we played, I can't remember if it was as a five-piece or a two-piece, but we were in a little bar, of course, and there was a group of travellers around a pool table and they were beating the shit out of each other with pool cues, belting each other round the head. I was in conversation with this very drunk lady who was probably in her 60s and she told me to speak quietly because I'd wake the cat. I said 'What cat?' To which she opened her leopard-skin handbag, and inside it was the cat.

That was Tipperary. In Tralee, the Micro Disney boys were chucked out of the pub for daring to allow a stripper to share the stage with them. Fun, but not really working out as music. Their obscure noise was "very unsatisfactory because it didn't involve people in what you were trying to do at all, they were just forced to stand there and watch this thing trundle past. The audiences we played to then weren't especially distant but they were, as a collective body, unconcerned." And so the sweetly melodic side of Microdisney was born. Not as a conscious attempt to be more crowd-pleasing or commercial, but as a reflection of the music Cathal and Sean had been listening to and loved. They never saw any contradiction between melody and punk. "For me, punk was buying the first Clash album and *Pet Sounds* on the same day," said Cathal. Brian Wilson was an obsession—where did those heavenly combinations of chords and harmonies come from? And they loved bits of Steely Dan and Frankie Valli and the Four Seasons. They realised jamming stuff was a waste of time for them, they needed to piece together the arrangement of chords first, then build the song (with a prickle of anger inside). Ideas and examples came from a tangled garden of a record collection, full of surprising corners and thorned flowers: John Cage, Miles Davis, Scott Walker, Lee Dorsey, Robert Wyatt, the torch singer Dagmar Krause and Arabic pop; lots of Bobby Womack and the country sounds of Merle Haggard and Gram Parsons. Microdisney had accumulated some skills, and the experience of those surreal nights in bars provided the motivation to try something different.

Micro Disney were given a leg up by 'Downtown Kampus' at the Arcadia ballroom. Elvera Butler was Entertainments Officer at the University College and had been looking for an alternative venue to the canteen for gigs. With her partner Andy Foster she set up the Kampus nights in 'the Arc' in 1977. The capacity of more than a thousand meant they were able to book the bigger acts—U2 played there nine times between 1978 and 1980—and there was the chance for local bands like Nun Attax and Mean Features to get noticed, or at least get free tickets to see the big names play, like The Fall, The Cure, The Specials, The Undertones, UB40, XTC and The Only Ones. Elvera looked after her Cork bands. The Kampus was an alcohol-free venue for customers, but she'd make them hot toddies with whiskey and cream, or take them over to the Handlebars pub opposite the train station (where they could renew their admiration for the huge moustache of the landlord). Micro Disney were never a fan favourite in those early days, playing material like

'Leper' and 'Come Back and Fla Me, Like You Did Last Year'[17] to a low-grade drum machine backing. Some indifferent applause was the best they could hope for, an improvement on the booing, bottling and 'feck off''s. They were known for their own misbehaviour. During one support slot for U2, Cathal had decided to get on his knees, make the sign of the cross and chant the words: "*U2 boy wanks at confession*". After that performance, Paul McGuinness, U2's manager, would only pay them half of the agreed £50 fee. Unpopularity, along with the alcohol and too much caffeine, was all fuel to Cathal and his need to rile an audience. He'd enjoy dressing up in a priest's costume and dark glasses and take a train into Dublin. If anyone thought to pay their respects or start up a conversation with the Father, he'd respond with a torrent of sweary feckin abuse.

Cork was changing dramatically. The jobs that the locals had devoted so many years of their life and loyalty to —having been raised to expect continuity—were vanishing. There was no place for old-time sentimentality any more. The company bosses, still seen around the city in their chauffeur-driven cars, seemed powerless to do anything about the changing business tide. In 1983 the Dunlop factory closed down, then in the following year, the Verolme dockyard. Worst of all, Ford gave up on Cork. The closures dried up the streams of money going into local supply chains of engineering firms, as well as the shops and cafés. Murphy's brewery was under threat and there were plans to shut Cork airport. Cork United went bankrupt. Woolworth's was closed, and the English Market was earmarked as a site for a

---

[17] Fla: the Cork slang for 'shag'.

multi-storey car park. Unemployment in Ireland rose generally from 7.8 per cent in 1979 to 18.2 per cent by 1985. With fewer gigs being played there were cutbacks at Microdisney, a return to the original two piece and the need to take on odd jobs. Music producer Jacknife Lee remembers going with Cathal and Sean as a 14-year-old to work at Galway Races "selling junk".[18] There were no recording studios in Cork and they couldn't afford to go to Dublin. Their song-writing reached a dead end, another consequence of the city's feeling of having sunk to the bottom of the world. "People seemed to be going through the motions in a consumer society that was blatantly on a burning foundation," said Cathal. "So a lot of those lyrics anyway were jibing at that. There was a song we had that we never recorded called 'Weeds' that was... 'Here we are, fully grown, gone as far as we will…' and the idea was basically that we were just detritus, really. A whole generation."

*

Sarah doesn't want to look. Dad is sitting alone in the living room with a glass of champagne in his hand, perched on the edge of the settee in his suit and Snowman tie. Everyone else has gone out onto the patio to look at Tony's satellite dish, leaving Dad on his own with the Christmas Album CD playing on a loop. There's a strange kind of smile on his face, as if he's listening to someone telling a good joke.

---

[18] Lee was a producer who worked with REM, U2, Snow Patrol, The Killers etc, Jacknife lost touch with Cathal for many years, but they reunited in 2020 to collaborate as Telefís.

It was her fault, because she'd told Mum she had to at least invite him for Christmas Day. This year everyone was going to be at her and Tony's place, a four-bed detached with a conservatory. They had the space, like they said. And Dad would be on his own otherwise. He was supposed to say no. Instead he'd turned up early with a bunch of flowers and a kind of wave in his hair. "What's he doing this for?" *Mum had whispered, spitting in her ear. Nothing bothered Tony, he'd sold his greengrocer's to a chemist chain and was bronzed and affable from all the golf and holidays in Portugal. A white-haired piece of mahogany in a Benetton pullover and chinos, he loved being the host, showing off his gadgets and filling up glasses with his better class of plonk.*

"*Just like old times,*" *says Dad to Sarah as they sat down at the table, laid out with Christmas candles, napkins and neatly-written placecards.*

"*Is it?*" *Mum responds. She's been drinking lots of wine in the kitchen.*

Tony is all smiles.

"*You'll want a top-up Adey, you're at university aren't you eh? You students.*"

"*It's not really a university,*" *clarifies Sarah,* "*it's one of those Institutes of Higher Education.*"
Adrian looks at her like she's belched in his face.

"*We take the same exams sis. There's no poor man's version like you might think. We read Nietzsche just the same way.*"
The pretentious dick.

Dad makes a show of looking around: "*Haven't we got crackers? We always used to have crackers—we had great fun —*"

"*We don't need things like that anymore,*" *says Mum without looking over, sending Tony to the kitchen for the electric carver.*

Dad becomes even more talkative during lunch, hardly touching his food. He doesn't think the Chunnel is a good idea because of the risk of "backdoor invasion". And then stuff about David Icke. He wasn't a totally stupid man, Dad tells them, because Icke had worked at the BBC for years hadn't he?—so maybe he was being, you know, sort of symbolic.

"When he said cosmic lizards from another dimension are filling our heads with fear, maybe it's you know—it's —"

"An allegory?" offers Adrian.

"Yes! Like you say. That's it—an allagry of what rich people are actually doing to us. He just couldn't, you know, say it out loud." That strange smile again as he looked around the table for approval. Sarah wasn't playing.

"David Icke, the Son of God—yeah—have you seen that shell-suit?"

Then the worst moment of the meal, when Mum brings out the cheese board with the grapes and the cheese knives and Dad laughs.

They go for a walk with Mum and Tony in their new cashmere-blend coats and scarves. Dad stays behind and watches the Queen's speech because that was what they'd always done. On his own with the glow of the TV and the five-speed Christmas tree lights.

*

Cathal and Sean went to London to make their fortune in July 1983. Like Dick Whittingtons with spotted handkerchiefs tied to sticks. They didn't expect anything other than success: they'd write the songs in the first month, bag a record deal then count the gold.

They arrived in a heatwave. A London so hot and sultry that Cathal was glad he'd not been drinking on the Innisfallen ferry out of Cork like the others and kept a clear head for once. Friends put them up in Willesden until they found a cheap flat to rent in Kensal Rise, the ground floor of a house owned by a West Indian family in North West London. Microdisney HQ: their home during the years of brain-altering chemicals and rising levels of desperation. "Everything was pretty pristine when we moved in, so it is with certain regret I look back on how it looked a couple of years later. We didn't completely wreck the place, but there was a lot more dust gathering in corners, shall we say."

Migration from Ireland to England had been a trend since early in the nineteenth century, but there were peaks and troughs, and the Eighties were another of the peaks. By 1986, the *Irish Post* newspaper, set up in 1970 for the migrant community in Britain, had a weekly circulation of 78,000. St Patrick's Day was marked with a week of festivals in London of Irish music and films. For some, migration had led to access to well-paid careers, leading to the rise of the NIPPLES (New Irish Professional People Living in England). But for many others it was the beginning of a descent into Hell, as recounted by the Microdisney song: "I will sing this song about an honest man / He never had a job, he barely had a home / And the landlord came to call / Just pack your things and go / This room is now on show." There were pockets of struggling Irish across the poorest areas of the city, mostly containing older, blue-collar Irish men. This group had a higher risk of early death than if they'd stayed in Ireland, because of the poor state of housing, and the drinking and smoking that helped them forget their poverty. Shane McGowan wrote a song for The Pogues about a Sixties' migrant, but it could equally have applied to 1987, the year it was written: "I got a job doing meals on wheels /

Round NW3 / I was scaring poor old grannies / For half a quid a week / I was drunk and stoned / Smashed and blocked in NW3." A dour and ashen ghetto life, familiar to Cathal and Sean. When *Melody Maker* met with Cathal in December 1985 they found him in a "neon-lit greasy café in downtown Kilburn."

> As the locals avidly pore over newly-bought copies of the *Connaught Tribune* and *Leinster Leader*, absently flicking roll-up ash into their egg and chips, a more recent Irish exile sits before me, a solid thick-set figure, a singer and writer, and a man of deep compassion. Only the black leather jacket distinguishes him from the nicotine and grit soiled Paddies, the whiskey and porter brigade who'll spend their days indebted to the turf accountants, their nights in alehouses lamenting the day they ever left the Auld Sod.

Drinking was a big part of the Microdisney life, the cheapest form of entertainment alongside taking acid and speed. Other hobbies included not getting enough to eat. Fatalism. Lonely walks through London's squares, past the homes of the wealthy; well-appointed venues of dinner parties, flirty career chatter and Tracy Chapman CDs. Returning to their rented room where there would be letters written in the dust on the window by kids: 'IF YOU'RE SO CLEVER WHY AREN'T YOU RICH?" "Well, I may be an alcoholic by the time I'm 30 but at least I'll be a far more interesting person than George Michael," said Cathal. Not that he was part of the Irish community either. The first time he went to see The Pogues he was "fucking outraged" by what he saw as a fake kind of party-Irishness; "I just did not get the Irish diaspora, its diversity, and its linkages to the rest of the community here. It took me years to fathom." Cathal and Sean did mix with musicians like Aindrías Ó'Grúama, the guitarist with Zerra One. In the winter of 1982, Aindrías had been given a preview cassette tape of Microdisney by friends, Gareth Ryan and Cormac Tohill of the Kabuki Records label.

> I was intrigued by what I heard, the two songs, 'The Helicopter of the Holy Ghost' and 'The Pink Skinned Man', by a two piece band with the same lineup as Zerra One at that time, string machine keys and guitar with backing tapes, but with fabulous singing in a Cork accent. The music was like nothing I'd ever heard before, and I was a fan from that moment on. When we heard that Cathal and Sean were planning to come to London we invited them over to our house in Westhampstead. We stole a chicken from the local shop and made a slap up meal to welcome them. We'd often run into each other at parties and gigs and got to know each other well.

Microdisney were working hard, re-writing old songs, but it was never a job with money or security attached. "We had this daily routine, we'd just go down to the telephone box with a fistful of 10ps and badger people every single day from various record companies. Eventually we booked a little rehearsal studio in Walworth Road which was completely alien to us. We went to this strange place every day called the Elephant and Castle which was completely peculiar." Within a year of their arrival they had recorded three sessions for John Peel. The main source of income turned out to be warehouse work at Rough Trade. "We had to re-sleeve a whole lot of 'What Difference Does It Make?' singles because of changes to the cover." A Microdisney album was finally recorded for the new Blanco y Negro label, who'd paid the band just enough to cover the costs of the studio time. Then Blanco decided they didn't want it. *Everybody is Fantastic* (1984) was saved by the intervention of Geoff Travis, a partner in Blanco, and picked up for Rough Trade (maybe only because Sean had remembered Geoff promising to do so if things fell through, and had kept him to his word). But the deal they signed wasn't one for a hot prospect, it could sometimes feel like a favour for a band that had mates in the warehouse. "I have to say that I don't know if they had the belief in us or not, I don't know, I've no idea," said Cathal. "The experience of boxing the records for The Smiths, and not being The Smiths, possibly might have had an influence."

From a distance, Microdisney looked like a success story. They'd made five albums and been signed by Virgin. The band could look almost glamorous in the pink-cheeked promotional photographs and videos. They'd bagged a slot on the same bill as David Bowie—and been guests on the *Tom O'Connor Show* (with Cathal sporting a lovely yellow cardigan for the easy-listening fans). Cathal was another of the

Cork entertainers who'd made the big time, like the tenor singer Walloo Dunlea[19] and actor Eddie Mulhare[20] who'd made their home town proud. In 2018, *The Clock Comes Down The Stairs* (1985) was recognised as "culturally important" with an IMRO/NCH Trailblazer Award, and the band's reunion concerts in Dublin's National Concert Hall and the Barbican in London were simple celebrations of a musical treasure. Because memories were short. There had always been an unhappy ambivalence to Microdisney, a contradiction between ambition and the need for some kind of integrity; between a musical identity and confusion, arrogance and shattered confidence. They needed a level of commercial success to keep a roof over their heads and to eat (rather than to become stars) and that meant dealing with the mainstream. "We were not making a living when we were on Rough Trade, but that was not the point of Rough Trade," said Cathal. "We built up debts all over the place, owing to one person (non-RT) who stole from us, and we owed the government, due to not writing things down. We had to get some money fast—hence Virgin." Lost in a hard-nosed, disinterested city, they had to learn as they went along. How they couldn't trust the enthusiasm of record labels ("Before I came here I didn't know what it was like to starve, and to be lied to in a very insidious and pally way.") and the importance of making tax returns. While *Clock* made number one in the indie charts, its sales only just covered the band's debts

---

[19] Walloo arrived in England from Cork after the Second World War, singing old songs and Italian airs to Irish immigrants in clubs before going on to star in BBC radio programmes and a career in the US.

[20] Eddie was known for playing the part of Professor Higgins in the original Broadway production of *My Fair Lady*, as well as TV roles in *Robin Hood*, *The Ghost & Mrs Muir* and *Knight Rider*.

and prevented bankruptcy. Most reviewers could hear the high grade of Microdisney's melodies—even the pop panel on *Saturday Superstore* made 'Town to Town' their pick of the week. But there was still very little radio play and no hits. The numbers said only one thing to a record company, and Microdisney were dropped by Virgin in 1988.

Contradictions, in the end, were never a commercial proposition. Beautifully dark and clever irony doesn't sell. Not even a Brian Wilson-like feel for a tune mixed with soul guitars and social criticism. Cathal and Sean themselves couldn't see any mismatch between the blithe music and the violence of the words, but they'd always known the rules: "Keep yourself bland, so folks will understand".[21] They went some way towards meeting mainstream listeners' tastes, but not without it starting to cause conflict. During the making of the last album, *39 Minutes* (1988), Cathal felt that his "artistic intentions" had been "edited". 'Gale Force Wind', he said, was an example of a song written just to please the label, an attempt at second-guessing what the mainstream wanted. Decisions were being made "by committee". "It was clear that the only way forward was to agree a new con-sensus on the music, its style and function, and it was also clear that there was no way for that to happen."

At the core of the tension was Cathal's Hellish vision of modern London. Microdisney "write strikingly melodic songs only to have them roared at the audience by the slightly terrifying Cathal Coughlan," complained Tracey Thorn. The band looked unwieldy on stage, like an over-

---

[21] From 'United Colours'.

loaded bucket of drunk and angry emotions; yes, attended to by a gang of careful technicians with Sean in charge, but that bucket was always just about to slide and slosh over. "The basic motivation for me writing lyrics is 'What do I hate most today?' and just take it from there, really," Cathal explained in 1987. Religion, of course, was a target; imperialism in any form, whether that was Roman, British or corporate; and the effects of the money culture on British society, its insidious energy. "Young would-be-rich cops and people in suits," added Cathal. "It's just an infantile way of expressing something fairly complicated. I think it's the best way to do it. I think the only way to make records is as if each one is going to be your last."

He was an outsider walking the streets of London, feeling like a member of the underclass in a period when an Irish accent was something to be wary of. He would recount the story of being stopped by a policeman who'd told him: "As far as I'm concerned, you're in this country illegally." There was more than personal animosity to this attitude. The Provisional IRA's campaign of bombing in London had targeted spaces crowded with ordinary people, in Hyde Park, Regent's Park, Harrods and a Wimpy bar in Oxford Street. So Cathal felt the eyes of people on him, listening carefully to his accent, his otherness sticking to him. A significant inclusion in Cathal's list of favourite films was Michael Cimino's *Heaven's Gate* (1980).[22] The film had been regarded as a bad joke by the industry and critics because of its mammoth budget overspend, but Cathal recognised what it was: a

---

[22] His other choices included David Lynch's *Blue Velvet* (1986) and John Schlesinger's *Midnight Cowboy* (1969).

stunning piece of cinematic art telling the untold story of how immigrants to the US from Eastern Europe had been targeted by local landowners for extermination. Cathal didn't think he could ever belong in England.

> The English are still told in their schools, 'you are the centre of the world. If someone else talks your language with a different accent, they're scum. If anyone claims to be British but they haven't got the same tone of skin, they're scum'. Being Irish, you experience it in its most pure form: because you're white, like they're white, and you speak the same language…They take the piss out of your accent. They fuck up your name all the fucking time. That's something which really, really, *really* gets on my nerves and is the main thing responsible for driving me into myself. I don't want to talk to anybody because they're only going to ask me five times what my name is. I always end up having to settle for something less than the correct pronunciation.[23]

Money and materialism, he felt, were like a sickly drug in Britain. "There's such a lack of values here that have nothing to do with pounds, shillings and pence—in Ireland you do have all this loathsome superstitious bullshit that the

---

[23] 'Car-hul Cock-lun'. John Peel got away with 'Cath-ul Coff-lun'.

Catholic church has nurtured, but at the same time people do have a certain appreciation of things that don't have anything to do with *direct gain* for themselves."

Cathal's nerves were becoming ever more raw. London, he believed, was overcrowded and filthy: "rats everywhere, rats do better than the people here"; other musicians were part of a dirty system: Paul Weller was "an idiot, a cretin… he makes Tory music for the upwardly, socially mobile"; U2 were "bastards, scum. Bono has political ambitions". But he could never go back to Ireland either. "There's a lot of things you have to ignore [in England]. It's OK—the government's fucking disgusting and pop music's disgusting, but it's a much better place to live than in Southern Ireland. It's much easier to find a place to have a good time and I don't think that applies just to London. Over there the only thing you can do is go down the pub and get pissed, which can be fun or it can be soul-destroying." London, he felt, was the only place he could be an artist, however tenuous the existence. He could at least feel moments of freedom—on the run with a head full of exile. "I'm sure I'd be a much different creature if I had managed to settle in one place and establish myself as part of a community. I often regret this. But the ongoing lack of geographic allegiance and sense of being established is a huge part of my work."

Playing live to an audience could expose and exaggerate the band's doubts and despair. The Microdisney shows were a "cabaret representation of constant depression" according to their lead singer. The tour through Communist Europe—Poland, East Germany, Czechoslovakia—was remembered mostly for the scale of the drinking, the lack of financial returns (and an incident on the window

121

ledge of a hotel in Poland). And back home wasn't any easi-er. "It's like pissing in the rain. You're in Derby, it's Tuesday night, you can barely talk so you have to drink a few brandies to get some sort of voice, take headfuls of coffee to stay awake and you're supposed to be doing something which is more than standing up on a piece of wood. The feeling is extremely enlightening really—you really know what you're doing is pretty artificial." Microdisney didn't often come off stage in a good mood, and then the drinking would start up again to take away the pain.

It was one live show, 'Intruder at the Palace', that finished the band, a slot on the bill with David Bowie as part of a benefit show raising money for the Institute of Contem-porary Arts at the Dominion Theatre. Cathal had already been mixing antihistamines with booze that day in July 1988 and was "stewing", because he was 28 and he had nothing. Virgin had told him Microdisney were being dumped and now he had to go out and perform for another audience. Well-heeled Londoners in the comfortable seated rows of the Dominion, far more interested in Bowie or even the Kronos Quartet or The Woodentops than a filler band called Mi-crodisney. And when Cathal arrived there was tetchiness and quibbling backstage because of a lack of time for sound checks. Bowie's contribution was an eight minute, multime-dia version of 'Look Back in Anger' with the singer dancing alongside members of the experimental La La La Human Steps dance group flown in from Montreal. A contemporary art performance. It was Microdisney, though, who provided the real human drama of the evening, with what Sean de-scribed as "a band in nervous breakdown filmed on TV".

Cathal started like a man in a fever, white and distracted and burning up, his arms and legs flailing, one shoulder hunched crookedly into the mic—but fighting the disease was doing him no good. So he slouched and lost interest, overcome by demons. Half-singing, using whatever ugly words came to mind; picking up the mic stand like he might use it as a weapon; smacking his forehead over and again with the microphone until it bled. Not his body anymore. The polite musicians of his band played carefully on, until the final song of the set faded out and they saw Cathal rush to the front of the stage—demon unloosed—and hold up his middle finger to the seated rows of London's benefactors, screaming: "*Fuck you.*"

Much later, Cathal would describe the night at the Dominion as an "unnecessary self-inflicted trauma". In hindsight he knew things with Microdisney weren't so bad (that his life was going to get worse), but at the time it felt like a nightmarish end. In his blackest moods Cathal had always expected the next day to bring destitution, prison or death. Sean, meanwhile, had been planning to get Don Was involved in producing the next album, but that wasn't happening anymore. There was no basis for moving past what had happened—and two years' on, when Cathal was interviewed by Dave Fanning for RTÉ, he wouldn't talk about Microdisney or Sean, or offer any conventional words of conciliation.

*

The Fatima Mansions came out of the wilderness. "I must lie down where all the ladders start," wrote Irish poet WB

Yeats. "In the foul rag-and-bone shop of the heart." It was a place of more drinking and confusion, but Cathal felt a bitter, bracing grandeur at starting from the very bottom of the ladder. "It's very seldom that anybody creates a decent piece of work unless they're put to the pin of their fuckin' collar, or down to the very last reserves of courage or confidence. My favourite records are by people who've been dragged through the mire, and they're just about on the point of giving up, *but not quite*." He was an outlaw on the music scene; an outlaw who now needed to live off his wits. He'd use cheap studios (no more shiny Virgin aesthetic), do the pub toilet gigs, make something more homemade and *meant*— because life was "too short to wait for people to get the joke". He was going to take direct action. Pay more attention to the changing tides of his own musical imagination and the places it could take him. "I liked the idea of acid house…. The house-trained rock bands didn't interest me at all. Industrial music from the US and continental Europe was the only current 'band' stuff I actually liked. I'm thinking The Young Gods, Einsturzende Neubauten, Ministry and Meat Beat Manifesto." But it was something lying in a quieter, almost forgotten corner of his Cork-made mind that got Cathal started again. "There was a particular Peadar Ó Riada record that I was pretty gone on. It was really eclectic, there were home recordings of him playing the piano with the fire crackling in the background. It was bloody-minded, quite a Lo-fi record, recorded in the church."[24] Cathal sang Ó Riada's 'Im Long Mé Measim' [A Ship I Am] for a flexi 7" re-

---

[24] *Peadar Ó Riada* (1987).

leased by Caff Corporation Records, the first release for the label set up by Bob Stanley of Saint Etienne in 1989 (CAFF1).[25] "My *blas* [accent] is *uafásach* [awful] and I wish I hadn't recorded it… it was the first thing I probably did." There's an important clue to the real Cathal in this obscure piece, in the way he reached back towards music untainted by London and the industry, that spoke instead to his private self. Ó Riada's music comes from an emptier world, where people's minds and ideas were made from their relation with elemental things rather than media noise, the moods of the green hills and the water and its mists; closer to the mysteries of birth and death; shaped by an austere race memory that's a universe away from the celebrity pages of the *Daily Mail*. 'A Ship I Am' is a hymn-like song. The lyrics came from a poem by Dónal Ó Liatháin, based around the image of a man in exile, alone and at the mercy of the open sea and its storms ("There is no harbour before me.… I wrote a book in a language from the sky / And there is nothing that would understand it… All doors are closed under lock and key / I will wait for you like a ship in a bottle / Let it escape as a whisper, like the rest of my life").

Cathal didn't become a demon on stage because he was nihilistic or unspiritual. He was someone who paid close attention to the workings of his inner life and ideas of right and wrong—which made him hypersensitive to how spirituality could be corrupted, how formal religion and its inhuman rules could be absurd; how modern minds were gener-

---

[25] The flexi disc was sold in some independent record shops but was mainly given away free in fanzines, *Honey Hunt* and *Far Out and Fishy*. Caff label also released singles by Pulp, Manic Street Preachers, The Field Mice, Television Personalities and The Lilac Time. The label was closed down in 1992.

ally arid, leading to an acceptance of pretence and deception. Cathal was looking for something closer to truth, for vindication. As well as a critic of others, it made him brutally hard on himself. While a cycle of booze and rage works fine if you don't care, when there's kindness and sensitivity involved it can make life a torture. The confessional line on 'Walk Yr Way', "Through aimless thought, through thoughtless deed, I joined with liars and thieves", is typical. "I was not very honest as a person," he claimed. "An important thing to keep in mind about me is that I am essentially a low character."

Working with other musicians gave Cathal a solid musical skeleton for his outcast's vision, and people that he'd come to feel responsible for as 'his band'. He needed one quick anyway. He'd been offered a short tour over Christmas 1988 in Switzerland. Cathal was going to play a mix of Microdisney numbers like 'Back to the Old Town' and 'Loftholdingswood' along with some of his new stuff ('The Door-to-Door Inspector' was one of the earliest Mansions songs), under the band name 'The Freedom Association'. Grimmo was first on the team sheet. He'd formed a new band after quitting from Zerra One, called My Baby's Arm: "Cathal heard an acetate of our second single at a party, liked the production and the guitars and gave me a call to ask if I would care to play some guitar on his new demos." Keyboard player Zac Woolhouse was a mate of Grimmo's who'd been playing piano in a Conservative club in deepest Hertfordshire. Drummer Nick Allum—who'd been a big Microdisney fan since *Everybody is Fantastic*—got the job through his hairdresser, Sue Hackett of Hacketts in Princess

Road, Kilburn. They'd been talking about music when she mentioned that her friend's boyfriend was that Microdisney feller Coughlan. Nick had completed "half a degree" in jazz at Berklee College of Music in Boston and been playing with a group called The Apartments.[26]

The music on the first tour of the proto-Mansions was "Microdisney-ish in those days, less MOR and more rough edges," said Nick. It was only meant to be a one-off project with rented musicians until Cathal got a call from Keith Armstrong. "One night I was at home getting pissed listening to 'Horse Overboard'," said Keith. "I called Cathal up and asked him what he was up to. He said he was forming a band called Fatima Mansions—I said 'can they be on Kitchenware?' and he said 'of course'." Keith loved Microdisney and Cathal's voice in particular. He'd once arranged a concert just so he'd have an excuse to have them on the bill (the 'Stolen Thunder Review' alongside Kitchenware bands Hurrah! and The Daintees). The *Viva Dead Ponies* line-up was completed by bass player Hugh Bunker, who'd been recommended to Keith by Neil Conti of Prefab Sprout. Hugh was a jobbing freelance at the time, playing with his first wife's show band the Fabulous Singlettes and picking up any work he could. But Hugh wanted to be part of a band. "Microdisney weren't on my radar, they just sent me a copy of the

------

[26] Berklee was known in particular for its jazz teaching. Alumni include Donald Fagen, Quincy Jones, Branford Marsalis, Keith Jarrett (and Bruce Hornsby).

Against Nature EP [the first Mansions recording] which I loved. I was chuffed to do it."[27]

*

Kitchenware put up the money for an LP. More than that, Kitchenware were prepared to get behind what was good and not just what would sell. "I've known them the whole time and their philosophy," said Cathal in 1990, "you do what you do, and then try and sell it, you don't try and pre-empt the vagaries of the right wing. You live within your means basically." 1989 was a very productive year for Cathal. He was no longer tied to days of rehearsal room bookings (he couldn't afford them) and there were fewer things to worry about when it was just him and a keyboard for doing the writing. And maybe it was this limitation and less the musical zeitgeist that made *Viva Dead Ponies* an experiment in electronica. It was around this time that Cathal had become interested in *musique concrète*, the effect that could be created from putting recorded sounds and electronic sounds together: noises that come from recordings of musical instruments, the natural environment and human voices, alongside created sounds from computer-based digital signal processing; a

---

[27] Hugh's brother Nick Bunker was signed up to play keyboards. Nick was part of the band that toured *Viva Dead Ponies*, and returned to play with Cathal on his solo project *Grand Necropolitan* (1996), playing guitar on 'Unbroken Ones'. Hugh's first wife, a classically trained singer credited as 'Dame Alison Jiear, Voice of God-as-She' on the record, sang the operatic interlude on 'Farewell Oratorio'. An Australian, Alison Jiear was trained at the Queensland Conservatorium of Music. She went on to sing in West End shows and with the English National Opera, Most famously, Alison reached the semi-finals of *Britain's Got Talent* in 2015 where she sang 'You'll Never Walk Alone' (the eventual winner was a performing Border Collie) and went on to record with Kylie Minogue and Robbie Williams.

collage of sound that didn't have to follow the usual rules of melody, harmony, rhythm or metre. In other words, it meant noises that were less contrived and more like the everyday environment of 'found' music, the traffic, the snatches of jingles, the atmospheres of places. Messy sampling. *Musique concrète* didn't have to be obscure or avant garde, as demonstrated by Meat Beat Manifesto's *Storm the Studio* (1989), which turned garbled natural sounds into a thunder of dance beats. The *musique concrète* idea plays its part in shaping the manic world of *Viva Dead Ponies*. There are gentle reflective spaces, walls of brick and concrete, motorways and speeding cars, a chugging along of people's lives and radio pop songs—smashed by sudden eruptions from the Hell underneath. Cute surfaces of consumer culture keep breaking apart to reveal the reality of a soulless system, a system that could become weaponised by nation states. Emergency pulses, rumbling approaches, shrieks and squirts. Trapped animals. A fairground carny sneer. A song like 'White Knuckle Express' doesn't attempt to be anything other than a stitchwork of light and dark: "[It] veers from ECM free improv[28] to a crazy twisted big band groove on drums. It was a bit of a tour de force live. Certainly not pop music," explained Cathal.[29] But he also made use of familiar pop

---

[28] A reference to the German jazz label (Edition of Contemporary Music) known for its experiments in "space, shadow and atmosphere". ECM releases included Keith Jarrett's *Köln Concert* (1975), and the classic of minimalism, Steve Reich's *Music for 18 Musicians* (1978).

[29] The verses of 'White Knuckle Express' were originally written for a "quite prominent female vocalist of some renown", in a version known as 'Collar & Tie'; her manager responded by asking if Cathal couldn't write "something simpler". "NAAAAAAAH," was his response.

genres, the most conventional and comforting patterns of sounds: white-boy soul, soft rock ballads, grunge, House music piano, ambient, psychobilly, demonstrating that what mattered wasn't the style but the substance. "We take one particular branch of music and scribble all over it. The rock band idea, that's what we play with—and the pop bit, we scribble all over that as well."

On the way to the pub after leaving Solid Light: Nick, Aindrías, Hugh and Cathal.
Courtesy of Hugh Bunker.

The songs came together as a single album of poisoned musical theatre. Each song is a story from someone's life rather than abstract argument or observations. Folk songs. "I have lyrics and a narrative that are either highly structured or chronological. Most people avoid that nowadays—it's been out of favour since 1975! But it's part of what I am, the tradition I come from insofar as I come from any tradition at all." The first drafts of songs were put onto tape at Cathal's place in Crouch End. Grimmo, Hugh and the two Nicks would go round and work through their parts in his front room. Some of the album songs were already being played live, as part of the tour for the *Against Nature* mini-LP, and at rehearsal sessions at Solid Light in Camden. "We'd be in one room making a big racket, and next door would be a pop band," said Hugh. "We'd get heads sticking round the door trying to see what the hell was going on."

Everything Cathal had written for the album—from epic verse to electronic doodle—was recorded, even though Cathal was worried about the budget (and later he'd claim that whole Mansions records had been made for the same cost as Microdisney rehearsals). *Ponies* was made using two studio spaces known for being cheap, one in Tulse Hill and the other above a cab office in Hackney. A mate of Grimmo's was brought in to co-produce, following the work he'd already done mixing the sound for the Switzerland tour. Ralph Jezzard was 16 in 1983 when he got to work with Grimmo and his band Zerra One on their anthemic rock single 'The West's Awake' at Wickham Studios in south London—a tea-boy and tape operator given the chance to be the assistant engineer.[30] Wickham moved to a derelict Victorian warehouse in Clink Street, on the same floor as Beat Farm Studios, the centre of London's acid house, Chicago house and rave culture. Britain's new punk. Here, Ralph worked with dance acts like Bomb the Bass and, after *Ponies*, went on to produce the huge international hit for EMF, 'Unbelievable'. In 1989, Ralph was already building a reputation as a hard noise merchant, bumping up the rock with elec-

---

[30] Ralph had also been playing bass for punk band Blood and Roses.

tronica and vice-versa.[31] "Grimmo asked me if I'd like to work with his new band—I thought Zerra One were great, but the Mansions were even better." Ralph hadn't heard of Microdisney and wasn't a fan of the classic indie guitar sound. "I was young, I had that punk kind of vim and was more into heavy music. I wanted to make the Mansions sound less indie and more massive. Like Ministry. Not the same, they couldn't be that—but I wanted the abrasion and not the jingle-jangle." Cathal and Ralph found they shared common musical ground. A love for the industrial-metal barrage of Ministry alongside early forms of sampling. "I didn't know much about Cathal before then, but he was one of the coolest people I've ever met. Very easy to work with—not that we had the time for any disagreements anyway." The ballad-like songs were less Ralph's thing. "I knew they were great songs and I didn't take any less care over them, it just wasn't my vibe back then. I was excitable."

Most of the recording was done at Gooseberry Sound Studios, a house in a residential suburb of South London. The original Gooseberry was set up by Peter Houghton in 1968 as a place for cheap demos to be made, making it popular among punk and reggae bands in the Seventies.[32] Band members lived within commuting distance—Cathal came in from Crouch End, Nick from east London, Hugh from Archway and Ralph round the corner. The studio was block-

---

[31] Ralph went on to be bass player with Grand Theft Audio in the late Nineties and also became the go-to man for catchy, gritty rock soundtracks for films and gaming. He reunited with EMF to produce their 2024 album *The Beauty and the Chaos*.

[32] The Sex Pistols recorded demos for 'Pretty Vacant' and 'God Save the Queen' at Gooseberry in 1977; Louisa Mark had recorded 'Caught You in a Lie' (1974), an early example of Lovers Rock reggae).

booked on a daily rate for three weeks, meaning they worked eight to 10 hours a day. Gooseberry's management set-up was much more erratic by comparison. The owners, a husband and wife team, were divorced. "The female co-owner, who I think, was a long-time emigrée from Eastern Europe, lived upstairs with her kindly, blazer-wearing, commodore-type second husband," said Cathal. The first husband had run off to Bulgaria to found himself another, younger partner. He was back, but was made to live with his new girlfriend in the shed in the garden, and was very much a low-ranking second-in-command. "The guy had this nose job done in Eastern Europe, and his nose was still splattered over his face with a bandage round it, and he'd come and knock on the door to ask for a cup of tea or something," recalled Ralph.

For a budget studio it was unusual in having a top-of-the-range SSL production desk.[33] "A big toy," said Ralph, "a good way to lure in clients. Good for automation and recall for mixing." Which would have been perfect if it had worked. "The automation depended on a minicomputer in the basement, and that kept going wrong," said Nick Allum. "The computer repair man was coming out all the time. It meant we had to use the old method of everyone taking charge of a fader and moving it at the appropriate time, and when the tracks were mixed there was no way of recovering the original recordings." Often frustrated by the delays, Cathal would get help from Vic Keary, the engineer on many of the Trojan reggae recordings, who was providing Gooseberry's maintenance as a freelance. But he was more of a

---

[33] Solid State Logic.

valves man. When the tech was working, young gun Ralph would do his best to break it again by overloading the amps in the desk to get the distortion he wanted, or sticking the bass and high watt bass amps in a cupboard with the mic and letting them blast and bleed. The "glorious abrasion" on the album was created by Ralph, said Cathal: "digital was new, so the mistakes were used as effects. If it sounds like it's breaking the song, let's use it."

The sessions were pre-planned in detail ("In the studio, Cathal was very focused and prepared—and great," said producer Victor Van Vugt of his experiences on the subsequent EPs and album). The first week was all about the rhythm section, Nick and Hugh, who were both feeling the pressure as they worked to the time sequences Cathal had assembled on his keyboard. "A 24 track tape was only 15 minutes and really expensive so we had to make sure it was one or two takes—three max—and that's what we did," said Nick who'd borrowed a drum kit for the sessions from Tom Fenner, the former Microdisney drummer.[34] "It wasn't romantic," added Hugh, "we weren't the Beatles riffing new things. We weren't exactly a quiet, well-mannered band either, there was lots of noise going on and it was a challenge to deal with the feedback and noise levels."

Sometimes Ralph would sleep at the studio to make the most of the day rate, doing the mixing alone. "We didn't have the budget to do anything but knock it out. But I never had to do any splicing, cutting or sticking tape back together because they were all brilliant musicians. If they hadn't been,

---

[34] Nick liked the Yamaha 9000 so much he bought one for himself— using it on all the subsequent Mansions recordings.

the album would never have been made. Cathal's singing was done in one take, a couple of drop-ins maybe, but it was a joy to record." Cathal could be self-conscious about the monster vocal lines to songs like 'Angel's Delight', that weren't so easy to do in the artificial space of a studio. "We used to knock out all the lights and he'd go nuts." Cathal joked about it later: "It was so, so easy to look photogenic when performing ['Angel's Delight'] back in the day! I owe my many modelling assignments since then to this. Got me on the ladder, this song—my arse…" It hasn't only been the songwriting that has gone unappreciated. His voice was always special, full and musical, with a protean virtuosity that could mange everything from hacksaw screams to a savoury richness and lulling caramel-brown sweetness. And with it, an actor's gift for delivering a joke or bitter aside.

Two songs needed to be re-recorded with the full band. 'You're A Rose' and 'Chemical Cosh' were originally both electronic-only. Keith at Kitchenware didn't think the versions lived up to what he'd heard played live—and later Cathal admitted 'You're A Rose' "sounded like an advert".[35] The six minute-long 'Blues for Ceaușescu' was recorded but not included because it was going to make the album too long for vinyl.[36] Not really a song about a Romanian dictator, but aimed directly at "that scumbag" Margaret Thatcher. There was a moment of felicity in the studio when Ralph and Cathal were trying to find a sample for the intro. After

---

[35] Those original recordings of 'You're A Rose' and 'Chemical Cosh' are still believed to exist somewhere. The outro guitar on 'Rose' is Nick Allum playing around on Grimmo's guitar.

[36] It became a single instead—giving Keith the chance to enjoy hearing US radio DJ's try to pronounce "Ceaușescu".

only ten minutes of radio surfing on shortwave they came across a Romanian station reporting live on the demise of Ceauşescu, and "the only solution is another revolution" was grabbed live for the tape.

The interlude pieces—written by Cathal on a keyboard plugged into Nick's Atari ST computer with MIDI studio software—were recorded at a studio in Hackney Road.[37] "A horrible place," groaned Ralph. Another cheapo studio, originally based in Victorian terraced houses which had been a club run by the Kray brothers, it was set up by jazz musicians Dill Katz and Colin Dudman, then run by bass player Ollie Crooke (a friend of Nick's from Berklee College days). The electronica was an important part of Cathal's plans to move away from standard rock and create an otherly sound and feel. The closing doodle, 'More Smack Vicar' included a "motif" that he wanted to include in every Mansions album (it had been on *Against Nature* at the end of '13th Century Boy'): "Sadly, the low-rent version of corporate approvals hell we found ourselves in for the US put an end to that." The Hackney studio, above the minicab office, was also where the synth-based 'Thursday' was recorded: "If you turn it way up and the wind is blowing the right way, you can still hear the 1984 Opel Asconas flocking to Clapton Pond in the kerosene twilight, in search of that Big Fare."[38]

In Cathal's mind he had been difficult throughout the recording of *Viva Dead Ponies*, he'd been unreliable, up and

------

[37] The production work here is credited to Cathal's alter ego Tíma Mansió (Brasil) for Beautiful Sexual Intercourses, B.V. Later the studio became known as The Premises Studios and went up in the world, booked by Nina Simone, Arctic Monkeys, Nick Cave, Amy Winehouse, Al Green, Franz Ferdinand etc.

[38] In Britain, unlike Ireland, the Opel Ascona was a Vauxhall Cavalier.

down. He talked about his "shenanigans" and the "forbearance" of the band. No-one else involved saw or remembers that being the case. What was he seeing that nobody else did? The medical profession might point to 'False Memory Obsessive Compulsive Disorder', a recognised condition that is more likely to affect people with a history of depression. But why put something so complex as the human mind into a box? To an extent he'd been hardwired, against his will, for feelings of shame and regret and the need to confess.

As with any album recording there was a lot of waiting around in the lounge. There were the problems with the tech and uncertainty about who'd play keyboards until Nick Bunker stepped in. There could be the occasional drinking session in the evenings, but nothing crazy. "Cathal would never let that affect the recording. You knew he was the boss, but he was never angry, there were no power trips. He was always gentle and gracious around the band," said Nick Allum. "You couldn't ask for a more polite person to work with," agreed Hugh. "I struggled to understand what he wanted early on—clearly his brain was engaged with lots of other things, he'd be fucked off by things happening in government—but he was a sensitive, nice person to be around." Keith would drop in to the studios and join them for drinks after. "To be honest I just let them do whatever they wanted. They were pushing so many boundaries there seemed to be no limits." There'd be noise everywhere, lots of joking around. Cathal gave them each an Irish nickname, so Grimmo was Sister Mary (while on tour, he would sometimes like to come down to breakfast in a dress); Nick was Nicholas Tiompáin Ó'Drumadoireacht or 'Timps' for short; Hugh was Cool Aodh (pronounced "Cool A"). He referred to himself as Cathal Ó Cochláin.[39] Nick Bagnall was 'the Duke' after Duke Ellington—or 'His Grace', as he preferred to stay above the fray of the Mansions' antics.

Grimmo always took his music around with him: a Seventies' tape deck playing Neil Young's *Harvest Moon*, Lou Reed and the jazz trumpet of Miles Davis. "The tapedeck drove me to distraction," said Hugh. Miles Davis was a thing for them all. In soundchecks the band turned into their alter-egos 'The Tower of Crap Horns', an atonal brass section.[40] Grimmo liked to do impressions of Miles' voice, that fag-ash whisper; he'd quote bits from the recently published autobiography and do a classic Miles-about-town line, point to someone's clothes and do a husky croak of "Hey—nice vines…"[41] And it was Grimmo who played the muted trumpet line at the beginning of 'Look What I Stole' (they had to get a tribute to Miles in there somewhere). They'd go to the local pubs for pints of Guinness, where Cathal would lead the conversation around politics, the latest doings of the Pope and the coming of the Poll Tax.[42] "He'd be reading his

---

[39] Backstage with Kirsty Wark before their performance on *The Late Show* in 1991, the band managed to persuade Kirsty that their lead singer should only be referred to as Cathal Ó Cochláin.

[40] Somewhere, accompanying an article by Dave Cavanagh for *Select* magazine, is a photo of the Mansions with trombones: The Tower of Crap Horns themselves.

[41] Miles Davis had caused permanent damage to his vocal chords by getting into a shouting match with a music exec while he was meant to be resting his throat after surgery.

[42] Officially the 'Community Charge', it was a regressive tax where the wealthy paid the same as lower income householders for local authority services. In March 1990, 200,000 protestors marched through London. There were incidents of riots in the capital (in Hackney, where the police used a baton charge), and protests in towns around the UK, including one of 5,000 people in Bristol (which was charged by mounted police). The Poll Tax was scrapped in 1991 and replaced in 1993.

copy of the *Guardian* in the studio," remembered Nick, "and later be railing against Thatcher and the Poll Tax in the pub —that's really what 'Door to Door Inspector' is about. He was angry and worried. When we used to visit his place in Crouch End we'd have to knock on the window, not the door, so he'd know we weren't bailiffs—or later on, that we weren't coming about his unpaid Poll Tax. On tour the conversations can be two-dimensional—have you heard this, do you like this band. It wasn't like that with Cathal."

The first choice for a title wasn't going to work. Keith was open-minded when it came to a lot of things, but they weren't going to get far in 1990 with an album called *Bugs Fucking Bunny*.[43] There was a story going round that when REM signed for a major label in 1988, Michael Stipe was asked why he'd chosen Warner Brothers. He'd replied: "Bugs Bunny!" A joke, but one that was like fingernails dragged down a blackboard to Cathal (wealthy pop stars enjoying being cute and trivial). REM would become a target again when The Fatima Mansions played New York in 1991. "Everyone was getting excited because they knew Michael Stipe was coming to see the band," said Keith. "They were saying how amazing it was he'd be there. I'm near the back and so I see Stipe coming in with his boyfriend—no-one else does—and they sit down. Grimmo starts playing trumpet for 'Look What I Stole'. He can't play and it's a racket. So after just half a song, Michael Stipe walks out. Everyone's going on about him—'is he here? is he here?', and I say, 'no, he's walked out'". Reportedly Stipe had complained about not

---

[43] Actually, planning to call the album *Bugs Fucking Bunny* was a story cooked up by Keith and Cathal for the music press. Too good a wind-up not to include.

liking 'art rock' bands. And that was the origin of the extraordinary cover version of 'Shiny Happy People' on the *Bertie's Brochures* mini-LP. "We had to get them back, so they did that kind of 2 Unlimited version."

The cover was a painting by Lawrence Bogle, a Newcastle artist who'd been part of the team working on Kitchenware covers for years (including Prefab Sprout's *Swoon*). "Except he'd become much wilder since then," according to Keith. Bogle plays a central part in one of Keith's favourite Mansions stories.

> I'd called Lawrence to make sure the cover image for the single of 'Only Losers Take the Bus' for the US was done, because it was very late and the Mansions' new label were waiting for it. 'They're desperate,' I told him. So I was at a pool party in LA with Radioactive, sitting around drinking beer, one of those classic rock n' roll kind of scenes, when a guy from the label rushes up. He says I've got to go straightaway. I need to go to the record company offices because there's a problem with the sleeve image for 'Only Losers Take the Bus'. I go across town to big corporate offices and I'm in the waiting room. A guy was smoking dope and passing it round— there was a lot of that going on—I didn't do much, but this time I took a hit before I went in, because I didn't know what was coming. So I was half-stoned by the time I get in

there, in this big office with a guy in a suit
and tie. A straight-laced kind of guy. He says:
'The Fatima Mansion artwork has arrived,
and I'm going to show it you.' What I didn't
know was that Lawrence had just split up
with his boyfriend and was going through a
bit of a crisis. He'd let out all his emotions in
one go. This cover had cocks all over it, big
cocks, spunking cocks, cocks up backsides,
cocks everywhere. It was a surreal moment.
So the suit says to me, 'I have one question
for you. Where's the bus?'

The cover of *Viva Dead Ponies* is cock-free. Instead it
illustrates the wavering margins between Hell and modern
life: a table at a wine bar occupied by members of a wealthy
elite. Well-groomed characters with manicured nails are
making clever conversation; a pally arm around the shoulder,
an elegant cigarette. The painting dramatises the unseen
through seething primary colours and wicked mutations.
The assumption of superiority and undertones of spite are
there in the phantom dagger, the spurting demon eye and
fingernails. And the scene widens to the blue world beyond
the wine bar, to what the power system means for ordinary
people, where minions are used in a cycle of shooting, killing
and persecution, to make sure the wheels of wealth generation keep moving. A hovering, hi-tech weapon is waiting if
anything in the system goes wrong.

*

Knock-knock.

"*What are you doing?*"

"*Well. I'm in the toilet sis. You can have two guesses.*"

"*I know you bruv. There's loads more than two things you'd do in the loo.*"

Adrian had fallen in love with student life. So hazy and unlikely it was like a dream. There were essays to write and seminars to miss, but still a dream. He'd been drugged by the glory of it, just from climbing the beer-sticky steps to the shabby heaven of the SU bar every night. He was in one big fat, beer-happy, beer-sad, love story.

Being home for Christmas was like falling out of a hole into proper reality again, where there was triple-ply, peach-coloured toilet paper. This was what an actual home was like, where the rooms were warm, the carpets were thick and soft, and even the toilet smelt nice. There was food everywhere—on plates, on trays, in the fridge—and food you wanted to eat, not ends of Mother's Pride and rubbery cheese. Booze came in funny small glasses and you sipped it.

Knock-knock.

"*Yes, hello, thanks. Won't be long.*"

He wants to stay there as long as he can. There was something reassuringly boring about it. The magnolia walls and their pictures of cats. The potpourri bowl with silver and gold baubles. A little toilet window that looks over a winter tree and the grey of the season.

"*What's wrong with Dad?*"

"*Eh?*"

"*Has he said anything to you? It's like he's here on a mission. And that bloody Snowman tie.*"

"*I think he looks smart sis. Better than that track suit he wore, you remember that? He's trying.*"

"That's what I'm worried about—trying what? Does he think he's in with a chance with Mum? That next year we're going round his place to eat tinned potatoes."

"No. No—he's not nuts."

"Isn't he?"

"Give him a break. It's not his thing. You know. People. Can't you talk to him?"

"About what?"

"Mum. So he knows where he stands."

"Who am I, Marjorie Proops?"

"You could be. You look like her."

"I'll think about it Turd."

Because she can't see him behind the door, Adrian smiles. She'd not called him that for years.

*

An angry LP by an Evil Man? Cathal is more like a Japanese demon. A statue of a howling monster positioned at the front gates of a temple to ward off evil spirits, his goggling face distorted by rage. Not representing a single moment of anger but a stance that demonstrates a readiness to keep on fighting. A vocation. "Our contemporary pop climate is, make no mistake, rich in many treasurable things but is almost bereft of any *real* intensity," wrote Andrew Mueller in 1991. "The furious are currently without franchise. The nearest Ride *et al* ever get is a kind of attractive diffident annoyance, the sort one feels when the Highgate platform indicator informs that the next Charing Cross tube is due sometime around 1997… So, we need Cathal Coughlan, and we need his mighty, mighty band. Cathal just about makes up for everyone.

Cathal gives the impression it would be substantially less time-consuming to list the things he isn't completely wound up about."

As we've seen in this potted history of the start of the Nineties and the rise in the status of commerce there were good reasons to be angry. Not just because of the unemployment, the greed, or even the Poll Tax. It was the lack of interest in truth, an unthinking acceptance of convenient untruths (leave the banks to it, they know what they're doing with your money; what does it matter if a CEO earns a hundred and twenty times more than the average employee?). Acceptance of the absurd because that was business, and business was paying the bills. Which is why the output of The Fatima Mansions sounds so much like it's set at the end of the world, in a pandemonium where no-one sees or cares what's happening. Cathal's foot is down hard on the pedal, or he's running carelessly down the stairs (one step, two steps, seven steps), he's an exile always on the move and getting away. Only the wilderness awaits.

Viva Dead Ponies—as the title song suggests—is a bloody lament for the lives of the underclass. The ones left with nothing and still kept under surveillance in 'Angel's Delight': "You roll down my street in your gleaming new car / I've got no secrets, cash or time left to give you". There's no basis for making moral choices anymore: "the rich man's militia photographing my block / Kill a cop. Why the hell not?" For not playing the game the way they should, the underclasses are visited by the Door-to-Door Inspector: "You made your choice when mocking the ways of true grown men / Now may your woman-love protect you / As you face this grievous punishment you've earned." Most worryingly, the Inspector is "rapping on your window"—which means he's figured out Cathal's signal. For the underclass every moment of life is a struggle, "folks use razor blades for toothpaste / And every breath is a holy war". It has been traditional for underclasses to look to religion as a refuge and solace, and in the West especially, to Jesus, the protector of the meek. Which is why Cathal wanted to re-imagine what "old Jeezus" would do if he really was to return to Earth: "When he's behind his sportscar wheel / And the windscreen glass is all gummed up with blood?" The blood-stained windscreen was a recurring image of Cathal's: the idea that modern life had become a racetrack for the privileged, an express highway where the underclass could easily find themselves smashed to oblivion. The Jeezus of 1990, of course, turns from religion to business, the only true faith, "he sells papers and beer in a shop in Crouch End". He's not any better off than anyone else, a bully, deluded by his own sense of grandeur ("If you can't shift this crate of Brillo pads by Friday, vengeance shall be mine").[44] Without a foundation of truth, nothing matters. There's the same potential slide into madness even for a son of God: "I have switched the fridges off / And I will burn down this whole stinking shop / I will get drunk *and I will break every little Islamical law*".

Heaven isn't a blissful place to escape to anyway, there's still hierarchy and more judgment doled out to even the meekest and most ailing characters: "Now she's ascend-

---

[44] Cathal may have had a particular seller of Brillo pads in mind. When asked by the *NME* for 'ten excellent excuses for suicide', he included Budgens supermarket in Crouch End.

ing into heaven with contentment on her face / And Holy God is there to greet and batter her into her place."

The album is much more than angry, there's wit and merriment and the macabre, as well as moments that are quietly reflective. The jokes can be dark, like those about death: "A holiday in a box, opportunity knocks"; bawdy: "Passion not spent, a man alone (with his hand)"; and nicely surreal: "On the day that I was born / There was no big flash and no great storm / But the man read the news in Dutch and warned / 'I'm gonna play 'Je T'aime' on my hunting horn' / In my cradle I was most impressed—/ So this is what you call success." And rather than ranting, Cathal's lyrics are filled with empathy for what grinding poverty can doe to people. The chemical cosh of drugs and booze, the constant insecurity, the sickness and jealousy, none of it makes for a load of saints, and as with any good novelist, it's not clear whose side Cathal is on. 'A Pack of Lies' is a vicious folk tale: the story of an immigrant clutching at whatever he can get. He marries a dying woman, pretending to be affectionate for sex, then dumps her when he goes back home ("They were herded on like cattle to a ferry at high tide / This unkempt, aging orphan and his helpless, dying bride / But he left her at the other shore crying on the deck"). Ordinary people bow to the powerful and their lies, and end up following their example of vicious greed. "The moral of this story is: this land's a victim-farm / Don't you ever feed a beggar here, *he'll eat your fucking arm*." 'Look What I Stole For Us Darling' isn't about shoplifting a tin of beans for the kids' tea, it's a horror film about a coven of bodysnatchers, flickering with a nasty sulphurous light. The lyrics are livid with desperation: "We discuss ways to die, ways we could have gone wrong / We don't mention the now / We can see no way out / We draw skulls on the walls / We draw blood from our balls / We play catch with the rats / Still the silence won't crack though we heave and we hack". They play at necrophilia for fun with a woman's torso. "*We used to be—human beings—not anymore / I'll have her washed and brought to you / So you, my wife, can know her, too*".

For the financially comfortable, the landscape of the album is a plastic city, a Legoland ("I weed my house, I wash my trees"). Shiny but unnerving under a "burnt-out silver sun", divided by walls of concrete. The busy, pulsing noises of the city are the sound of anxiety, the lesss-than-human. And the countryside that had once been home to the lower classes of old has been reduced to a ruined in-between: "It rains for miles out there / On mud and tar and still air / And the fungus-lined gap between stinking towns".

The hyperreality of the album is governed by petty officials who are both pathetic and dangerous. Five years before the first airing of the sitcom *Father Ted*, 'Mr Baby' depicted a very similar kind of priesthood—made up of feckless servants of an organisation they don't understand or want to understand. "See the priest in gleaming nappies / Gurgling and burping child at play / Signing warrants, blessing firing squads / Are the pleasures of this baby's day". The closing piece, 'More Smack Vicar' has an Alice in Wonderland feel, capturing the absurdity of the traditional scene of priests going round to parishioners homes for afternoon tea (on estates like Fatima Mansions). The church, the state, police, bailiffs. Cathal's lyrics are obsessed with the violence that exists within seemingly benign and traditional systems of power. It can look like paranoia when he talks about the CIA, the Pope, the US President, the Poll Tax inspectors—as if they're all in on the same plot. But maybe we just don't want to think about it. As Thatcher implied in her final speech to Parliament, there was a need for surveillance and violence if capitalism was to be protected from evil. Evidence of the approach was already there in the response to the coal miners' strikes of 1984. The miners were "the enemy within" she said, and that legitimised the use of police violence.[45] Institutions had become very good at making extreme ideas seem normal, demonising reasonable opposition. "They will have it known you're mad if you don't fit their equation," sang Cathal.

The album's mood can be rueful and helpless. "If the past is a wreck then all who sail in it / Make me realise it's time to move on / But all the ships and the planes have gone / I'm in a savage place with a timid song." The ballads and quiet pieces of electronica were always an essential part of Cathal's idea of the Mansions, acting as echoes of those long walks around London's streets and backways.[46] Cathal would do acoustic shows in-between those of the full band at places like Brownies bar near the Marquee, where he'd play songs

---

[45] At the 'Battle of Orgreave' in June 1984, protesting miners were charged by mounted police and beaten with truncheons. The chair of the South Yorkshire Police Committee called it "deplorable; sheer hooliganism by yobs in uniform". In 1991, the police force was found to be guilty of assault, wrongful arrest, unlawful detention and malicious prosecution, and made to pay out £425,000 in compensation to 39 miners.

[46] When *Viva Dead Ponies* was finally allowed on music streaming services, Cathal complained about what happened to 'Concrete Block'. It was far too loud. "But of course the streaming service overlord/undertakers don't give 2-fux anyway, so they are the great normaliser of history…"

such as 'Wilderness On Time' and 'Bertie's Brochures', when Nick Allum would play piano.

There's a fulcrum to the anger and macabre cynicism in the LP, and that's Cathal's sense of truth and beauty. It's there in the *musique concrète* approach—a form of listening to sounds which French filmmaker Jean Epstein described as the "phenomenon of an epiphanic being". Because along with its noise, *Ponies* echoes some of the gorgeously dark theatre of Scott Walker's *Scott3* (1969). As a writer for *Rock and Roll Globe* put it, Cathal was "a man who knew exactly what to love, what to hate and how to draw a line between the two with a colourful precision worthy of any of the great expressionist painters." He was careful not to be a literary poseur, but the lyrics are crafted and poetic. They were written out by hand for the inside cover of the album (as he'd also done for the Microdisney album *Crooked Mile*).[47] Like so much Irish literature, there's an unusual richness to Cathal's use of language, it's full-blooded, extravagant and racy. As if he couldn't write any other way, having drunk in a national culture built on myth and stories that worked as a defence against oppression. Words needed to be rich and dark to keep the blood stirring and strong, to be used as a way to reach a more difficult, ransacked, boarded-up beauty. So there's a poetry of atmosphere on the album: "At the platform's end, where the crowd grew thin / And the light was

---

[47] There's some ad libbing in what he's written: 'Angel's Delight' is just "perfectly intelligible" either flagging that it's all about the performance or his caution at putting the words down on paper. And he didn't bother with 'Thursday': "naah". The extras are saved for 'Farewell Oratorio': "Beastly, beastly... but still, though... Lullabye of Legoland – rockabye my little angels – 20th century casualty – not a fashionable nationality [something not decipherable about "God from us"], and an aside to 'Chemical Cosh': "I've got your number, also, H.M Rentboy, plus which I know how to write it on paper – I even own some paper. Jesus, I'm rich."

dim on our shoes / Where we sat there so tense/ Not to touch though we meant to (I think) / There was no will, no spell / To breach the night and stop the talk / She tossed her hair and home did walk." Robust metaphors: "The frost-damp town wore a fat-guts frown"; "What do you do when words collapse / And all that's left is broken glass?". And a complex, worked out poetry of ideas: "Well, now accept you're just a person / Not the touchstone, not the face / Of the ages past, their grandeur / And the death-wish of the Master Race". Often there's an intellectual collage going on, even in a song as blunt as 'Angel's Delight' (a title that implies both religious doctrine and a popular instant pudding). The lyrics involve serious questions about the nature of morality—who gets to decide what that is, who upholds it and how—alongside images of militarism, torture devices and heaven's revenge. "It was my way of throwing a brick," explained Cathal. "At the time, people were being jailed in England for protesting the Poll Tax. And I was having a lot of difficulty with government agencies. And I was living in a bad area with lots of burglaries and the police did nothing. The 'kill a cop' thing was just my brick through their window." Unlike Ice-T who was the subject of record store boycotts and torrid media and political attention because of his 'Cop Killer' in 1992, no-one seemed to notice Cathal's brick as it sailed past.

"Cathal was a giant. He was a great writer," said collaborator Jacknife Lee. "His perspective was really unique. Even when I met him when he was twenty, he was writing things like 'Helicopter of the Holy Ghost', he was intellectually so far ahead of everybody else. He was intimidatingly smart and gifted, conveying these images that were so tangible."

*

While the early Eighties bands of *Like Magic* would see themselves on the anti-rock side of Romantic idealism and sincerity, ideas of 'goodness' became muddled and difficult by the Nineties. Business and the cultural mainstream had been steadily co-opting the model of what made shiny happy good people through inescapable campaigns of marketing and advertising. With the conviction of Puritans, they insisted people should follow the path of careers and consumption. The worst blasphemy would be to contradict the value of money.

Among some people, that association was prompting feelings of ambivalence and ambiguity—and a certain sympathy for the Devil. Who 'owned' goodness? It was easy for culturally dominant forces to slate whatever contradicted their happiness mantra—or they could do their work as randomly as they liked, according to Cathal's 'Evil Man': "The city was evil, some country was evil, the hippies were evil, the writers were evil, the homeless were evil, the workers were evil, the summer was evil, independence was evil". Growing up meant understanding that nothing was that simple. Sometimes there were just different agendas. We're all capable of weakness and mistakes, and imposing ideals of good could be as repressive and inhuman as a regime of the bad. During the government of religious extremist Oliver Cromwell, the job of communicating this contrary message was taken by John Milton via his portrayal of Satan in *Paradise*

Lost (1667).[48] "Satan, cast down to hell by a vindictive and smiling God, comes before us with all heroic magnificence," wrote Milton's biographer AN Wilson. "Around this character he had thrown a singularity of daring, a grandeur of sufferance, and a ruined splendour, which constitute the very height of poetic sublimity," according to Samuel Coleridge. Another poet, Charles Baudelaire suggested that a "hidden Lucifer figure" was "enthroned deep in every human heart". The best art recognised this truth and "expressed the blasphemous element in human passion".

Against this kind of setting, Cathal makes even more sense—the man described by Andrew Mueller for *Melody Maker* as that "horned Sinatra"—and when he sang: "Of course I burn with an evil burst", "I'll be good 'till Thursday comes / Then burn all good away". It was a role that stuck with him. Sitting down with his laptop to take part in Tim Burgess's Listening Party for *Ponies* in 2021, Cathal knew what his audience were expecting: "It's morning in the Big Satan house… Aah, let the fresh air fill your lungs… along with the manganese and dioxins."

Paddy McAloon enjoyed playing the rakish devil. He liked 'Horsin' Around' and telling 'Blueberry Pies'. For him, music was a "wild thing with mischief to prove". The one intimate, acoustic song on *Jordan*, 'Mercy', is written from the perspective of the Devil. Lucifer also sings 'Michael', about trying to make things up with God: "help me write a letter to you know who". Paddy stands up for the Devil against binary thinking: "if you are on the side of good / Now where

---

[48] It shouldn't be forgotten that Cromwell initiated and led the invasion of Ireland to suppress Catholic forces, leading to massacres of Irish Catholics.

does that leave me?", and "without mercy where is goodness?". The sympathy had always been there. Paddy knew
the Devil had all the best tunes; and when he came a-calling
he was "charming, articulate, urbane". The original cover of
Protest Songs (1989)—designed by Lawrence Bogle—included
a scrawled pair of devil's horns on Wendy's innocently wistful face. Together, *Viva Dead Ponies* and *Jordan* formed a Kitchenware diptych for 1990, a Paradise Lost adventure that
illuminated a dull year with colour and curiosity, with Devils
and Angels. "We'd done really well in the Eighties by being
fearless and I think we regained our early fearlessness, combined with Paddy and Cathal's artistic confidence," said
Keith, "but to be honest, I don't think any of us were doing
anything we hadn't done before. We just knew more. I was
always trying to give all our artists the confidence to express
themselves."

While the critics might have thought they witnessed
the Angel Harriet descend from Heaven ("*we don't deserve
them…* with our pollution, our litter, our bad manners, our
belches: *we are not fit for this*—this snow-voice, this chorus, this
deity, this love. They are everything we hoped and prayed
they would be."), we know better. It was the Devil in Harriet
that made her go down to the shed. And The Sundays' attitude is clear in a song from *Blind.* "Love to be good / But
we'd rather be bad / But how was I supposed to know
that? / Because God made people / That was the luck of
the draw/ We do what we want." From the Go-Betweens'
perspective there was 'something of the night' about Peter
Milton Walsh. Certainly he was a songwriter looking for
beauty in the night, but more often than not he was finding
something unsettling. Like this from 'What's Left of Your

Nerve': "then you turned up angel, my innocent one / With your suitcase of knives… the next time I see you / You're skinning the dog." The Trashcans knew their way around Hell. How many times had they been pulled over by the police on the M666 after they'd been showing off their private parts again?

*

"When *Viva Dead Ponies* came out I remember thinking I'm not going to make a better album than this, and I don't think I have," said Nick. At the time they all needed the money and Hugh's first thought was that maybe it "wasn't a commercial album" but might play better in the US. "I was extremely proud of it—you can't put it in a box, there's nothing else like it." John Mulvey in the *NME* gave it a 9/10: "*Viva Dead Ponies* stands as 1990's most varied, inexhaustible and downright malicious white-knuckle ride. *Viva Dead Ponies* makes the entire, and not inconsiderable, recorded work of Microdisney look like a warm-up exercise." Morrissey made it his 'Album of the Year' in *Melody Maker*, and he probably wasn't joking. While recognising the achievement, some reviews, like this one in *Hot Press*, could be distracted by the anger. "Fatima Mansions really do summon up the repressed hate-filled nightmares behind the dreams of poppy love. All the familiar keyboard cliches of the dancefloor get warped in Fatima Mansions' festival of folly. 'Thursday' could be the Hitman and Cher, 'You're A Rose' is a malicious transmutation of Bros… there are moments like the opening 'Angel's

Delight' when Coughlan's anger gets unmoored and his abuse unfocused."

The album could be too extraordinary to stomach. An obscure jag in the smooth reinvention of indie rock that was underway, the move towards grunge, shoe gaze and Britpop, because Cathal had followed his imaginative instincts rather than any plan. He wasn't going to be "tuneful, cute and giving" anymore. The Microdisney effect. He didn't ever want to have that feeling again, of having gone halfway towards pop acceptability and then been rejected anyway. How many more chances would he have? "See, that's how we make our living / In a hall full of corpses, we'd smile and bounce on / Some say it's aimless bullshit / But they come from big houses and budgets / And, although I don't look it, I'm getting really fucking old" ('White Knuckle Express'). "I think he had a weakness, in that he created sabotage quite a lot," Jacknife Lee has suggested. "Sabotage was one of the genetic codes of Fatima Mansions, you can hear it in the songs. He didn't give a fuck if people liked him or not which is not what happens now in music." It would take distance and a separation from its context for *Viva Dead Ponies* to become lovable. In 2022, *Louder than War* declared it to be "the Fatima's DEFINITIVE musical statement and a true tour de force magnum opus of utter spellbinding brilliance. No other album released that year quite matched its sheer diversity of styles and its compulsive magnificence." Cathal has talked it down, as an "outsider gesture that got somehow inflated. All things went wrong during and after", but has also admitted it's a favourite, "the one where wasn't so much of a blueprint".

*

Playing *Ponies* live, the Mansions blew everyone away. "They were the best live band I've ever seen. Bono once said the same," said Keith. "I remember them at the Bull & Gate in Camden playing their biggest gig so far. Cathal came on stage and stared at everyone. He just stood there staring at

Straight out of the limo and onto Venice Beach, Florida: Cathal, Nick, Hugh, Nick Bagnall and Aindrías. Courtesy of Hugh Bunker.

this crowd of hundreds. Whole minutes went past, then he said: *'I've been all around the fookin world… And I still can't find my*

fookin baby' and the band launches into 'Chemical Cosh'."[49]
Touring might not have been glamorous, with no budget for
anything other than B&Bs, lots of drinking and junk food
(and Sister Mary turning up in her dress), but they were
some of the best times, said Hugh. "We were a real rock and
roll band but we wanted to try to express music correctly,
make sure our shit was wired down with no mistakes or
messing about. Playing with Cathal was a fantastic experience—his interaction with the rest of the band really got us
going."

After *Ponies*, the music kept coming, but this time
with a different sound for the mini-LP *Bertie's Brochures* (1991).
Nick introduced Cathal to producer Victor Van Vugt, who
he'd been working with on tour with The Apartments.
"Cathal wanted to make a more acoustic record after the
experiments with electronic music," said Victor. "He was
always taking a new direction. It all suited me—especially as
we recorded it at a church studio round corner from where I
was living. I'd just done a Billy Bragg album there. I'd go
hold of this ex-BBC microphone which sounded amazing
with Cathal's voice. It was only later that I realised it had
been broken all that time."

Then the business world caught up with the Mansions, like it was always going to. Cathal had signed to the
US label Radioactive Records, a part of MCA. "He insisted
on signing the contract in the Blind Beggar pub in Whitechapel, because he wanted to get the slick record executive to
go to a shitty East End pub," said Nick. They'd get to experi-

---

[49] For anyone not a Lisa Stansfield fan, this is a reference to the chorus of one of the
biggest hits of that year, 'All Around the World'.

ence the smell of stale beer and an aura of menace and despair. The Blind Beggar had been top of William Booth's list of places to preach about salvation and the evils of drink, and where Ronnie Kray shot Georgie Cornell in the head.[50] Like Cathal, Keith knew what they were getting into. "Radioactive was a deal of convenience. We always thought of Kitchenware like Malcolm X, you know 'by any means necessary', and we'd run out of money. That meant dealing with the devil. Radioactive's Gary Kurfirst, yeah, he was a real number." Kurfirst was a hustler who'd started out in the Sixties music scene around Greenwich Village as a promoter and manager. He'd set up the New York Festival and the first east coast shows for Jimi Hendrix and The Who. A tall, balding man with a straggling tail of leftover hair and chocolate-brown eyes. He knew some tricks as a negotiator—but he was also known to be passionate about the music he liked, for which he'd move mountains. His clients included the Ramones, Blondie, Talking Heads, the B-52's and Eurythmics.[51]

Mansions records were being pushed out in the US, there were bigger support slots on tours and then Radioactive put all the money up for the making of *Lost in the Former West* (1993). The new contract changed the way the band worked, because now they were on a retainer rather than getting a flat fee for jobs. Nick spoke for the band in sorting out a gentleman's agreement over royalties; if there were go-

---

[50] Now it's a gentrified tourist attraction where a record industry boss would enjoy buying £10 pints of craft beer.

[51] Gary Kurfirst died aged 61 in 2009 while on holiday in the Bahamas.

ing to be supersized US sales then the band should get its share.

Radioactive, of course, only ever saw the investment into Cathal and the band as a loan. It had to be paid back somehow. With Cathal's sabotage approach that wasn't going to easy—and the deal started to affect the music, said Hugh: "It felt like *Lost* was more for an American market with the heavy guitar riffs. They brought in the Talking Heads producer for some sessions [Jerry Harrison]. He spent a lot of time in the studio trying to sell his house, which really pissed me off, it was bizarre." Radioactive themselves started to lose interest. "Things got bad in the later days when we were touring with Weezer and Live. It didn't feel right opening for them at all, but there we were travelling 14,000 miles across the US in seven weeks. We were promised a tour bus, but instead we got a transit van with a trailer. It almost killed me." If these kinds of hints weren't strong enough, the label then stopped sending the band money to cover its touring expenses. "We ended up having to go to down to Radioactive's office. We were going to sit there until we got paid," said Hugh. "In the end they said okay, we'll wire money but you'll need to go to a Western Union office for a money transfer. I went in a taxi with Andy, our tour manager and guitar techs Barry and Roger to pick up a very large amount of cash. The Western Union was in the worst part of town, there were people just hanging around on these dodgy streets, wanting cash badly. Barry stayed in the cab with orders to keep the engine running while the rest of us fetched the money."[52]

Radioactive were a disaster for Cathal. They wouldn't release any more records and the Mansions were left with financial debts and an accumulation of legal fees as Cathal tried to get out of the contract. "It's the same old story," said Victor, "they keep on saying 'we don't hear a hit, we don't hear a hit', so you have to go back and keep writing songs for another year. Cathal would have made his own *Metal Machine Music*[53] to get out of the contract if he could have done. You're fucked when labels don't let bands go. It's filthy. There's no other way of making an income, just doing fuck all. It's still like that, you can't tour if there's no record. I wish he'd not joined Radioactive. With his ambition as a songwriter he would have sat side-by-side with Scott Walker, easily." Cathal and the Mansions belonged to Radioactive, and they weren't planning to do anything with them unless Cathal wrote some hits, which he had no incentive to do. There was no more band.[54]

Physically and mentally Cathal had been burning up: working out and exercising so that he could drink even more heavily and not feel the effects so badly, not sleeping, allow-

---

[52] A series of events that provided the title for the Mansions live CD 'Western Union Steak-out'.

[53] Lou Reed's legendary white noise album from 1975.

[54] Aindrías has been a teacher of History and English in Germany. Nick is a professor of research methodology in the Sociology department at Essex University (and continues to play with Peter in The Apartments). He played on many of Cathal's excellent solo albums, including *Black River Falls* (2000) and *The Sky's Awful Blue* (2002). Hugh works for the Environment Agency, and played bass on *Grand Necropolitan* (1996).

ing his intensity to build and build and burst in his performances.

> I was living fast, planning to die young and I
> was probably gonna take a few people with
> me. I didn't think beyond the next step and I
> bitterly regret that because that was how I
> really fucked up my life and other people's.
> The fact that I didn't give myself or anybody
> else any reason for hope meant that there was
> just limitless scope for destruction. I was nev-
> er gonna last anyway, nothing was ever gonna
> last.

As an indication of Cathal's state of mind, he compared his
time touring in the US with Cormac McCarthy's *Blood Me-*
ridian (1985), a novel that follows the story of a teenager in
the nineteenth century who falls into a routine of violence,
taking part in casual killings and joining a gang who hunt
down native Indians to scalp. The book resonated with his
feeling of being consumed by negative emotions until Hell
became the norm. The blood-boiling performances had
come with a price. "I was being more aggressive on stage
than ever before and I was hurting myself, physically, to a
point where I was having trouble doing anything else. The
set we've been doing is in-your-face the whole way through."
Cathal began to practice meditation which included an
awareness of breathing technique. He became teetotal, a
vegan and a habitual runner—as a way to save himself
rather than become Mr Perfect, and the lyrics to 'Chemical
Cosh' spell out a rationale why. Those were still the days

when being a vegetarian marked someone out as eccentric. "I remember us wandering around Chicago looking for oatcakes," said Keith. "He was wasting away." "He was the only vegetarian, teetotaller I'd ever met in my life," said Victor (the man who'd spent 13 years on tour with Nick Cave and the Bad Seeds, The Go-Betweens and The Pogues). "It really calmed him down, he was a different Cathal Coughlan." In early 1992, Cathal split up with up his long-term girlfriend, his source of security and continuity. Gone. That same year, the *Valhalla Avenue* album came out to unenthusiastic reviews and Radioactive decided not to even release it in the US. He was starting to wonder whether he could, or should, be writing songs any more. Keith and the Kitchenware family encouraged Cathal to move up to Newcastle, to get away from London and its bad associations and be part of a more grounded music scene. Somewhere he could swap dirty jokes with Wendy of the Sprouts. "He thought Newcastle and the Geordies were funny, the dialects and words that only people in Newcastle would use. It was like a theme park and he enjoyed himself. Another reason for coming up was that he fancied my secretary, Julie. It was love at first sight for those two, you could tell when Cathal first walked into the office." Julie, an American from Detroit, was the office goddess. "Julie had such a great voice. We always thought she was like the secretary in the film of *The Producers*. People would ring up just to hear her voice and get to speak to her. She'd be chatting away for ages and we'd say 'Julie, is that for us?'— 'Oh yeah, it's for you'." There was a Kitchenware wedding in the centre of Newcastle in 1993 with the Mansions, the

Sprouts, the Kane Gang, the Daintees and Hurrah! Also joining Cathal and Julie at a pub afterwards.

His new home and lifestyle meant less dependence on getting recognition as an artist. Nothing, though, would soften the intensity of the Coughlan gaze. Even the likeable Geordies weren't going to get away with unthinking consumerism.

> Living in Newcastle, which is such a football town, the dichotomy between people's class allegiances and what they subscribe to through football really fucking pisses me off no end. You've got intelligent people who know what they're doing paying hundreds of pounds for season tickets to St. James' Park. People who hate the Tory party and everything it stands for and their season ticket money is going to this fucking millionaire arsehole called John Hall who gives money to the Tory party and has had a knighthood from the Tory party.

By 1996 Cathal and Julie were back in London, living in Whitechapel. Still under the yoke of Radioactive, he took a degree in Digital Publishing and in 2002 got a job as a Technical Product Manager working on BBC websites. "I thought, okay, I am not going to be dependent on any of that [music industry funding] in the future, so I figured out something else I could do to pay the rent, and I kind of split myself in two really." "He hated it sometimes," said Nick. A (beautiful) song written at the time, 'Goodbye Sadness' includes a glimpse of Cathal's attitude to our zombie-like absorption by everything digital: "Technology stuff would mop those lives up / Computer graphics and digital bluff". But the balance worked for him: "you realise you have to keep going, you do what you have to do, and you get the work out to some people, somehow. In a way, rightly or wrongly, I think I have chalked up a lot of problems in my life by trying to make a whole living out of music."

*

Someone had told her Cathal Coughlan had once been in music, but Arabella hadn't really thought about it until now, when she was about to work with him on the *Children in Need* platform. Then she'd discovered exactly why you should never Google your boss.

The trouble was, it kind of made you stare. They had a catch-up meeting on cloud storage planned, a one-to-one, and Cathal would be waiting for her in one of the break-out rooms. He'd be there first, with his laptop, notepad and pen. A slender, gaunt-faced man who'd look at her from over the top of his bi-focal reading glasses. There was a lot of pressure on the digital side when it came to scheduling and guarantees of continuity, but it never showed in Cathal. He was a picture of calm. When things went wrong, as they always would, his only reaction would be a look of wry amusement. This was the man who'd managed the big 'all or nothing' stuff for the corporation, like the first online voting platform for *Strictly Come Dancing* in 2004, and the years of making sure the voting platform for *Sports Personality Of The Year* wouldn't break. But now Arabella also knew he was the singer who'd stuck the Virgin Mary up his bottom at a U2 concert.

"Hello Cathal!"

"Hello."

He's looking through some notes, underlines a couple of things and then closes the file. He looks tired.

"Where did you want to start?" asks Arabella.

"Well—you're new to the team, aren't you."

"Yes. Great. Looking forward to it."

"So we'll need to start with the real essentials."

"Essentials? Great!"

"Yes. You see, basically, we're planning on diversifying our role at the BBC."

"Are we? That sounds, you know, exciting."

"It will be. Because we're going to get our own pro-gramme commissioned. Try and up the old quality levels round here. And we've figured out a way to ambush the Head of Commissioning at the exact moment he's got the optimum amount of money to spend, and the minimum amount of time to work out how to spend it."

"What do I do?"

"Well, you need to help us decide which idea to pitch him. We've been brainstorming these things for weeks now. You might have thought it was all high-level meetings round here, but not really. So. Are you ready for this?"

"Can't wait Cathal."

"First we want to do *Wiki Hospital*."

"Oh—I love it!"

"Well, hold on there now—*Wiki Hospital* is where we set up our own hospital with real doctors and nurses and things. There are real people who come in as patients with their actual emergencies and diseases. But all the treatments in our hospital come from ideas and theories we get from User Generated Content on the Internet. You know, alternative treatments."

"Oh—God."

"But what do you think. Is it going to be a ratings winner?"

"I don't know —"

"The other one, basically, is a reality TV concept called *Born to be Wild*. We get some newborn babies and leave them in the forest with a hidden BBC Nature camera crew and then see what happens. Any good?"[55]

"Bloody hell."

"It's got that thing."

"Thing?"

"You know—'peril'."

"Yes, yes I think they really have."

"Anyway I'll leave that with you Arabella. We must lower our sights from the future of the *telefís* and move on to the cloud."

"Before we start, I was just going to ask, one thing —"
"Sure."

Cathal takes off his glasses and rubs his eyes.

"Sorry Cathal, nothing, no, never mind. I've, I've been looking at some suppliers…"

---

[55] These ideas are from an actual pub conversation involving BBC tech managers. *Wiki Hospital* was Cathal's idea, *Born to be Wild* was Matt Verrill's.

*

Cathal was ill with sarcoma, a cancer of the bones and soft connecting tissue, for a number of years before he died on 18 May 2022 in the Royal Marsden Hospital in Chelsea. He was 61. After Microdisney and The Fatima Mansions, he'd gone on to make solo recordings that bear comparison with the best work of Scott Walker and Tom Waits. Maybe Cathal's proudest moment came in 2000, when Scott Walker himself booked Cathal to appear in the Meltdown festival he'd curated. Cathal kept hold of a handwritten note that Walker had written to him.

Cathal was a mostly forgotten man. Even at his height, Coughlan was a cartoon character for the press and the industry as a whole. A scary bloke in a parka with a Wilko bag who'd shout at passersby. Spouting a dark poetry with a clarity and depth of vision few people could be bothered to try to understand.

If we'd had the chance, wouldn't we have done something more? made sure he'd known it had been worthwhile, that he wasn't forgotten? It's too late now.

3.

"Is there one spell can bring, the once and future king?"
Prefab Sprout, *Jordan: The Comeback*
(August 1990)

A skinny boy leaves the field of battle, a matchstick of skin and bone in a jersey top.

Patrick has already forgotten the wet playing fields and the smell of trodden grass that's rank and green in the air around him, because he's walking off the pitch at St James' Park and there's a riot going on. He's just bagged the winner against Leeds United. Bobby Moncur had stopped a pass at the back and lumped it to Tony Green. He'd shimmied and threaded the ball like a needle through cloth—and who was there, taking it in his stride so smoothly? Supermac. And bang. Bottom corner like a rocket.

Okay then, not like that. He'd run through and chipped the keeper, yeah, in a perfect drifting arc, teasing everyone until the net bulged. And now Supermac's walking through the lads, they're clapping him as he heads out through his own personal exit to a waiting Rolls-Royce. He doesn't even need to go to the showers —[1]

"*Ow! Christ*—"

A slap on the head.

"C'mon Loony man—"

The boys are running away from him, too far in front to hear his choice of words for them. He wasn't shouting after the bollocks, he'd tell them later. Patrick's never short of something to say, his tongue poised and ready for action, a skip in his step.

There are soft lakes of cloud on the horizon, one grey Galilee after another. A moment of lemon sunlight falls on St Cuthbert's Seminary and illuminates the plain elegance of its Georgian edifice. It looks like a workhouse run by the most reasonable and agreeable of Enlightenment thinkers. On either side of that imposing building is a neo-Gothic chapel, close enough to visit in your pyjamas if you wanted to; each of them a mini-Heaven thick with gleaming symbols and clusters of mystery, and an immediate response, or reproach, to the earth-bound thinking of the Georgians.

It's one of those mellow autumn afternoons that are both limpid and faintly smoky with chimneys. Early enough in the new term that faces are still looking strange, even the ones that had been so familiar just a couple of months before. They were carrying on with the football match out on

---

[1] Between 1971 and 1976, Supermac (Malcolm Macdonald) scored 95 goals in 187 appearances for Newcastle United. To the tune of 'Jesus Christ Superstar', fans would sing "Supermac, superstar, how many goals have you scored so far?". Opposing fans had another version: "Supermac, superstar, wears frilly knickers and a see-through bra."

the field, the shouts and screams lingering high above in the cool air. Patrick stops to look behind him, back over Northern hills to the clouds that have turned into a great ridge of ash topped by rose-coloured peaks. He's dreaming of a living room with a coal fire. A colour television set and a bag of salty chips while he sits and watches the hot, ruby scenes of a TV studio; Marc Bolan with his glossy ringlets and dirty sweet guitar singing 'Hot Love'. The devils always had the best curls. A tempted angel, Patrick was going to keep growing his hair until it gave up and curled. How could anyone be a priest and take the vow when there was Lyn Paul and her honey waves of hair.[2] That lazy curl of honey only girls had, that even God didn't know how to make. And if he didn't, who did?

There it was again: an ache of confusion brought on by the idea and thrill of music. Knowing something was out there he needed to find and be part of. An exciting confusion because he'd fallen in love with some-thing and not some-one.

*

It's been a strange kind of love story. A love that wouldn't leave Paddy McAloon alone, like the red shoes of the fairytale. He was always fascinated by the intimations of melody and how they made him feel. The ineffable moments

---

[2] An early crush of Paddy's was a member of the New Seekers, who'd had hits with 'I'd Like to Teach the World to Sing (in Perfect Harmony', 'Beg, Steal or Borrow' and 'You Won't Find Another Fool Like Me'. Lyn Paul (originally Lynda Belcher) was Rod Stewart's girlfriend.

that together could be a kind of innocent, everyday spirituality. There was a secret in there somewhere.

The religious education that was one part of his upbringing might have suggested the need for an unworldly quest (looking for something more than the getting and spending) but not the ultimate goal in itself or the way to get there. There are similarities here with Cathal, in the way religion was everywhere in their young lives, often imbibed without noticing; and how neither would swallow religion whole. With his hatred of power systems, we've seen how Cathal gobbed it back out. Instead of taking much notice of official theology, Paddy began to make a rudimentary one of his own, starting with home-made records cut out of paper, with the name McAloon and lines of schoolboy poetry written on the label in the centre; and by writing songs in his seminary bedroom on the guitar he'd borrowed from home.

It was this kind of reverence for songwriting that would make him a unique figure in pop. There was no way round the winking flashbulbs of the music industry to begin with; so there was an early version of Paddy as an Eighties pop star, the young man with the big eyes and tidy bone structure who would shake his hair to make the girls faint. But he was only ever a reluctant, halfway star. For him, the interviews, photoshoots and live performances were a sideshow compared with his vocation of devising the means of producing a magical shiver. With his soft, singsong Geordie accent and thick-tongued way of speaking—holding up his chin as a kind of guard against the expected cynicism and bemusement, a squeeze of a smile in his eyes—Paddy was too gentle, too earnest and too subtle a character to pass through the inane rituals of publicity without a hitch. A misfit because he seemed to be so impossibly benign. "In a Merchant Ivory film, Paddy McAloon would be the gentle, cardigan-wearing priest who urges two shy lovers to make that twilight tryst," suggested Caitlin Moran in *The Times*. "In the swishy musicals of the 1930s, he would be the book-loving millionaire who funds the off-Broadway show and comes up with the hit song at the last minute, when the original composer accidentally breaks his brain in a golfing incident. He wouldn't get the girl, though—the supporting cast never manages to get the girl." A large part of the Eighties business model for music was based on the twitch of fashion. Few people were buying just songs, they were buying an image, a reflection of something about themselves they wanted to exhibit, to carry under their arm or pull from a bag with casual confidence and an unseen lift of an eyebrow. Because of this, cartoonishly cool characters were always going to work better than Paddy and Co.

"God, a lot of people hate Prefab Sprout," wrote *Record Mirror* in 1985. "A friend looked at their picture and cried, 'Pentangle', another, 'hippy', and yet another, 'wet'. Together all three summed up their attack thus: 'pretentious', 'wimpy' and most finally, 'music for nice young men who can't quite get it up'." And *Jamming!* magazine in the same year, when *Steve McQueen* and the band were most in vogue with the critics, concluded: "Few bands can inspire such instant vitriol as Prefab Sprout—condemned as too clever-clever for the pop kids, too wimpy for the alternative scene and too ridiculously named for either." One of his earliest interviews, with Jools Holland on *The Tube* in 1984, demonstrated how, from the very beginning of his career,

Paddy knew what he was up against. A stupid system. Mostly good-natured, but stupid. You can see the thought process, like a gathering together of clouds, as he's asked about the Newcastle pub scene (looking like a postgrad student in his beige jumper). Paddy knows he's not delivering the jokey patter the production team are looking for; but he's going to think about the questions asked and provide honest answers. He could do funny, no problem. He could do thoughtful insights all day long. Sharp opinions, sure. But he was frustrated by the situation and why a genial intelligence in itself wasn't entertaining enough; and why were his lyrics considered so darned clever, and just clever in a bad way? He wondered whether it was because he was from Newcastle rather than London or Manchester. No-one wanted a provincial smart-arse. At least until he entered the *Jordan* era, Paddy had tried to work out how to present himself and to explain what was wrong with prevailing attitudes. "In my opinion the term 'Street Credibility' has destroyed a lot in music. Professionalism, instrumental skills and theoretical knowledge are becoming insults. 'Passion' is used to hide ignorance and as an excuse for a lack of ideas. And those who can't write a decent song now 'experiment'." And he wasn't going to put up with being accused of pretension by *Smash Hits*.

> I reject that totally. To me it's having fun, being playful. Which doesn't make you easily understood on Mike Read's show [the Radio 1 breakfast programme]. That's not being snotty about it, it just doesn't. You aren't going to appeal to somebody who's looking for

a lyric like 'I Just Called To Say I Love You'.
It's going to take a little more thought. I like
putting words down like a piece of prose. I
love sounds and tunes and shapes of songs. It
sounds academic—I don't mean it to.

It was no different for the Sprout's siren, Wendy. She would
never mention that she preferred Mozart to chart music in
interviews because she knew she'd be made out to be insuf-
ferable.

Maybe because he wanted to counter the image being foisted onto him—and because he was honest—the rev-
erend Paddy wasn't always 'nice' in interviews. He knew how
to stick the boot in. Paul Weller, he said, was an example of
how standards of songwriting in the Eighties had fallen to a
new low. Bob Geldof was a "tenth-rater". Sting really should
have stuck to his day job (there was always demand for
teachers after all). He couldn't stomach Elvis Costello's
wordplay, or Lloyd Cole's French philosophy references
("That's so sixth form!"). Paddy liked Roddy Frame's early
material, but didn't want to be lumped with Aztec Camera.
"They've got their heads well up their arses, haven't they?
We're of the same age group I suppose and we tend to stay
in the same hotels, but that's as far as the similarity goes."
There were no good female songwriters at all, he said—
maybe Carole King at a push. Not Joni Mitchell. Whitney
Houston's voice was plastic and lacked soul.

Paddy believed most people were deaf to his band's
radical edge. Listen more carefully, he told them, it's viol-
ently unconventional. Uneasy listening. Just because the de-

livery could be gentle didn't mean the music was safe. "The press completely misunderstood what we were about so we just allowed them to meander on. The crucial misunderstanding has always been that volume, speed and a metallic guitar can somehow be equated with passion, commitment and strength. It's ludicrous." Rock and roll guitars, after all, stopped being the outsider music of rebellion some time in the Fifties; and so much indie music was just obscure and unengaging.

> There's nothing small about Prefab Sprout. Nothing bedsit. We get grouped in that Aztec Camera sensitive songwriter bracket, the Everything But The Girl wimp tag. We've got nothing in common with these people. Their music's tame. It's polite. It's mild-mannered. It comes knocking at your door. We've got passion, but not delivered in the same way as U2 or something—get a good riff going and turn it up full blast. That's so traditional your mother would like it.

He was never going to win the argument with a press and listening public that struggled with subtlety and complexity, so Paddy began to detach himself from the conversation instead. "I'm always more thrilled by a destructive piece than a flattering one," he said in 1985.

Paddy was simpler, more human and more interesting than the media image. A down-to-earth, English gentleman of the North. Someone who preferred home and familiar company. A glass of brandy and a little cigar to smoke

175

while he laughed at Finbarr Saunders and Terry Fuckwitt in *Viz*. He was maybe old-fashioned in some of his tastes, certainly in the maturity of his ideas and in his bookishness. Producer Thomas Dolby once said he thought of Paddy as a 75-year-old in a 35-year-old's body. But the gentle manner is that of the free-thinking bohemian, not a dewy-eyed vicar-in-the-making. He's living in his own head: a hard, snappy, cultured place that's disinterested in the shallow commercial world outside. The drivel of clichés. Paddy can be explained most of all by his honesty. He's been relentlessly, courageously—and, for some people, awkwardly—sincere. By not faking a pop disguise, by talking so much; and, most of all, by keeping faithful to a fundamental ideal: that boyhood reverie which had nothing to do with being fashionable. Why should it have to?

*

Prefab Sprout wasn't a Newcastle band or a Durham band. It was a Witton Gilbert band. Coming from an industrial city would have meant a whole scene and a bullying framework of influences and expectations around what to play and how to play it; as would a student city like Durham with its picture-book medieval and Georgian streets. Instead the Sprouts were made in Witton Gilbert, a village in the rural hinterlands of the County Durham coalfields—a green enclave hidden within a surrounding ring of black mountains in the form of the old coal and steel works, the mines and quarries; saved from attention by its association with names like Tyneside and Teeside only meant to mean industrial rivers and grime. The northern Pennines, though, are a relatively untouched and special landscape of ancient moors, drystone walls and outcrops of sugar limestone. Miles of hills and grassy meadowland are spotted with the colour of wildflowers, frothing each summer with clover, sorrel and meadowsweet. Hidden within those secret dales there are old stone villages with their little bridges and busy streams; there are otters on lonely riverbanks; red squirrels in the birch and oak woodlands.

Beauty and desolation are often close neighbours. Unlike Hardy's Wessex, the north Pennines have received fare less tourist board attention. During the Seventies and Eighties the region continued to have its own kind of insular culture, made from a hybrid history of industrial decline and small-scale farming. People were self-sufficient and blunt; they knew the fancy doings and fuss on television were not for them. There was a whole generation of unemployed coal miners and steel men stuck at home, only going outside to visit the pub, attend to their racing pigeons in the backyard or discuss the odds on whippets. The jobs that were still available—the milkman, the postie, working in a local shop or factory—would be less well paid than the old industries, and the wife might have to do a bit of this and that to help the family get by. It was the pinched existence that Paddy parodied in "Til the Cows Come Home': "Where's he working? He's not working / Thin as the smile I wear / Cold as the beaches you comb". Witton Gilbert was a typically unromantic kind of place. Instead of being the result of a grand plan of residential development it was a hodge-podge of Victorian workers' houses and older cottages mixed with modern in-fill. An on-the-way-to-somewhere-else place, looking out on a line of empty hills. A place of making-do dreams. Like a coal fire and a proper tea to come home to; a foamy nut-brown pint in the Glendenning Arms; some tasty street-corner gossip about the new folk up at Louisa Terrace.

The three brothers, Paddy the oldest, Marty and Mickey, lived on Front Street, the main through road that carried traffic between Consett and Durham, in a bungalow next to the little petrol station run by their dad. Tommy McAloon had taken a temporary job as a maths teacher at Langley Park Secondary Modern to afford the loan he needed to build the McAloon home (and little Paddy had helped to lay out some of the bricks). Tommy was following in the footsteps of his own father, who had left his job in the coal mines to run the village sweet shop. In the last term before he left teaching, Tommy's class were given a special project to design the sign for the garage, the big blue and yellow sign on the roof that would become a familiar landmark at the bottom of the village: 'McAloon's of Witton'. It was the family's little empire: a bungalow and filling station on one side of the road and a repair workshop and storage shed on the other. Much of the garage's income came from fitting tyres, but Tommy was a canny businessman and a charmer. The truck drivers who passed that way got to know him well, and Tommy arranged a deal where the fuel tanker drivers would come to McAloon's at the end of their route and sell the leftover petrol at a discount. The flimsy wooden cabin sold cigarettes and chocolate bars (which needed to be locked away every evening). A café had been planned for Mum to run on the other side of the road, serving teas to truck drivers and motorists, until she became pregnant with

Marty. For many years after having her three children, Mary McAloon would help out with cleaning the church at a nearby village, Our Blessed Lady and St Joseph in Leadgate, which was famous for being one of the Augustus Pugin churches and an important place of worship for the region's Irish Catholics.[3]

Home was important. How many indie pop stars would have their cool new producer round for lunch with Mum and Dad, as Paddy did with Thomas Dolby, to talk about plans for *Steve McQueen*? Or want the cover photograph for the album taken in their back garden? The 'rebels' who sneered at anything quiet or safe or homely, who couldn't see what was good about family, were childish. And it wasn't only the obvious rebels, the punks and the rock kids who were doing it. The rise of youth culture since the Fifties had been driven by a spirit of reinvention, of breaking old chains, of spending big and getting out. Paddy lived at home throughout the years of his biggest fame, including *Jordan*, and looked after his elderly parents until he was 54.

Tommy and Mary had children fairly late, and the boys could see the difference in manner and interests compared with their friends' younger parents. Tommy in particular was a good-humoured man, but the humour was a light coat worn by a man with stern Catholic principles. His truck driver pals would say he "had the demeanour of a priest." "He repaired cars, he supported people, and also sought to save souls from the demon of alcohol. He drank too, but in moderation, like a serious person. He was a serious person." Paddy sometimes liked to refer to him as a 'Victorian Dad'

---

[3] Mary would occasionally be cleaning alongside Sting's grandmother.

(although nothing like the version he'd know from *Viz*, beating his children and struggling with his arousal from the curves of table legs). His parents weren't fans of pop music in general, and when the mood was tetchy, Paddy's obsession could become a source of conflict: "they'd attack me… 'Do you think you'll get yourself through life trailing that stupid tape recorder with you?' I still remember that phrase perfectly. I spent my life with my cassettes, they found that extremely immature. I often felt hurt."

Home came with an air of old-world peace and grace. Years passed gently with the cycle of traditions, like the blossom of the cherry tree in the springtime garden; the evenings sitting together listening to *Sing Something Simple* on Radio 2 (featuring 'Slow Boat to China', 'The Skye Boat Song', 'I Left My Heart in San Francisco' etc); Mum and Dad playing the piano that was kept tuned and polished in the corner of the living room along a modest collection of records by Cole Porter, George Gershwin and Liberace alongside the *West Side Story* original soundtrack. Inspired by the folk revival of the late Sixties, Mum had got herself a Spanish guitar to play (soon to be purloined by Paddy); she'd bought Paddy his first vinyl singles (like T. Rex's 'Ride a White Swan'), and talked with him about pop songs on the radio. The family would go over to Auntie Gronear's house and the boys would nag at her to play the harp for them. And when Marty was old enough to have a small guitar of his own, the brothers would try to jam together. This is why, even when the Sprouts were in full swing, the songs and the music would be discussed around the McAloon dinner table —and why Thomas Dolby was introduced to the family.

Witton Gilbert was one element in what became a powerful formula for creativity, because it was a place where it was safe to dream, and become an eccentric. "As a kid I felt protected by this desolation, by living in a place with so few people," said Paddy. "Many people dislike the North, Newcastle, they speak of it as a depressing place, grey, boring, but I really like it, it's less threatening than London, the big cities. There's a more human scale to life. In big cities you lose yourself, you tend to slip into conformity so as to be accepted, where here you can be yourself, it's quieter." And it was a place where dreaming was also a necessity, to counter the boredom of living in a one-horse town and a way of charging the rural landscape with urgent Romance. "There were rumours there were huge places in the world, full of people and lights. One day I would go there. America really looked like heaven on earth. But no-one knew anything for certain"; "I thought I was lucky. I lived inside a film. I lived in a garage: what could be more cinematic than a petrol station and a road?"

*

A lot has been made of how Paddy attended the St Cuthbert's Roman Catholic Seminary in Ushaw. It was a good story for the press to latch onto: how the quirky young songwriter had chosen pop over a life in the priesthood. But while the facts might have been true, the assumed implications never were. Pupils had traditionally needed to have a solid Catholic family background to join St Cuthbert's, but by the time Paddy applied in 1968 the school had started to take lay pupils. Paddy went to the Seminary because it was only a few miles away, his Dad had once taught maths there, and an uncle had himself been a pupil. In other words, it was a reasonably ordinary boys' boarding school for 11 to 18-year-olds. There might have been Mass in the mornings, but that was followed by double Science, rude jokes and football. There was some incidental talk that Paddy might eventually find his vocation in the church; it would have been easy for family to imagine him giving sermons from behind a lectern, he'd been such a natural performer as a boy. Most likely, though, his parents would have seen that their oldest son, a frail boy in NHS spectacles, might not have been suited to the Langley Park comprehensive.

Even if it meant only seeing Mum and Dad twice a term, Paddy was drawn to the Greyfriars, Malory Towers, Mr Chips glamour of it: "I thought it must be great to have a tuck box!" At St Cuthbert's he liked English but struggled with Maths, regarding himself as one of the slower ones in general. Around the school Patrick was known most of all for his guitar playing. Radio was banned as a worldly temptation, and instead there were *samizdat*-style tape recordings of music like Simon & Garfunkel being passed around. The boys were encouraged to make their own music. Paddy took piano lessons in the dorm where he lived and joined the other boys with guitars for tuition from Father Jim O'Keefe. O'Keefe was still in his early twenties, an impish-looking, kind and committed man (and suitably, for the man who would take Paddy into the underworld of music, he had dark curly hair). He'd been on a placement living among homeless people in Liverpool before joining the school. Paddy's first dorm song was 'Tramp', co-written with fellow twelve-year-old Frank Dykes. Songwriting quickly became his passion as he tried to understand how it was really done, like taking apart a favourite toy—what was Marc Bolan's secret? —and he spent hours badgering Father O'Keefe to explain every possible chord formation in God's universe. Paddy also became one of the polite and presentable schoolboys who'd be taken round to play Beatles tunes in old people's homes and church events (arranged by Mary), and he started a band, fairly furtively, with two school friends, called Grappled Institution.

Summer holidays meant helping out in the garage. And after the years of living in the dorms at St Cuthbert's[4] and a grimly frugal sixth-form experience at St Joseph's, Paddy was happy enough to settle there. Filling cars with petrol. Writing songs. Reading. Mooching around in his bright blue beret and raincoat ensemble. Dad, though, had other plans for him. He rang up Newcastle Poly to see what places they had and immediately signed his son up for a Humanities degree (English and History). Paddy has had little to say about his student years—unusually for him—and what should have been a liberating period, a leap into a world of freedoms and creativity. In the village it made him a curiosity. "The attitude of people [in Witton] is very hard, it leaves very little room for things like poetry, artistic ambition. The simple fact that I was a student already fascinated them. That was something vaguely exotic, artistic for these people." He was also becoming self-conscious about his lack of experience with women. "I was probably about 18 or so when I

---

[4] St Cuthbert's was in serious decline throughout Paddy's time there. In 1968 there were 400 pupils but only 17 when he left.

first met girls… girls, it's mysterious really, isn't it? What do
they think about? What does go through their minds?" During term-time, student Paddy lived in the attic room of a
house in Whitley Bay for £5 a week. "I lived like some
starving artist in a garret, except I wasn't starving. I used to
cook tins of beans inside a kettle, which is not to be recommended for anybody… I would write these unusual songs
and dream about what was going to happen with them." His
study time was mostly taken up with reading. "I devoured as
many books as I could, no matter what they were. Detective
novels, magazines, everything. I loved them more for the way
they were written than the stories." And he learnt about
Modernism, the value of a cut-and-paste style, as well as the
actual nature of artistic revolution: "figures such as Picasso
and James Joyce, people who'd gripped the twentieth century
by the throat and redefined it in a new perspective… I was
interested in doing something revolutionary too but I kept
the sentiment to myself because I soon learned there are
very few things which are both revolutionary and good."

Paddy returned home when Dad suffered a cerebral
haemorrhage and needed help with running the garage.
Tommy returned to teaching Maths at a school in Durham.
Stepping out of the graduate race suited Paddy anyway, because looking for another kind of job didn't appeal, unless he
could be a librarian: "It seemed lovely. The whole day with
my nose in all those books." So there he stayed. In the grey
days of Witton Gilbert, drowsing and dreaming with his gui-

tar, his books and a notepad, living off benefits and filling the occasional car with petrol.[5]

*

When someone is happy living inside their own head, they see a whole world in a grain of sand. Their little bedroom could become a microcosm of cathedrals and stars, leaping with fountains and fireworks. When Thomas Dolby visited the McAloon home to talk about *Steve McQueen* he was led into a bedroom that was "twice the size of a single mattress". There was a single bed propped up on a stack of pages of lyrics. "[Paddy] sat with a guitar and played me songs from sheets of paper." He'd worked slavishly on the songs, both because it was an endlessly exciting process of experiment and discovery for him—and, as he would admit, he wrote slowly.

> I don't go on holiday, I don't ever sit around reading, I just like to work on my writing all the time… A typical day begins with me getting up at eight, switching on the keyboards before my Weetabix and then embarking upon a tight work schedule through until six, seven, maybe even eleven at night. I don't think a lot of people understand the sheer graft that goes into song-writing, particularly

---

[5] For a far more detailed account of Paddy's young life and the making of the band there's the excellent biography by John Birch, *Prefab Sprout: The Early Years* (2017).

when you're striving to be different, seeking
to be unique.

He was an addict, getting high on the act of creation. "I love
it. I go to bed and I'm so excited that I want to get up
straight away. I'm not a particularly good Catholic, but every
night I'm really grateful I'm doing something I love. I just get
so bloody thrilled, you know."

Paddy's rooms have been famous for being a mess.
There'd be the bed, then always a keyboard and a drum machine in there, the remaining space stacked with old letters
and magazines, maybe some ancient recording equipment
and snake-coils of leads; and above the heaps of musical detritus, a picture of the composer Pierre Boulez on the wall.
Until he was married, Paddy spent most of his time in these
kinds of rooms because he wasn't interested in the social side
of the business, in being part of a gang of finger-clicking
musos sharing tales. The only way he would stay in touch
with the music scene was by listening to Radio 2 in his morning bath (and you can imagine some of the faces he was
pulling while applying the Head and Shoulders). "I know the
Charlatans and the Stone Roses," he said in 1990. "But I'm
not really drawn to cover versions of old John Kongos songs
['Step On']. And besides, how much radically new, different
stuff do you get on the Simon Bates show?" He preferred not
to use the telephone or socialise if it was only for the sake of
it. He didn't like talking about family or girlfriends in his interviews. But he wasn't a hermit, and was obviously someone
who could be great company whenever he emerged from his
room. Again though, Paddy was happy in his own head—he

was that lesser-known personality type, the happy introvert. There are many benefits from being a cottage industry of one, from feeling small and self-sufficient and proud of it. Because that way you can make everything for yourself, in your own way, rather than relying on the larger world around you and its prescriptions of what's important (power, sex, money?) and what's cool (club music and buzzsaw guitars?). As Paddy once explained, he didn't need the supposed glory and glamour of London or New York to feel inspired: "I carry whatever it is that makes me write around with me." He'd been hardwired by Witton for simplicity: "It is nice to live where you feel you belong, somewhere you were brought up. To walk out on the street and know instinctively what your part is on that street." Paddy could get his fix of the big world by taking a trip into Newcastle as an ambling *flâneur*: "When I've written something I'm happy with, I'll go to Newcastle and walk around Woolworth's. I get a big kick out of that. I never buy anything, I just like all the bright lights!" And this, remember, was Newcastle: an urban and industrial sprawl dominated by six giant bridges over the River Tyne; with its districts of boarded-up houses, metal grilles over letterboxes to stop the firebombs; where kids sniffed glue and hunted for supplies of Temazepam, their 'wobbly eggs' and 'jellies'; the city best known for its great shifting tides of weekend drinkers moving from the Bigg Market down to the Quayside and back; where there were bouncers on the door of curry houses and kebab shops. But for someone like Paddy, Newcastle was glittering with life and warmth and character, through every kind of time of day and weather.

There was no musical schooling involved. For many years Paddy had only a rudimentary idea of rules and nota-

tions, and learnt as he went along, turning to computer software to look after things like bars and staves. So it was a
home-made alchemy. Songs were written up as lyrics with
the chords written above each line. He would use his own,
idiosyncratic and painstaking methods, and invented termin-
ology for his notes, like "con fuoco" or "avec biff" to indicate
a spurt of intensity. "I'm like a kid, I make riches out of zero.
Mentally I've got this huge pair of scissors—God, that
sounds like Julian Cope—with which I cut and shape the
world and share it with people"; "I think of songs as objects.
You're turning the world to your shape. I'm not a very arty
person; it's just a workmanlike thing to do. It's like making
an ashtray a song. It serves that sort of function"; "there's a
pure pleasure in the way those shapes move in a way that
you perhaps think they couldn't do to produce something
pretty." Until 1984 the shapes were put together on a guitar,
then afterwards a Roland JX-3P synth, while struggling to
coordinate his left and right hands on the keys.[6] At the same
time Paddy studied how other albums were put together, like
David Bowie's *Station to Station* (1976). He constructed whole
suites of songs based around a single idea (which is why *Steve
McQueen* includes 'Goodbye Lucille #1', there were eight
more Goodbye Lucilles).

An equal amount of time was invested into the lyrics.
"I'm neurotic about the actual words, I word each word very
carefully. But at the same time that doesn't mean every song

---

[6] His original cheap guitar (bought for around £18 and borrowed from Mum in 1968),
got smashed in 1984. Because he didn't know what to do with what was left of the
guitar, he burned it. "I wished now that I could just stick it on the wall somewhere in its
fragmented state." Paddy has never been a guitar geek. Asked by a specialist guitar
magazine about the model of his Gretsch, he said it was an "orange" one.

you write has to be a serious statement, you can talk about a light-hearted subject, it can be in a light-hearted manner." He ended up needing to juggle different concerns: how to avoid platitudes, not deal in social comment, not be over-refined or preciously poetical, but still deliver something meaningful—which meant he was trying to tread a fine line while still wanting there to be a natural flow of inspiration. "When you begin to write, the best things are when words come flowing one after another. At the beginning I start with inspiration and then I'll explore how to express it... I like working this way. Sometimes there's only an idea and I sit down and write about it slowly. Or there can be just a single word which I gradually breathe life around. Sometimes there is a flood. But the best things are always born from happy coincidences."

Hello Paddy: on stage for the *Jordan* tour in 1990 with Neil on drums, Paul Harvey on guitar. Courtesy of John Birch.

It was a life-absorbing project that led to a gloriously unpredictable songbook; where every cliché was scrupulously dodged and every melodic line seems to grow in branches and tendrils that bud, bloom and drip honey. It's music made from colours and feelings that lie some way outside the spectrum of standard pop music. And Paddy is like a writer who's only been capable of the most delicious prose, producing one lovely sentence after another. His original, often curious and errant melodies seem to arrive in such a gentle way, coming unforced, like the fall of an evening dew.

Another consequence of Paddy's dedication has been a small mountain of unrecorded and half-finished material. His manager, Keith Armstrong, has confirmed the rumours and legends. Yes, there are Tupperware boxes—a single box for each project—filled with cassette tapes, lyric sheets, chord charts, floppy discs with MIDI files and rough video recordings of songs as they were played; and all of them are kept simply in the garage of Paddy's family home: an archive of a songwriting history that is unlikely to ever be used for commercial release. Paddy has never needed to scratch around for songs to fill up an album, he's been able to pick and choose from a library—having written around 50 songs before 1980, and then 12 to 15 each year for many years after—and mostly just decide not to complete or record them at all. He's always been happy to talk about his unrecorded albums, not in a promotional way or to be a tease. Maybe only to justify the decades he's spent as a songwriter in his little dump of a room. He's talked about plans for a 30-song cycle covering the history of humanity since the Garden of Eden called *Earth, The Story So Far*: "I wrote one tiny little song about Adam and Eve; a song about the man who invented the wheel; Jesus and his mother; Adolf Hitler and his mother, and as I got into it, I thought, 'This is great: this is the best thing I've ever done in my life.'"[7] *20th Century Magic* was going to be an exploration of the celebrity-fixated mindset at the end of the Millennium, with songs like 'Twilight Of The Pimps' about the Dome (including the line: 'Dear Tony, It's a bold idea / We could use an unloved dome round here'), 'Elegy For a Ramraider', 'Geoff & Isolde' and ' Zero Attention Span'. There was his own Christmas album, *Total Snow*, which he wrote for producer Phil Spector as a follow-up to his Sixties' Christmas classic (including the song 'Madman on the Roof'). "The stories are about Christ born in a stable, a king that nobody recognises. The songs try to question the idea that everyone has of Christ. It's emotional. I want to make an album about the modern Christmas." There's an album of waltzes; a kind of gospel album, *The Atomic Hymn Book*; a soundtrack of bolero dance tunes for an animated film, *Zorro the Fox*; a musical based on the life of Michael Jackson called *Behind the Veil* (featuring 'Only the Boogie Music Won't Let You Down' and 'Me and Mr Lightning Boots'); and most recently, he's talked about *Femmes Mythologiques* and a Prefab Sprout dance album, *Jockey Of Discs*.[8]

"I've worked so hard, it's been to the detriment of other things," said Paddy, as long ago as 1985. "Relationships have suffered, I don't mind saying that. But I know if I don't work hard I won't get that golden moment. I know I

---

[7] The title track turned up on *Let's Change the World with Music* (2009).

[8] There are any number of one-off tracks that Paddy wrote, including a hurried attempt at a James Bond theme tune for *Tomorrow Never Dies* (1997): "They didn't use it... they were quite right not to, it wasn't very good... it just went round and round."

can go even further, but to do that I have to narrow down my interests." Not much had changed, 12 years later, when he turned 40 in 1997. "I should have been married with children for a long time, and instead I lock myself away in a studio imagining the stars. But at the same time I wouldn't exchange these seven years in my little village, away from the music business and the crowds, for the world."

Why did he do it? For the golden moments when the shapes came together in beautiful ways; and because he was a happy introvert, the type who could find people an intrusion into their private, star-lit haven of thought. But to lock yourself away for so many years?

*

Adrian hated smoking and did it anyway. Especially when he was pissed again, sitting on an empty cask outside the fire escape with Chris and a bottle of Grolsch. The fags completed the made-up look of bitterness he wanted to feel. Him: world-weary, careless and shabby in the cold night air.

The fire door bangs open and there's an escaping blast of Student Union, a mess of body heat, perfume and 'Groovy Train'. Monkey comes along with it, in a denim jacket and flared jeans. They all nod and Monkey takes a cigarette from the offered pack.

"Wankers," he says.

"Eh?"

"The wankers who sing Dexy's. They were doing it again in there, linking arms and doing that whole wanky performance."

"Monkey, have another drink, mate, you're doing the thing."

"What thing?"

"The thinking-thing-thing——"

"You know, when they sing 'WE ARE FAR TOO YOUNG AND CLEVERRR', I want to stab someone."

"Do it Monkey, we'll give you an alibi. A shit alibi from pissheads."

"There should be a Dexy's tax, so every student has to pay the bills for the real people who work in supermarkets, drive buses and clean places like this shithole."

"Well, yeah. It's called income tax," says Chris. *"And anyway, you're one of them. Your parents are rich, mate."*

"Rich? Not me. I'm getting another loan out, I might even have to get a job to stay living round here. I'm working-class me ——"

"You going in? They're playing the Mondays."

They all make a show of getting up and moving round the fire escape to the side of the building and its row of floor-to-ceiling windows. A hazy layer of condensation, rolling balls of red and purple colours; silhouettes of arms in the air; and never enough light to make out faces or who's with who, just flashes and outlines.

Another SU night of games and codes, thinks Adrian. Girls dancing near you, sometimes not; looking over, then looking somewhere else; dressed up or with a different hairdo; not sitting with their usual gang; drinking more, laughing louder, ignoring you when they know you're there. And why. What did it mean? It was a Cold War in there. And always worse for the poor buggers on the edges of things. The Klingons who moved around looking for a group to attach themselves to, practising their opening lines and their biggest brightest smile. But for the grace of God and all that.

Adrian finishes his bottle and thinks about lighting another fag.

"You going in then?" he asks Chris. He knows what Chris is looking at, both absently and intently. One of the first-year girls in a navy blazer with brass buttons, jeans and a big-buckled belt. Her boy-

193

friend is up from home, standing with her, making out he's having a fine time. Sweating more than anyone.

"Did we ever think this was coolio? I'd rather be down the Arms with the townies."

They leave and go back to the house and make toasted cheese sandwiches with the Breville, play Kick Off *on Monkey's Commodore 64. There would always be other nights, thought Adrian.*

*

None of the five bands wanted to be connected with the left-wing politics that had seemed so natural and necessary in the early Eighties. "I thought that if anyone was in the public eye, in popular music, playing to youngish people, they almost had a duty to express some kind of a political belief, to do a great deal of good," said Harriet of the The Sundays, looking back to memories of a concert by Everything But The Girl, who'd recently visited the Soviet Union and performed at a Festival of Youth and Students there.

> I imagine to some degree you can, but to some great degree also, you will also end up playing in the Academy in Brixton to a lot of people in donkey jackets, saying 'Sandinista', which are very noble sentiments that I wouldn't sneer at, but we thought about what we would do, before writing songs, and we just felt we could do more ultimately through this kind of legendary 'mood' and certain mundane down-to-earth, non-glamoured

> words which is a valuable or valid thing in
> itself, as opposed to 'you do this, you do that',
> because you'll be playing to a labour club.

"Those slogan songs are dangerous. Pop music like that reinforces in 17 and 18-year-olds a way of thinking that's wrong, a black and white, blinkered way. I worry about that, and the fact that you can take the money and run. I'm not apolitical but I'm cynical about the whole politics-in-pop-music thing," warned Paddy, back in 1985. People needed to think for themselves and do something, not just wear a badge and jump around at a benefit gig, absolving themselves of responsibility. "I've never felt that politics works in a song," said Peter Milton Walsh. "Opinions change rapidly, even faster than in journalism. Politics is much narrower than life. Songs about life, now there's a good idea! But songs about politics… It's like taking a photo of a very beautiful actress and only keeping a close-up of her dress." Not even Cathal's lyrics are political in the sense of commitment to an ideology. He didn't agree with John Peel's description of Microdisney as an "iron fist in a velvet glove", because it suggested an 'agency', something single-minded and premeditated that wasn't there. They weren't "subversive" either: "That's quite an academic thing, don't you think? To set out to do such a thing is not very much in itself. The idea is to make very good records with an awful lot in them, something with a bit of substance."

Rather than political, each of the five was trying to be authentic. And that was more important and difficult than before, given the smothering influence of mainstream culture. The means of communication were being consolidated steadily into fewer hands, meaning a diminishing number of independent voices, like those of regional newspapers and pirate radio stations, or anyone not validated by their appearance on a mainstream channel, a national paper, on TV or a station like Radio 1. We were becoming less likely to know why the local swimming pool was being shut; or why permission had been given for another housing estate and retail complex on the edge of town; and more likely to be engrossed in Italia '90, the *fatwa* on Salman Rushdie, the lip-syncing scandal of Milli Vanilli; more interested in photos of Julia Roberts in *Pretty Woman*, the finale of *Miami Vice* and the new series of *Mr Bean*. Besides his ownership of *The Times*, *The Sun* and the 20th Century Fox film company, during the Nineties, Rupert Murdoch launched what would become Sky TV in Britain, and Fox News in the US. By the end of the century he would own more than 800 media broadcasters in 50 countries. There were other global media empires—like those of Robert Maxwell and Conrad Black—and they were all doing the same thing: making fortunes from selling influence over consumers and voters. People were being plugged into supplies of entertainment/messaging that were now geared more towards vested interests (communicating the importance of business and fashionable consumption, the game of life, the numbers) than understanding and appreciating reality or challenging untruths. Newspapers had ossified in accordance with owner demands (the broadsheets around business and politics; the tabloids, show business and sport). Many *Daily Telegraph* journalists, for example, were known to be anti-Conservative, but were expected to adhere to editorial direction from the board. There was a shift towards more short-term reactive news over longer-term investigation and analysis—making news teams more reliant on PR-managed leaks and briefings. Areas of life that couldn't be linked to advertising promotions—aspects of a culture that weren't connected to a new product or event—became sidelined and irrelevant. Business, government and the media needed each other. And as a consequence, the reality of the late Eighties and Nineties was more consciously and intensely mediated, becoming devitalised and sometimes distorted. The clammy fingers of commerce were all over every kind of media. This isn't to suggest a conspiracy based around a conscious set of strategies necessarily, but the consequence of an accumulation of developments: self-interest, business planning and its cycles of success and rewards.

The music press was also changing. Many of the journos of the old champions of indie, the *NME*, *Melody Maker* and *Sounds,* had moved on to titles like *Smash Hits* and *The Face,* and would soon be on their way to the more grown-up music magazines, *Q, Select* and *Mojo.* The new titles had more of a cool, professional tone. All that childish passion, the breathless feeling that music was important, that it could make world and break someone's world if only for one night, had been replaced by quick-witted irony. "While it did its job very well, I found [*Q* magazine] rather smarmy," said Barney Hoskyns, "it took away the danger, glamour and mystery of music for me, because its tone was never to take anything seriously." *Q* knew its market was older consumers and that meant keeping heritage rock on the cover, Dire Straits, Mick Jagger, Elton John, Pink Floyd. Meanwhile, the coverage of indie music was sliding into a laddish, comedy version of itself. Madchester was a gift. Like when the *NME* tracked down Shaun Ryder to a resort in Barbados, where he and the Happy Mondays were meant to be recording *Yes Please!* and found exactly what they wanted to find: "Shaun sits on the toilet with his pipe, smoking a rock of crack." When *Q* finally shut down its print publication in 2020, its co-founder David Hepworth wrote an open letter to the music industry: "You're going to miss the music press. Why? Because it did one thing you failed to value. Through its lens it made your acts seem exciting and larger than life, even when they weren't." Maybe it wasn't the industry's fault that the music media had fallen into decline (had *Q* ever really made music *exciting*?). Cynicism and materialism, in general, was in. If music didn't mean anything, why would anyone want to spend their time reading about it, what was there to think about other than new releases, who was on tour and the commercial successes and failures?

Music had turned into a wallpaper product. In the Eighties, fans had got used to the idea of having a personal and intimate connection with the artefacts of music; saving up to buy a new album, bringing it home from a record shop like a thing of legend, knotted up with anticipation; they'd spend time just looking at the cover and the inside images, trying to find sense and relevance in the lyrics, and then play the songs over and over again until the record became soaked into their story and be forever associated with the places and happenings of that moment in time. By the Nineties the experience was far more about the external look of things: the perception and reputation of the music and how it made other people see us—like when we were dancing—rather than an internal dialogue. In his book *About a Boy* (1998), Nick Hornby was expressing a very typical attitude of the age when the main character Will (played by Hugh Grant in the film) squirms and feels pity for someone who plays piano and sings for him. Because they're being sincere. "There was nothing between her and the songs, she was inside them. She even closed her eyes when she was singing."

Irony—the knowing little smile—had become contagious in British society. The Establishment didn't like it for obvious reasons. In a speech in 1994, Michael Portillo talked about a "self-destructive sickness of national cynicism", and not just among the unwashed, "too many politicians, academics, churchmen, authors, commentators and journalists exhibit the full-blown symptoms of this new British disease." Attacking national institutions had become easier for newspapers that were part of global organisations with no stake or responsibility within any single nation; not that those institutions were helping themselves. The Nineties were notable for a series of scandals involving the sticky beaks of politicians and civil servants using their positions for financial gain; in 1993 half of police forces were found to have a case 'clear-up rate' of less than 20 per cent. The official religion of Britain, Christianity was an accepted target for mockery. ITV's Sunday 'God-slot' show *Highway* was cancelled in 1993, and its early evening audiences immediately surged as a result. Even Gordon Brown, the son of a Church of Scotland minister, agreed that mentioning God was now "a disaster area". When it came to the new religion of business, no-one expected there to be evidence of scruples anyway—business and principles just didn't mix. It was accepted that the new billionaires would be shady, that the mechanisms of speculation and cheap credit would lead to spectacular debt, bankruptcy, unpaid bills and half-finished building sites. When Robert Maxwell was found to have taken £400 million out of the pension fund for *Daily Mirror* employees, no-one was that surprised. If institutions couldn't be trusted, what and who could? Probably only yourself. Audiences fell in love with phone-ins and talk shows, where everyone could have their fifteen minutes of fame and become an instant celebrity—as seemed only right in a classless society—and a free market for opinion was born. The BBC's speech station, Radio 5, was launched in 1990, followed by Talk Radio in 1995. "Opinion-making is this country's most virulent growth industry," said the playwright John Osborne, one of the Angry Young Men, in 1993. "Phone-ins proliferate, choked with calls from the semi-literate, bigoted and barmy. We are becoming a nation of babbling back-seat cab drivers."

What had happened to our interest in the mysteries of life, the possibility of larger and more meaningful truths? So often in history there had been a revolt by young artists and writers against the humdrum thinking of older generations and the way they'd allowed a dimming film of grey to fall over their eyes, narrowing their perspective. Like the Romantics, the Pre-Raphaelites, America's Transcendentalists, and the radical poets of the Twenties and Thirties, who'd all believed they were seeing the world fresh again. Instead, by the Nineties it was the younger generations who were embarrassed by anything earnest, by beliefs and loose emotions; the only source of joy seemed to be status, celebrity and possessions. According to Clive Aslet (a traditional Tory and editor/publisher of *Country Life*) in his 1997 book on British identity, Britain hadn't only been aiming to be classless but culture-less. The village fete of England, where the locals would dress up and come together to eat and drink, had been replaced by one big car boot sale, run by individuals only interested in flogging stuff from their pitch. Culture-less Britain had become a place of bad manners, relativism, nihilism and 'road rage'. This view was obviously a generalisation, when many British people, if only a minority, had been able to live without becoming slaves to mainstream culture and its consumerism; decent people who were well aware of what was happening and been trying to find their own independent ways of living. It's a contrary impulse we see again and again in the stories of these five albums, and shows through in lyrics and interviews. So Paddy had a poke at the celebrity scene in 'The Ice Maiden': "Welcome to the glow of high octane affairs / Esperanto style and blonde dishevelled hair"; and Cathal summarised the underlying problem with cynicism: "Resignation, irony, under scrutiny, so events can slip / From memory of history, a voluntary dictatorship"; and The Sundays rejected the bandwagon of Madchester. "Well really what the movement is saying is, 'Nothing is important. Get down to the disco, get off your heads, drink a lot and have enormous trousers and a big top with a hood on it'… I'm not sure it's really healthy. There's a lot of it that seems to fit in with Thatcher's ideals—go and spend a lot of cash on training shoes, and such. Like it's really important to look good amongst your so-called friends. I mean, there could be a healthier attitude."

*

The five bands of this book shared a sympathy for the golden age of thoughtful pop songwriting of the Sixties and Seventies—with a quality of style and sincerity that had since been downgraded and relegated into a category of 'classic' but 'old'. The music industry was committed to business models based on cycles of new trends and new products, making sure music fans would be relentless consumers, meaning no place for conservatism. So it was 'yes' to Vanilla Ice, 'no' to Glen Campbell. "The first record that really made me love music was 'Wichita Lineman'," said Paddy. "I still think it might be the greatest record I ever heard. It's not that I yearn for the past, but when I listen to records like *West Side Story*, *Pet Sounds* or any number of Jimmy Webb or Beatles records, I'm not sure what any of us have to show that's an improvement on that basic model." Songwriters like Scott Walker, Brian Wilson, Jimmy Webb, Lou Reed and Paul McCartney were only in their forties in 1990 and still actively writing material, but they were now considered to be an irrelevance by the tastemakers.

As Peter put it, the influence of good songwriting can be intravenous. "When you hear the first Velvet Underground record it just goes into your bloodstream, you'll never forget it. You'll never have that feeling about it again because it's the wildest, freshest, thing you've ever heard... So a lot of the things I like tend to be like that... I love Jimmy Webb, Hal David, Burt Bacharach... It's like infinite melody I love." Paddy, in particular, was conscious of the heavy workload involved. "I just don't detect the melodic inventiveness now that there was in the past, and a lot of it's down to laziness," he said in 1984. "People are suspicious of the craft… 'craftsman' is used in a derogatory sense. Bands like the Alarm can't wait to be elevated beyond having to write songs —they'd rather be at the front of an army of followers."

There was work to be done. "The essential task as far as I saw it was to break pop out of the format of standard 4/4 time [the standard Western time signature of four quarter notes per bar] and move it somewhere else." Importantly though, he wanted his songs to be for the masses, part of the everyday currency of a culture and not specialist museum pieces: "Music is the soundtrack to your life. It sounds corny, but it's there. People use my records in the same way they use Lionel Richie or Queen's records, and you can't be snobby about it." He was happy to fall in with the advice of Muff Winwood, the A&R man at CBS Records who'd originally signed Prefab Sprout: "You've got to reach the *Sun* reader"—as long as there was no compromise in terms of the singular personality he'd brought to the music. "I don't want people to say, 'It's their 15th album, and they're doing the Town & Country tonight.' I'd rather have it said, 'He's been at home for 16 years, writing the big one.'"

The bands weren't just clinging to classic songwriting because it was technically 'better'. It was a vote for beauty, a recognition of the importance of music that contained something more than the sum of its parts, a tune and lyrics. Songs with sincerity and a pang of emotion to them—not sloppy or glossy emotions that can be packaged up and sold, but the more obscure, haunting, nagging kind. Because you might not be able to change the world through politics any more, there may well be no God, but you could instead appeal to

human instincts and a shared wisdom that didn't rely on a
manifesto, belief or philosophical theory, or maybe even
need to be signalled and articulated. Maybe it was only in
music and not in art or written language that this particular
kind of nameless beauty could be reached, making songs like
'Wichita Lineman'—or 'Summertime' from *Porgy and Bess*, or
Brian Wilson's 'God Only Knows'—timeless and unforgettable.

This is what drove Paddy. "I know exactly why I love
[music] so much, but I find it difficult to explain. It's not like
a novel or a poem. You can use words to talk about words.
That's much harder with music. It is the secret of how music
affects body, soul and spirit. I love this mystery and I never
want to give it away through explanation." Because music
was capable of expressing a truth that could only be felt, a
truth about what makes us human in spite of all the dehu-
manising influences of the modern world; or that could at
least be a medium that encouraged susceptibility and response, as opposed to being numb or calculating or ironic—
in other words, the kind of role that in the past had been
played for so many people by religion. Paddy knew there was
something inside, a receptivity, that could be reached in spite
of the blanket standardisation of consumer culture. "I believe man is a spiritual being. Anyone who has any sense of
humanity must concede that a man is more than just what
his body allows him to be… Respect for life is something
spiritual, beyond a belief or not in God."; "And if there is no
God, as [French symbolist poet] Mallarmé would say, the act
of making things is an attempt at a kind of secular religion

in a way… to create things—works of art—to try to find value in what they have. That's what I think."

The evidence for the existence of a divine art wasn't difficult to find for Paddy, it was everywhere, in everything from the Clash to Stockhausen. He started out listening to Radio 1 in the Seventies, latching onto the sounds of T-Rex, David Bowie and the Beatles. In press interviews he'd be self-conscious about how he was going to be labelled and pre-empt it.

> Who do people expect me to like? [wondered Paddy in 1985] Some ridiculous band like the Byrds or Steely Dan, who I like, but it's a complete and utter myth… I've got a lot of Steely Dan albums but I've got all of Led Zeppelin's albums… I thought I'd throw what I hoped would be a few spanners in the works by mentioning Stephen Sondheim, hoping that other songwriters would check out someone in a different field of writing who wasn't going to be hampered by bloody rhyming couplets of "maybe/baby", you know the whole boring disco plodding schtick. So I mentioned these and now I'm labelled as the Tin Pan Alley man or the intellectual of musicals or something. Bernstein, yeah, but there again with a man like him I would rather go to Stravinsky and Ravel and listen to some of their records.

Stronger drugs were available for a disciple of musical highs. When he was 17, Paddy wrote to the "father of electronic music" Karlheinz Stockhausen, asking him whether he used a piano for composition ("anybody with any acquaintance with Stockhausen would know that, Jesus, you don't write something like 'Gesang der Jünglinge' or whatever on a piano").[9] Igor Stravinsky and Maurice Ravel would provide their own thrills, but his principal hero was Pierre Boulez, another composer who experimented with electronic music. Boulez was a romantic figure for Paddy because he'd also been sent to a Catholic seminary by a religious father, he'd repudiated his faith and devoted 13 years of his life to writing strange rebellious music in his attic rooms in Paris—an exotically dramatised version of his own story. Boulez was a lonely figure, hacking a route through music history with his confrontational manner and compositions that used newly invented forms of electro-noisemaking as well as African drums, harps, vibraphones and guitars; the kind of music that demanded concentrated study to unpick and reveal some hidden pleasures. Paddy once met Boulez after a concert in London and shook his hand, telling the Frenchman he was a fan but had struggled with his book, *Boulez on Music Today* (1971). "Throw it out ze window," advised Boulez.

When it came to his own writing, the model was more Stephen Sondheim and his alternative take on musical theatre, who Paddy described as "a god". "I first noticed him on TV, being interviewed by another clever dick, André

---

[9] Paddy had found Stockhausen's address in Cologne in a copy of *Who's Who* in Wigan library. The composer replied with a signed photocopy of the first page of one of his musical scores: "cordially for Patrick McAloor [*sic*]".

Previn. Previn introduced him as 'the greatest writer of the 20th century', fact! Sondheim didn't bat an eyelid." "What I like about Sondheim is that he can put a set of precise emotions into a song lasting a certain number of minutes. If he had an odd-shaped sentiment, he would construct an odd-shaped melody to accommodate it. There was never any sense of it being a happy accident."

Paddy could be just as enthusiastic about pink-sprinkled confections of pop ("Because I have a sweet tooth"). He especially loved a good pop eccentric. The older Elvis; the little-boy weirdness of Brian Wilson; not the Stevie Wonder who made *Songs in the Key of Life* but the visionary of *Journey Through 'The Secret Life Of Plants'*.[10] In 1985 he claimed the song he would most like to have written was Prince's 'Little Red Corvette'. "I want someone to astonish me. So I tend to prefer the Michael Jackson aspiration to a kind of Disneyland of the Soul. So what if Prince is out of touch with the world, when he's so clearly in touch with his music? There's a capacity in him, or in Jackson, to astonish, to tip over the paintbox and come out with something you've never seen before." He could be a pop scientist.

> Quincy Jones says that Rod Temperton, for instance, writes like Bach and that's true. He's got the knack of weaving melodies, of counterpointing seven or eight of them without cluttering up the song… It's amazing. From a

---

[10] *Journey Through 'The Secret Life of Plants'* (1979) was a soundtrack to a documentary film about the ability of plants to 'think' and 'communicate', and has been one of Paddy's favourite LPs. The film's producer described each visual image in detail and Stevie Wonder wrote music to suit, with some of the first uses of a digital sampling synthesiser.

> tiny, simple framework these people are at the
> peak of Western consciousness, all pervasive,
> defining the times like all great songwriters
> do.

But Paddy only liked bits and pieces of pop. Chic worked, he said, because the band was so tight in keeping those chicken-greased tunes together; Michael Jackson made seductive music but the lyrics were made of fluff; too often Prince seemed to have started with a beat he liked and then written a song to suit it: "I wouldn't want to write like him, even if I could… I'd feel like a bit of a cheat."

Is there a simple complexity or a complex simplicity to the lyrics? Paddy explained it like this: "People think I'm some sort of crossword fan compiling intricate puzzles for people. I like that to be there. I like some of the little tricks, but I hate the pun world. I hate word play—I like language that has some sort of emotional weight. I don't think 'is this a nicely turned phrase?' I think 'does that have any emotional significance?' Life is very complicated and I think music should reflect that. That doesn't mean music should have 2,000 layers of meaning. It does mean you can feel two things at once." In other words, Paddy was trying to tell the truth, and the truth is often a contradictory thing. But he was taking language seriously, both how it worked and what it said.

> You're trying to describe something that is
> really not describable, for example the
> concept of love, and before you know it, you

throw a whole bunch of words at them which only make it less clear. Your mind works so much faster than the words you have available to you. At the same time you've stumbled on another interesting paradox: I'm making it clear that language doesn't work by using the same language…

If something spontaneous said it just as well—'be-bop-a-lula' or 'She was just seventeen / You know what I mean'—then that could be even better: "Some of the lyrics I've got are more direct and a bit less intense and I've got songs that are just a laugh. I work on instinct, on feeling; a lot of people have failed to pick that up."

It's important to watch out for the 'Blueberry Pies' because Paddy got bored with fielding the same old questions from journalists. Like when he said that 'Prefab Sprout' was the result of him mishearing a line from an old Nancy Sinatra song, "hotter than a pepper sprout" in 'Jackson'; and posed on the motorbike for the cover of Steve McQueen, parodying Prince's flamboyant *Purple Rain* cover with his own, much damper, North of England version. Or saying that he would never write a song called 'The King of Rock 'n' Roll', when he'd already planned to release one. Paddy especially liked to subvert media illusions: making up a fictional PR pro (Emma Welles) to write liner notes for *Swoon* (and inventing the back story that the album title meant 'Songs Written Out Of Necessity'); writing out crib notes for Griff Rhys-Jones during a record review programme on radio so he could sound the most knowledgeable of them all; and getting brother Michael to do some interviews with Australian media when he was feeling ill. CBS sent Paddy a fax afterwards saying thank you—they'd been some of his most candid and successful interviews so far, it said. The song 'Paris Smith' includes a dig, made in debonair style, at the favourite obsession of music journos: "any music worth its salt is good for dancing… But I tried to be the Fred Astaire of words."

*

We've looked at a few of the aspects and mechanics of Paddy the songwriter, if only what he's wanted to put on show, via a misty viewing window onto the works. Rather than any blueprint for Sprout-music, all we've really been left with is McAloon himself. A man who's wanted to be admitted into the pantheon of the greats, but only on his own terms—accepted for the right reasons. "Most people are too bloody stupid to know that you can think and that doesn't take the heart out of you. I'd love to have a string of number one hits but I couldn't do it if it was at the expense of my writing." An irreducible Paddy. With songs that didn't spring from the fertile fields of all those influences, but from nowhere, like the wild flowers of his corner of the Pennines, growing in spite of the scars and stains of industry.

In a culture besotted by the popular media, Paddy wanted himself and his songs to remain unmediated, to exist as they'd been created in his imagination (or in the Witton Gilbert garage) in their raw, crystalline form. That meant not having to be interpreted or re-interpreted by the music press, and not having to exist as a character in one of the media's long-running soap operas; not having to tour and play live versions of songs that would only ever be corruptions of the original; and not have to be subject constantly to the whims of public opinion. Which is why so much of his work has gone unrecorded, left unmediated and untainted. Staying as innocent as young children.

*

With all of this in mind, it seems strange there was a band at all. But the band experience and the people in the band were essential to the existence of any Prefab Sprout songs (and making sure Paddy's room didn't become a place of dust, littered with the crisp black shells of his unhatched chrysalids).

The best version of the band according to Paddy was the one that first played in the workshop across the road from his dad's garage in 1975. With young brother Marty on bass guitar and Mick 'Fish' Salmon from a few doors down the street on drums. Even though it sounded like chaos to the ears of passer-sby, like village milkman Tommy. "Ah yes, I remember the McAloon boys. My kids used to play with them when they were little. God, they were dreadful when they started." A zippy, jaggedy collation of new wave coloured by Paddy's ever-widening stock of cultural interests, like: "Igor Stravinsky / he's not what you thinksky", and "oooooh Don Quixote". "I was young—eighteen or nineteen," recalled Paddy, "Martin was only thirteen or fourteen, and our drummer would be that age too, so you couldn't even go and play in a pub. We were waiting for everyone, myself included, to get 'up to speed'. This was one of the most exciting things because you were discovering your 'newness'." They'd play for hour after hour just to feel the buzz of creation. "We started from zero and played every night for three years. I mean it, every night, and we loved it, you know, screaming hoarse." Mickey would have been in the band too (the Brothers McAloon) but his head was full of cinema and the sounds of the Sex Pistols, Public Image Limited, Sham 69 and The Jam (he had "a whole different generational thing going").[11] By 1978, the garage band was Prefab Sprout rather than the Dick Diver Band,[12] and not one of Paddy's other options, 'Dry Axe', 'Village Bus' or 'Chrysalis Cognosci'—a name he'd originally dreamt up when he was 13, when he'd been putting words together to see what magically profound composites would appear. It was around this time Paddy sent another one of his letters to a hero, this time Brian Eno. "I'd read that he was forming a label, so I've got this rejection slip from Obscure Records. It was written by Eno: 'Dear Patrick, I've listened to your tape, it's not really what I've been looking for, but thanks anyway. Sorry I've taken so long in getting back to you, but I've been very busy.' I didn't know it then, of course, but he must have been working on *Low* [with David Bowie]. So fair do's, really."

The Sprouts took up residency at The Brewers' Arms in Durham in 1980, an ordinary boozer to the north of the city centre, looking doleful and domestic behind its net cur-

---

[11] Youngest brother Michael was born in 1965. He had plans to be an actor and went into a career in cinema.

[12] Dick Diver was the lead character in F. Scott Fitzgerald's novel *Tender is the Night* (1934), a Bright Young Thing from the Jazz Age who descends into a spiral of alcoholism and unhappiness.

tains, just one of many pubs on the same slow-climbing hill road out of town. It was here they launched into their set of urgent but wandering guitar songs, all for the benefit of twenty or so regulars. "I stuck my vocal mic into a guitar amp and shouted at the top of my lungs. In terms of a three-piece band, I don't really want to compare, but we might have been close to The Jam." Quick, jittery versions of songs like 'Faron Young', 'The Golden Calf' and 'Bonny', with Paddy's glasses sliding further down his nose as he waggled out the next chord. The Sprouts would also support many of the bigger acts playing Durham University and get slots at small venues around the area, like the newly opened Spectro Arts Workshop in Newcastle, the Arts Centre in the new town of Washington, and Annabel's nightclub in Sunderland. Ticket prices on the door ranged from 30p to 50p. But in Paddy's view, live performance was adding nothing to the songs. The PA system was a pig and his guitar would keep on creeping out of tune. "We were really snobby about playing in pubs, we thought we aren't going to play in any pubs where people would really require drinking music," said Paddy. "We're not going to have them shouting 'Whiskey in the Jar' when we're just doing our things." Not that they had much choice. "We felt we were more like jukeboxes than anything else," admitted Martin. "All those people who were standing in front of you drinking beer made you feel a little sick after a while." A single-night tour would have been enough for Paddy: "We'd do one gig in front of thirty people in a pub, and then I'd say—right, I've done it now, that's it. Now I'm gonna retire and go back to the songwriting." Playing live was just taking time away from his life's work of writing the big one; and he didn't want to be pushed off course by audience feedback, by the way they seemed to droop and lose interest when the slower numbers began.

Then Fish went to university and left the band.[13] He wasn't just the drummer but a big part of the dynamic, stoking the enthusiasm for rehearsals in the workshop. Martin suddenly became even more important in keeping his older brother on the straight and narrow. Often Martin would be labelled as the band's joker: "A big clumsy youth with blonde curls and cauliflower ears whistling words like a pressure cooker full of sarcastic steam," wrote *Best* magazine in 1985. The lanky bass player who was just happy to be taken along for the ride. But Martin was also the steady beating heart of the band, the good-natured Catholic who took casual jobs to make money to pay for studio time; who sent out the cassettes, arranged the gigs, hand-drew the posters with wax crayons, and made the early approaches to record labels; the one who was there with kind, conciliatory words when the rest of the band were in a bad mood; who was humble enough to stay in the background of interviews, accepting Paddy was the main man. Martin put serious effort into learning pieces of music, taking one at a time, and also writing his own songs, like 'Rock 'n Roly Poly' as part of his brother's *Puddings* suite. Paddy had been truly blessed with a brother like Martin. "Many people ask us if there are conflicts in the relationship between Martin and me as there often are in groups where brothers work together, the syndrome of the brothers Davies of the Kinks, for example. I see very well how such things can occur: as we grow up, our

---

[13] Mick Salmon died in December 2023. Martin and Paddy attended the funeral.

personalities assert themselves and our desires and tastes differ. Luckily, we don't have such problems. We also take care we don't see too much of each other outside the periods when we have to work together."

It was the three months that Martin spent working as a nightwatchman that paid for the first, extraordinary single to be recorded in 1982, 'Lions in My Own Garden (Exit Someone)'.[14] The session also led to the arrival of Wendy Smith into the band, a 19-year-old who'd moved with her family from Hartlepool to Newcastle. First impressions of Wendy are of a quiet and mysterious-looking girl from next door; the one who'd keep her distance in the street, propped up against the red-brick with her arms folded. Watching. But what was she thinking? Flicking back her long blonde hair and looking serious, like the troubled daughter in an Ingmar Bergman film.

Wendy was the waif-like girlfriend of one of the earliest of Sprouts fans, John Sunter, who'd been at gigs so often they'd recruited him as a roadie. She'd had singing lessons as part of her drama course at New College in Durham, and, unlike the rest of the band, she could read music. To begin with, Wendy's job was to collect the handfuls of ten pence pieces at the door until Paddy saw her potential—not so much as a backing singer but to supply an aural atmosphere that a keyboard couldn't manage on its own. "My idea was that she should colour the sound. She has a very melodic

---

[14] A song steeped in romantic associations. A girlfriend of Paddy's had left Newcastle to study in what would have seemed a faraway and mysterious place, Limoges in France. The single was initially self-released on their own record label Candle, which had the strapline of 'Wax that won't get on your wick'. A thousand copies were pressed in the first run, making them highly collectible items   although, reputedly, Martin still had a whole box of them in his loft in 2011.

voice, it has a very sort of beautiful tone to it." 'Smitty'—
with her strong Geordie accent and glaring black-rimmed
eyes—was their Northern minx. Like a "defrocked nun"
suggested *Record Mirror* in 1985. Not interested in the pop life
that so many young women her age would have jumped at:
"Records always seem boring or just really really awful.
That's about the range of it really. I don't really listen to any
records except Sprout's records of course, I'm not really interested… I NEVER go out. Paddy stays at home with his
drum machine and I stay at home with me little piano… I do
like going out but I don't get much opportunity and Newcastle's not the greatest place to go out in the world." Wendy
was more into fashion, or at least, the best that Newcastle
could offer. "I buy a lot of my things in London. I think the
best shop up here is probably Marks & Spencer They've got
the best jumpers and everything. And Warehouse and Next."
Her studio flat in the city centre was a hoard of clothes and
"anything that's nice, even things like nice sweet packets".
On her walls, alongside some serious art, was a pull-out
poster of Wham! taken from a copy of *Smash Hits*. With no
plans for making a name for herself in music, Wendy was
happy just spending time with the band, taking the piss, giving them the famous 'Smitty stare' or a clip round the head
if they were getting on her nerves. She was known for her
wicked sense of humour. Wendy told *i-D* magazine she was
so keen to be featured on the cover of a fashion magazine
she'd shave her head and pose naked. Driving through Paris
during the *Jordan* tour in Paris in 1991, Wendy pointed out a
couple of French *gendarmes* astride their Harley-Davidson
motorbikes to a *Melody Maker* journalist. "I want to be arres-

ted by a policeman in a leather uniform," she said, sighing theatrically and licking her lips.[15]

They were a little family, happy sharing the band routines, in-jokes and breaks for junk food. For Paddy that often meant bars of dark chocolate, fry-ups, fish and chips, burgers and curries. And for Wendy, anything else in reach. "I have to eat tons of food just to stay at seven stone. I seem to burn it all up in nervous energy." By this time, the McAloons had put the Witton Gilbert garage up for sale and moved to the nearby village of Leadgate. A bypass had drained the traffic away from Front Street and lost them petrol sales. Tommy was also now having to deal with the onset of Parkinson's Disease. The majority of the household income was now being made by Mary from her work as a housekeeper for the parish of Our Blessed Lady and St Joseph. The family rented a nineteenth-century Gothic house that was close to her work, a dark and musty place that had been part of a nunnery and a school run by the Sisters of Charity of St Paul the Apostle.

*

Keith Armstrong was the young manager of an HMV store in Newcastle's Northumberland Street in 1982 when Martin popped in with a few copies of 'Lions in My Own Garden'.

---

[15] It's not important to this chapter—and really none of our business—but we're naturally interested in whether Paddy and Wendy were a couple. Hints in interviews suggest that between 1984 and 1988 they were, in a low-key kind of way that would have suited Paddy's sometimes solitary routines. They were such good friends that people would still think of them as a couple in 1990 during the recording of *Jordan*. Paul Gomersall, the sound engineer on the album, certainly thought they were—until he himself became Wendy's boyfriend later that year.

The shop was a cavernous space with a heavy red carpet and grey-speckled walls, lit by rows of spot-lighting and HMV's trademark neon signage.

> I always listened to every record that came in [said Keith] so I'd know what I was talking about, especially the post-punk indie, from Postcard, Mute, ZE in the US. When I heard 'Lions' I thought it was absolutely brilliant. We tracked the band down and asked them to come to the basement of the HMV office and play. Recording demos wasn't such a thing then. There were five of them, the two girls [Wendy and another friend who sang on 'Lions', Feona Attwood]. There was this Montgomery Clift-looking character who I assumed was Paddy, the singer. But that turned out to be Mick Salmon. Paddy was the one hiding at the back in an overcoat and old cloth cap. I remember the first thing Martin said to me, before they'd even started playing, was "we're not changing the name". That hadn't even occurred to me. They then came to the Kitchenware offices in Clayton Street and played for about three hours without repeating anything. There were many of the songs that would be on *Swoon* (as well as 'Bonny' which I tried and failed to get on *Swoon*). They were magnificent live, so unique and exciting. Lyrics in particular are

> my thing and Paddy blew me away with his. I
> told them I thought I could sell more copies
> of 'Lions', if they'd give me a chance.

Keith had played guitar in punk bands when he was at school. A business degree at Newcastle Poly took him into the kingdom of HMV, where he became the company's youngest manager, taking over the Derby branch. But he was soon bored stiff with being stuck inside the same four walls of retail every day, stuck with the plastic-wrapped products. Alongside a fellow HMV-escapee, assistant manager Phil Mitchell and his schoolfriend Paul Ludford, Keith started to hire space at the Casablanca Club and Tiffany's Function Room, getting a new generation of indie bands to play Newcastle. From the very first gigs in the summer of 1981, 'The Soul Kitchen' was hot. 17-year-old Roddy Frame appeared for the first time outside of Scotland. Orange Juice came, New Order, Josef K, The Fire Engines, The Bluebells, Blue Rondo (tickets: £2). For a city more used to retro-rock and bars filled with mullets, the year of Soul Kitchen was a small revolution. An excited, optimistic, pocket-sized scene where fans could get away with wearing plaid shirts, bootlace ties and sailor hats, and being interested in more than their next snog and bottle of 'Broon'. The shows—promoted with straplines like "the only fun in town" and "Fancy Newcastle now?!"—included a mix of live performances and contributions from local artists, painters and photographers. Audiences would get to bring along their coolest indie records to play. The bands themselves were on a better deal, because they didn't have to pay middle-men for promotion. With his neatly barbered hair, big brown eyes and leather jacket,

219

Keith was the face of a new scene, pushing an approach that mixed principles with realism. Keith had learnt a lot from an HMV training course that exposed him to the world of sales reps and radio pluggers. So the next step had to be Kitchenware Records, a way to fight against the blandness of chart music, the scowling "inverted snobbery" of indie labels, and the idea that you had to be in London to make a success of anything. A more sensible version of Postcard.[16] As Keith explained—in his steady, always persuasive way of speaking—the big industry model was "pretty crass", totally dependent on achieving sales targets in order to fund the next project, with no time for dealing with bands as human beings. A&R had ended up as a function only looking for copycat versions of proven sellers. The Kitchenware model would be different. "We became, I think one of the first 'dependent' record labels'. We did deals with whoever would fund our artists but kept full creative control. We were more interested in integrity than money." They'd go for exciting, niche bands (who wouldn't just be picked off for their mainstream potential); look after them properly, guarantee big label distribution, and build relationships with influencers in places like the BBC. Get the G&Ts in. "Everyone involved with Kitchenware is positive about what we are doing. It's important to us to have pride, even when things seem to be going against us. We are searching for the spirit that you

---

[16] Keith admired what Alan Horne had done at Postcard and the freshness of the music, but could see what had gone wrong. "One of the problems with Postcard was that Alan wanted to be as big a star as Edwyn Collins. He also tried to impose his own musical tastes on his bands too much. He'd get them to do cover versions of his favourite songs, which was too close to manipulation for my liking. If anything, I try and get them to bring out and exaggerate what is already there."

found on records like 'Young, Gifted and Black', 'Be Young, Be Foolish, Be Happy' and 'Say It Loud, I'm Black and I'm Proud'. It's not only the spirit that is lacking in most music today, it's the spirit… missing in this country." The first signings to Kitchenware were Newcastle's tuneful rockers Hurrah!, followed by Sunderland's Martin Stephenson and the Daintees (a gang of characters who made the most of life on the dole, doing the rounds of busking, setting up a band co-op for rehearsals and picking magic mushrooms as a sideline enterprise), then soul boys the Kane Gang.[17]

The morning Keith splashed on the aftershave and headed down to London, he promised Paddy he was going to get him £100,000 for the first LP, *Swoon* (which had been recorded for £5,000). He was meeting up with the A&R at CBS Records to talk about a little-known regional band making obtuse, wordy pop that was like nothing else; a band fronted by a one-off genius who might not want to do promotional tours. Somehow, Keith came back with the £100,000 contract, plus an eight-LP deal and artistic control left in the hands of the band. It wouldn't have been so straightforward if the A&R had been someone less enlightened than Muff Winwood, who was willing to make his

---

[17] Kitchenware stayed true to its mission in Newcastle and lasted longer than most other indie operations, earning itself a new lease of life in the Noughties with bands like Editors, Smith & Burrows and Sirens, an all-girl hip hop band from Newcastle who had hits in Japan and the US. "I hoped Kitchenware would give people from Newcastle the belief that they could push boundaries in the same way Manchester and Glasgow had. I was a young punk rocker who thought that anyone could do anything if they believed in it enough. I guess we helped get music released that otherwise may not have been heard. If Kitchenware could be remembered in the same way as labels like Beserkely or ZE, I'd be chuffed." Soul Kitchen now exists as an enterprise "devoted to developing young artists from outside of London and helping young non-musicians assist them in doing it."

Not a dream after all: Stevie Wonder was in the studio to record his harmonica
solo for 'Nightingales' in September 1987, with Keith, Wendy, Paddy and Martin
(playing 'Alfie' on the piano). Courtesy of Keith Armstrong.

own judgements and take risks.[18] It led to a remarkably free
hand for Paddy. Would there have been a recording career
for the Sprouts if that hadn't been the case? "I would let
them record anything, the songs were so good," said Keith.
"He didn't really need A&R, I always believed it was just a
case of getting Paddy in the right place, the right studio with
the right people, and everything would work by itself. He
never played a song to me or Muff that was rejected."

---

[18] Mervyn Winwood (nicknamed Muff after the TV character Muffin the Mule) was
brother of Steve Winwood and bass player with the Spencer Davis Group ('Gimme
Some Lovin', 'Keep on Running'). He also signed the Psychedelic Furs, Terence Trent
D'Arby, Sade (and, er, Shakin' Stevens). He'd been a record producer working with
Sparks, Traffic, Mott the Hoople, Kevin Ayers and Marianne Faithfull.

They were the first ones to say unreservedly 'yes' to us [said Paddy of CBS]. They liked our musical style. I'm never at any time being pressured from them. They don't come knocking on the door wanting a follow-up single to such-and-such, they take them as they come. They will eventually have a lot of good singles, I hope. They know we're an acquired taste, they aren't trying to spark with us like Shakin' Stevens. Everybody criticises the major record companies for playing safe—well they are not playing safe with us. The money was good but any money which gets you off the dole is good money and if you've signed up with someone on a long-term deal you've got to make sure the money is good.

Paddy just happened to be in the Kitchenware offices and picked up the phone when a drummer rang to offer his services. Neil Conti had heard a performance of 'Don't Sing' on Richard Skinner's Radio 1 show and been "blown away". He'd also read that the band was reliant on a temporary drummer, Dave Ruffy (of the Ruts and Aztec Camera).

I used to hang out in London with Mel Gaynor, an excellent drummer friend [said Neil]. We were both frustrated at being told to play like 'some-other-established-drummer' when we worked in recording studios and agreed that it was probably better to join a band and hopefully get to play our own style. So he ended up joining Simple Minds and I joined Prefab… By the way, that ridiculous story going around about me calling and saying I was a better drummer than their current one is complete rubbish. Paddy and I had a great chat and it just felt easy and natural when we all got together a few weeks later to play some songs.[19]

The release of *Swoon* (1984) meant a one-way trip into the pop-media universe. There was excitement around what the Sprouts might achieve ("I remember someone at Rough Trade saying to me it would be good if we sold 5,000 copies," said Keith. "I said why won't everybody want a copy? Our ambitions were always huge.") But the bigger dream suffered a small death.

Once you make a living from music, the atmosphere shifts. People around us said after *Swoon*: 'That did OK for a record that didn't cost much. Where's your next one?' And suddenly you're not bashing out songs in a rehearsal room, it's me in a room trying to ensure the band's got a good supply of material… I didn't enjoy being in a band. As a teenager, pop music answers some fantasy

---

[19] Luton-born Neil (1959) played piano from the age of six (his cousin was the keyboard player for Mott the Hoople, Morgan Fisher), but switched to drums when he was 12. Neil played on the first five Sprouts albums, and has also played in bands for David Bowie, Mick Jagger, Robert Plant, Annie Lennox and Youssou N'Dour.

part of your mind. And the reality of it—being in the back of a van going to venues—
was so far away from the fantasy that I just
rejected it.

The Sprouts had their five minutes of cool. John Peel called
them "subversive MOR" and there was a series of cover features putting them in the quirky guitar indie bracket—but it
was only a passing moment. Paddy quickly realised they were
in the papers because they were new, not necessarily because
they were believed to be good. Even with *Swoon* an *NME*
writer suggested the vinyl should come with a "free axe" for
smashing it to pieces. The sweet, melancholy marvel of *Steve
McQueen* (1985) didn't lead to any place of security or creative peace. Just demands for bigger, more frequent contributions to the product and promotion cycle. Paddy's argument
was that popularity was possible without being the same as
everyone else. Robert De Niro didn't do interviews, so why
should he? Keith did his best.

We were having dinner with the label [CBS
had been bought by Sony by this stage],
around the time Paddy was saying he was
done with touring, he wouldn't ever go out on
the road again. The bosses were getting us
drunk—but I always had a rule that no matter how drunk I got I'd always write down
everything that was said in a meeting like
that. An exec made some outlandish promise,
like five extra per cent on the record deal
money. I made sure I reminded him of that

by mail the very next day—and of course he said he didn't remember saying that. Paddy had eventually agreed to a tour during the dinner, but then afterwards he stuck his heels in. Sony ended up spending a lot of money on Deacon Blue instead, to make a point to Paddy about the importance of playing live.

Nothing much about being a celebrity was good for Paddy. "I was too shy to talk to people. Everyone would stay at the Columbia Hotel, and my brother Marty could talk to anyone. But when I saw Noddy Holder at the bar, I just thought, 'That's Noddy Holder!' like any fan would and go shy."

The Sprouts ended up as a tangle of contradictions because they were so reliant on a prolific talent who kept a tight lid on what he shared with the world. A genuinely novel, radical artist who also longed for a big hit single, to make that one classic piece of jukebox vinyl. They weren't going to become a more commercial proposition by touring, so Paddy had to at least write a pop hit. Lighten up. Drop the clever-clever lyrics.

A few months after 'The King of Rock 'n' Roll' had taken the Sprouts into the Top Ten and sucked them into agreeing to a performance miming on *Top of the Pops* in 1988, Paddy bumped into one his heroes, Paul McCartney. He'd been invited along to a McCartney Productions party celebrating a Buddy Holly anniversary (McCartney owned Holly's publishing rights). Paddy had done really well with that last single, McCartney told him, because he'd got the kids and the grannies with that one: "That 'hot dog, jumping frog' is going to be your 'Ding-a-Ling'." Here was the grim truth of pop. All those solitary years as the Galahad of songwriting, following his quest along the sun-dappled byways of music, searching for just the right kind of beauty, had come down to this. He was going to be remembered for a novelty hit. A video with dancing hot dogs and frogs in tuxedos serving drinks by a pool. "Well," said a hesitant Paddy to McCartney, "that's not really representative of what I do, man."

The year of hot dogs was a kind of ending, a break from the pop dream. There was going to be no tour to promote the album. Instead Paddy headed back to his room, thinking about what it had all been for, telling the world: "I've abandoned hipness altogether."

*

Jordan: The Comeback would contain sixty-four minutes and nineteen tracks of music (once five had been cut out). It took seven months and around $500,000 to record and mix. Think of how this compares with the albums of *Like Magic*, most of which were recorded in the space of two weeks. Even the famously tortured perfectionists of the Blue Nile spent only five months on *A Walk Across the Rooftops*. *Jordan* was a grand statement—but a statement about what?

Producer Thomas Dolby had met up with Paddy in a café in London to talk about what he wanted to do with his new bunch of songs. They both had colds and Paddy was pink-nosed and ripe with the smell of Vicks vapour rub. So, asked Thomas, what's this one about? Our most mercurial of songwriters was looking drawn and intense and his response was a fit of coughing into his hand. Finally, Paddy ran his fingers through his curtains of hair and came up with as short and simple an answer as he could manage: "It's about Elvis and death."

Paddy's shorthand. There was really no single all-encompassing concept, the album was just meant to be big. Big and excessive. He'd been working on a "mad musical idea" which he'd abandoned, "and so I was freed up to do some random things". He was still in the mood for widescreen, technicolour fantasia. "I picture my songs as nuclear-powered Walt Disney film themes—but they never come out like that." Maybe he'd come across Hal Willner's *Stay Awake* (1988), a gorgeous re-working of the Disney songbook that makes full use of the dark wonder and fear at the heart of the old Disney films;[20] or liked what he'd heard on another recent, sprawling album of surprises, Prince's *Sign O' the Times* (1987). What was *Jordan*? Thinking retrospectively, Wendy's suggestions reflect how difficult it's been to put the album into a box: "An abandoned musical. A concept album. A rock opera. A hymn book. An epic poem." Sony took one look and knew exactly what it was: too long. Keith fell out with execs when he insisted that *Jordan* had to stay at the full length and be released as a double album. "It would have been a killer single album, but then it also wouldn't have been the artistic statement it was meant to be."[21]

---

[20] Featuring contributions from, among others, Tom Waits, Michael Stipe, Natalie Merchant, Sun Ra, Ringo Starr, Ken Nordine, James Taylor, Sinead O'Connor, Los Lobos and The Replacements.

[21] Paddy and Keith wanted it to be a double album, but Sony put their foot down. It wasn't until the remastered vinyl version in 2019 that the album appeared as it was intended over four sides (except for the release in South Africa which was always a double. The country's pressing machines couldn't put so much material onto a single disc).

In making sense of what was going on, we shouldn't forget the Brian Wilson factor. There had been a remarkable article by Tom Nolan in *Rolling Stone* about the Beach Boys and the legendary *Smile* songs that Paddy had read repeatedly over the years. In his piece, Nolan told the story of a distracted genius. Record producer Terry Melcher told him: "[Brian] isn't *fashionable*. He's definitely not fashionable in any sense of the word as it might apply to anything. We all have certain modes; we're wearing Levis, we're not wearing gingham pants. But *he might* be wearing blue-and-white-specked ginghams when you get to his house. And a red short-sleeved T-shirt with some food on the front. It wouldn't be a shock. He's just so involved in that one thing that he doesn't see any reason for concessions on any level. They just don't exist. He's really an unusual guy." And at the same time, a prodigy.

> He writes *fantastic* melodies. He's like a classical composer. Brian can do a Bach thing. Give him 90 pieces and he'll give you a Bach thing; then give it to an expert and he'd have a hell of a time finding the difference… If I could write melodies and chords like Brian Wilson, I'd take those fucking songs and make up demos of the tracks and send them out to Hal David and to Lennon and to McCartney—I'd send 'em all over the fuckin' world, and take the best one. That's what he should do. 'Cause he's good enough. He's better than *all* those people. He knows more

about music than *anyone* who's at all present
on the music scene. He knows a *lot* more.

And who does this sound like?

> He was moving so quickly, he had so many
> projects, it was hard for anything to set in. He
> wanted to do an album of music built from
> sound effects. They were taping water
> sounds, fountains, faucets, everything. He
> wanted to use the water noise as note pat-
> terns, chords spliced together through a
> whole LP. He wanted to do a comedy album.
> He wanted to do a health food album.

It was an inspiring, maybe also reassuring portrait for another fixated songsmith to read, even when it came to describing
the eccentric side of Brian: his purple house in Bel Air, the
slide he'd had built from his roof that curled into the swimming pool; how he'd stuff himself with burgers then head
off to work behind the counter of his own health foodstore,
the Radiant Radish. Or even the neurotic, sometimes desperate state of Brian, the crying and breakdowns, the obsessive behaviours and delusions. At one point he'd believed
there was a halo over his head no-one else could see; and
that rehearsing his track 'Fire', with the musicians wearing
toy firemen's helmets, had caused an actual blaze downtown.
    In his plans for *Smile*, the follow-up to *Pet Sounds*, Brian
had wanted to make an epic about the making of America;
in an American way, with lots of humour, so that the plain

goodness at the heart of things would just keep on bubbling through. "His musical theories were based upon emotion," wrote Tom Nolan. "He could sit down and write a chart, anytime, but when he described the music it was always in artistic or literary allusions, colours, mental responses. *Smile* conveyed a tremendous amount of real, really deep happiness. There was glitter and sunshine, yet there were profound shades of blue like yawning caves or climbing through thick ivy."

From Paddy's 'Rollmo' home studio in Leadgate came a set of demos.[22] Anyone who hadn't heard the final mix might think the demos were a finished album in themselves. Many of the arrangements and some of the starlight atmosphere was already there (as well as curious details, like the 'yippity-yoppity' accompaniment on 'The Wedding March'). These weren't vocal and keyboard sketches waiting to be coloured in, but Paddy himself didn't consider them to be anything other than raw material, the straw for Thomas Dolby to work with.

Muff had called up Thomas Dolby in January 1984 after hearing his thoughtful response to 'Don't Sing' on Radio 1's Round Table show. Here was someone who wasn't afraid to go against the tide of opinion on a record review

---

[22] 'Rollmo' was Michael Jackson's phrase. Or at least what Paddy had dreamt Jackson had said. "I was stuck in the studio with him and he's there with his brothers discussing the recording session [for *Bad*]. Michael says, 'Ah, you want to give it a little more *rollmo*.' When I asked Michael what it meant, he said, '*Rollmo* is a term we picked up back in the Motown days—it's a little bit of magic you've got to add to it, whether it's in the recording process or whether it's something to do with the deal you make. *Rollmo* makes it a little more special.'" The dream also featured songs planned for the next Jackson album, to be called *The Flimsy World of Film*. Paddy was disappointed not to have remembered enough of the songs to pinch them. In a retelling of the story, Michael had explained it differently in the dream (which makes you wonder whether the whole thing isn't blueberry-flavoured): "Oh, it's something that we borrowed from our legal affairs adviser, that's when a deal is extra sweet… *Rollmo*."

panel that included a young DJ Steve Wright and 'Miss Bee-hive' Mari Wilson.

> One after another, these records came up
> that I thought were terrible [said Dolby] and
> the others would wax lyrical about them and
> say, 'Oh, that great new one by Haircut 100'
> or whoever it was… and I was very uninter-
> ested. I was starting to feel like a real killjoy
> when on came 'Don't Sing'. Right from the
> opening bars, with the acoustic guitar and
> harmonica, and the first line, 'An outlaw
> stand in a peasant land', it just grabbed my
> attention and so I said really nice things
> about it.

The 25-year-old Dolby was a synth *wunderkind* who'd been brought in to add a funky electro edge to albums by the likes of Foreigner, Def Leppard and Joan Armatrading, but was best known in the UK for his single 'She Blinded Me With Science' featuring 'deranged' TV scientist Magnus Pyke. Paddy met Thomas and he was invited up to the rural Goth-ic environs of Leadgate. "I'd heard him pick 'Johnny and Mary' by Robert Palmer, a Marvin Gaye song, one by the Band, a Beatles song, the Beach Boys… Similar tastes, and I thought, why not?" said Paddy at the time. "Besides, he's a keyboard player and I'm an amateur one myself, and I knew he was well up on keyboard technology which is important as I want to learn about music." Most of all, the Sprouts and Kitchenware liked the idea of working with someone from commercial pop. Thomas was their Trevor Horn or Quincy Jones, just a bit more budget-friendly.

> I can picture him at 60 with a wealth of experience, and not snobby [said Paddy]. He gets a lot of good offers from people but if he hears a band that he likes who have no money, I suspect Thomas would go and do that. We had CBS, but I know he really did it because he liked it, liked the idea of it… He's known as Mr Boffin, but he's Mr Performance to tell you the truth. He works on the basis that if the feel is right then you can excuse the odd error. He brought back some of the live dynamic we'd lost along the way.

Working together on *Steve McQueen*, Paddy was struck by how hard-working and committed his young producer was, "a sweet man" who as soon as he'd finished one track would be off playing his piano and working on new ideas, trying out other new combinations to get the best from the material. Thomas was a revelation, "the Brian Wilson of the synthesiser" said Paddy; he'd record extra little pieces of piano or cello colour to add in, identify interesting undercurrents of rhythms, all as a means of "building up pictures in layers" that became beautiful arrangements of counterpoint. From the beginning, Thomas saw what he could do for the Sprouts —not by injecting more of a Dolby flavour, not changing anything—but by being "someone to boss them around a little bit". Give them some expert objectivity. That included being the curator who decided which songs to record and the craftsman who knew how to "massage the structure" of songs and bring the smooth edges and polish that could transform the overall effect.

> I saw they had a unique individuality, a fascinating lyrical approach, the *sound*, and interesting chords… much more complex chords than mostly happen in pop music; reminiscent of Steely Dan, Stephen Sondheim, George Gershwin, Brian Wilson… just really unusual pop music. Paddy's words are so expressive, so emotional. Wendy's voice was sort of very deadpan; I thought that that was a very interesting vocal sound. It's not often that you come across a new vocal sound that you haven't heard before, it was very distinctive, very intriguing. But I suppose none of that would have mattered were it not for the fact that to me there are a lot of rough edges about the way that they'd arrange the songs and some of the song structures and so on, which I think had come about because of the method that Paddy applied to writing his songs. He was 'lyrics first'. He'd write the lyrics and he'd sit there and strum, and if it was appropriate to have a bar with five beats in, or a phrase with seven bars in, he would just do it that way. He'd just strum it until it was time to come back in with the vocals.

Working with Thomas upgraded Paddy's knowledge and approach to making music, and the demos for *Jordan* were made with Dolby—his standards and methods—in mind. He'd been turned into a studio-based creative. "In the past I would write a song, hand it over to Thomas Dolby, and he'd make something out of it," said Paddy in 1990.

> Now I want to write the song and get the at-mosphere going at home with the computer, what have you, do the arrangement and then hand over to Thomas or the band and then say 'Look, this is what I am trying to do.'…
> To give an example 'Jesse James Bolero' exists on the album very much like in the demo… I wanted it broken up in terms of the ar-rangement, lots of different instruments play-ing small parts. I can only get close to that if I work at home. That's a very recent thing for me to be involved with. It's to do with having more technical equipment at home than I used to have. And to do with taking control, not only with writing the songs but also defin-ing the sound world you wanted to be in.

As it turned out, Thomas wasn't available to work on *Jordan*. He was living in the US and had recently married the actor Kathleen Beller, famous for her role in the soap opera *Dyn-asty* as Kirby Anders Colby. Hearing the demos changed his mind—two songs in particular, 'Wild Horses'[23] and 'Jesse James Bolero'—and he flew in to London (where he caught that cold). Paddy was clear he didn't want another *Steve Mc-Queen* with its "glassy, shiny" sound. *Jordan* was going to inhabit a universe all of its own.

A marathon journey of recording began in June 1989 at Thomas's own studio, The Think Tank in Fulham. There was no turning back now as the forthcoming album and its title had already been announced as part of the press release for *Protest Songs*. Paddy's home demos, C-Lab keyboard tracks, were poured into Thomas's Fairlight for the pre-rehearsals used to set out arrangements ahead of studio sessions.

> Some of Paddy's demos by then were becoming so excellent that I was starting to say to him, 'Look, I don't know if you actually need me. If I were you, I'd just put out two albums a year and do them yourself at home. They won't be quite as polished, but at least they will see the light of day and it'll keep your costs down.' But Paddy never really subscribed to that point of view, even after the internet came in.

For all the essential quality of the demos, they have something flaccid and pale about them, you can hear the sounds

---

[23] "It's unique among my songs, as it was written entirely on a sampling keyboard, an Ensoniq Mirage." Hot Chip have spoken up about the brilliance of 'Wild Horses' and its swung rhythm, using samples and loops which were ahead of its time (and were part of the original demo).

of a cheap Casio keyboard; there are rhythms that seem insistent and blunt rather than part of the whole. Not that there aren't fascinating moments. Like the pathos of Paddy's single voice singing 'All Boys Believe Anything', the more ABBA-ish take on 'The Ice Maiden', and the smoother, stripped-down ballad version of 'Scarlet Nights'. The weakest demos, in Thomas's mind, were 'Carnival 2000', 'Michael' and 'Scarlet Nights', "all of which I radicalised". The final Dolby-fied version of the songs is like a landscape filling with the warmth and colours of summer.

To spare Thomas from living in one hotel after another, the band moved into a residential studio, a 17th-century farmhouse in the North Downs of Surrey that was an oasis of meadows and woodland. There'd been good reports about the place from Hurrah!, who'd just recorded their first album there.[24] "It was a large, sprawling, comfortable residential country retreat with tennis courts, swimming pool, great chef and very nice friendly staff," said Neil. "The technical staff were very adept and had even built some of their own recording equipment. We were still in the era of recording to tape, of course, which I think gives the record a nice compressed and warm sound, rather than the cold digital era that came after." All the drum tracks were recorded at Ridge Farm.

> I had a smaller drum kit custom-made by a
> great London craftsman called Eddie Ryan,
> which I'd used on a Level 42 tour in the

---

[24] Ridge Farm was set up in 1975 by the lighting man who'd worked on live tours with ABBA and Queen. It was the UK's first residential studio. Despite being a favourite of many Britpop-era bands, the studio closed in 2003.

USA. It had a tighter 'soul' sound than the big Gretsch on the previous albums, as I thought it would fit the style of the Jordan songs better, especially tracks like 'Machine Gun Ibiza' and 'Let the Stars Go'. We had the drums set up in a smaller space than before to get a drier, more intimate sound, and I liaised with Paul Gomersall, a brilliant engineer, on mic choice and placement.

Then they had to move on. The middle of June came with long days of heat and sunshine and the air conditioning stopped working. Being shut in a studio was sweaty enough and Thomas fell ill with a lung infection. The Sprouts headed for another country retreat, this time The Farmyard in Little Chalfont in Buckinghamshire, which they knew from mixing *Steve McQueen*.[25] It had a real 'olde worlde' country feel, said Paul. "A great place to hang out in as well as work. Friends came and went for the duration." Martin had become a dad during this time and was dropping in and out.[26] Paddy himself was always in or around the studio, but left Thomas in charge when it came to recording Martin and Wendy's tracks. (Like any close family, they didn't always take advice or constructive criticism from each other that well).

---

[25] The 18th-century buildings of the Farmyard had been the home of actor Dirk Bogarde before becoming a studio in the late Sixties. Yes, Genesis, the Rolling Stones and Simple Minds had all recorded there. Farmyard closed in 2013 and is now a luxury holiday rental.

[26] Jonathan McAloon, who has made a career for himself as a literary critic, contributing to the *Financial Times*, *Times Literary Supplement*, *The Guardian* etc.

The months away from his new wife and home in Los Angeles, much longer than he'd planned, were also getting difficult for Thomas. Paul remembered the times when the air would turn blue, when Thomas would get so engrossed in programming the fine details of songs he'd forget to save what he'd done and the computer would crash. "Thomas has an incredible aural memory so was able to recreate what he'd done pretty quickly. I did start to remind him after a few times of it happening though." "I did have occasional differences with Thomas," said Neil. "He could be moody and downright cruel sometimes, but good art is rarely made without a few sparks flying, so I'm at peace with all that." Gripes and tensions soon dissipated during that golden summer. They were always a bunch of friends spending time on a project together. "Paddy is one of the funniest people I've ever worked with," said Paul, "incredibly sharp witted, so I would say there was never a dull moment. If anything was starting to get a little strained, one of us could always break the tension to get over it." The Greek heritage of George Michael and his "wonderful sense of hummus" turned out to be a running joke (Paul had worked as engineer on Wham! records like 'Careless Whisper' and 'Last Christmas').[27]

At Farmyard though, Paddy and Thomas felt some of the equipment was going to let them down: "the gear they had was coming to the end of its time. We started to second guess ourselves on the vocals because we weren't sure whether we getting an accurate sound—the SSL [Solid State Logic console] had a few problems, it had been used for five or six

---

[27] The joke about George Michael, it should be said, was originally Boy George's.

years—and when you get paranoid about your vocal sound you tend to lose the plot a bit." Vocal tracks were scrapped and the journey continued at Sony's own studio in Whitfield Street, just off Tottenham Court Road in London, where most of the vocals and keyboard parts were recorded. "Thomas always listens to the room to tell what microphone we should use to achieve a certain sound. For 'Machine Gun Ibiza' we needed a harder, dryer sound; whereas something like 'Paris Smith' on the original demo I'd used chorus on the voice—something you'd never do—and Thomas liked that, so we used Dimension D [an effect that 'widens' the sound and adds extra stereo] so that it swirls a bit." The relationship between the two of them was the foundation of everything. "A lot of other producers might've tried to rein in such an ambitious artist, but I got the impression that Dolby quite enjoyed the challenge, even though it was a mighty task," said Neil. 'Carnival 2000' took some re-working. "It's got a lot of time signatures and lengths of phrase; it took us a while to come up with a groove that really worked and accommodated the song," said Thomas. The recording wasn't helped by the horn section's band leader, Gary Barnacle, whose new-fangled chunk of mobile phone kept going off. The third time it happened, Paddy reached for the talkback button: "How are you going to get home on the underground train, Gary, with that saxophone shoved up your anus?"[28] 'Scarlet Nights' was another re-make. Initially,

---

[28] The Phantom Horns were the trendy horn section for the Eighties. Gary Barnacle had played sax, flute and clarinet for everyone, from The Clash and The Damned to Spandau Ballet, Level 42, Phil Collins and David Bowie etc.

Thomas spent a day programming a hip-hop style beat, but this was vetoed by Paddy.

Backing vocals featured the one and only appearance of 'The Ning Singers', a group made up of Wendy, Martin, Neil and new mum Bernadette McAloon, who recorded 'All Boys Believe Anything' in the studio kitchen.[29] Thomas included his own voice for effects on 'Looking for Atlantis' and 'We Let the Stars Go'. The romantic, old-school sexiness of Jenny Agutter was also added courtesy of Thomas: "Jenny Agutter was actually my last girlfriend before I met my wife, so she graciously agreed to add that little bit to the album. It was kind of perfect because she was, for English men of our generation, such an iconic figure from our adolescence, and not necessarily in a lustful way. It was more like you wanted the first girl you fell in love with to be like Jenny Agutter." The guitars were recorded by Paddy with the help of his "unofficial guitar consultant" Dave Brewis of the Kane Gang.

> Yeah, he sells me his guitars. The ones he doesn't like, I end up with! I mainly use the Strat, which is a 1962. Dave sold me that, and it's a lovely guitar. Then there's a Martin dreadnought and a Gretsch. I've got a Chet Atkins nylon string as well, which I used on 'Carnival 2000' and 'Paris Smith'. The sustain goes on for forty days and forty nights with those, and they go out of tune so easily.

---

[29] Bernadette McAloon is Martin's wife, a good friend of Wendy, a published poet who has worked as an arts and mental health practitioner in Newcastle.

You've really got to stroke them. The intona-
tion's pretty good—but you've just got to
tickle it. I also have a little £75 nylon string
Ibanez guitar, that I used for the rumbly
acoustic on 'Looking for Atlantis'.

A critical moment for the album, its overall balance as a set
of songs, came in the last week when Paddy was waiting for
the Fostex B-16 tape machine to rewind. It was then he
picked up his guitar and started to strum, singing the words
that had wandered into his head, "I remember King David,
with his harp and his beautiful, beautiful songs". 'One of the
Broken', 'Mercy' and 'Doo Wop in Harlem' were all written
on the spot, in the studio. "I don't know what the record
would have felt like without some of these things," he said
later.[30]

Thomas had always known when to leave Paddy's vision alone.

There was always a sense with Prefab that—
and he wouldn't be sanctimonious enough to
say this—his music is really righteous and
there's a sort of unspoken rule that you don't
bend over backwards to be poppy or to get
on the radio, or to 'fit in' with other things
out there; that there is a core truth to the music, which we are all servants to… Paddy, to

[30] The tracks that didn't make the final 19 include (the excellent) 'Who Intrigues You
Now', along with 'Meet the New Mozart' (which turned up on *Let's Change the World with
Music*—Thomas had struggled with the line "One day there will be / A more conducive
century"), and (most probably) 'Snowy Rents a Dog'.

> me, was always a quiet, sensitive and studious
> man with a streak of exhibitionism that
> would occasionally come to the surface…
> We're very, very respectful of each other and
> we're each other's number one fan, really. He
> puts up with me… I can be a bit opinionated
> and stubborn sometimes, but somehow the
> chemistry sort of works. As a producer, you
> have to be willing to subsume your own view
> to that of the artist, because they're not my
> records, they're his.

Thomas knew that even for Paddy, *Jordan* was different.
There were "lofty goals" involved, it was "a literary work,
like *Ulysses*".

The final push happened in Los Angeles because the
newly-wed Thomas needed to get home, even if it meant
paying the air fares for Paddy, because by this time the recording budget had run dry. The work was done at the
glamorous beachside home of the new Mrs Dolby, with
Parisian mixing engineer Eric Calvi helping out on the desk,
fresh from working with Miles Davis. There was lots of
swimming and the chance to spend languorous LA nights
being rock stars. "Because we had a two-month break before
mixing, it gave us such a fresh perspective on it," Paddy said.
"I suppose in comparison to a lot of people's records we're
quite brutal in mixing the vocals loud, and sometimes that
isn't always a great thing, but if the lyrics are good and
you've sung it alright, then let them hear whatever it is you're
doing. It's like what your mam would say about not hearing
the words, so you mix them up."

Art student Wendy was given the job of briefing the cover designer Gerry Judah. Judah's day job was in the theatre, a stagehand who'd get involved with making props and painting scenery. His passion was for sculpture and making statement pieces for public spaces and events, which he went on to do for the big London museums, the BBC, and for Michael Jackson and Paul McCartney concerts. Wendy suggested a rippled, watery theme, "a painted backdrop with the words *Jordan: The Comeback* in lights in reverse reflected on the water… Other objects related included, i.e. glitter added to the water or a leaf floating by. Sky reflected in the water." One idea was to use an anilyne dye (a powder) or oil in the water to add colour and texture. Something un-slick and unexpected—"photographed experimentally by young photographer". Wendy stressed the quadripartite structure of the piece, the individuality of the four sets of songs on the album, and how it needed emphasising in the inner sleeve design. The basic idea was translated onto the cover, but it became a plastic impression rather than a real mood, the tranquil frailty of Wendy's idea—the natural world versus the electric sparkle of pop—was lost.

*

Having to walk a mile along the dual carriageway made you see things differently. Cars were king. Soon as you got out of your shiny, pine-scented machine you discovered the grass verges were only cosmetic, and every place was un-walkable, even for someone in the lowest of heels. A countryside of McDonalds bags and bottles of orangeade that definitely weren't orangeade.

Sarah looks back to her car behind her in the distance, still steaming, one wheel awkwardly on the road. It'd probably be alright, as long as she made it to the garage before dusk, and then she'd have to think about the money. No thinking about that that now. And definitely no thinking about the pinstripe suits that had turned up at work. Everyone knew they were management consultants, not clients—they smiled too much.

Drivers roar past, seeing her Metro dumped there. A black Golf stutters and slows down for a look. On its boot is a Teenage Mutant Ninja Turtles sticker, "I'm Michelangelo!". Truck drivers glance over and look away in case she's thinking about a lift. It wasn't the Seventies any more, when a girl could reasonably expect to push out her chest and stop the traffic.

It was times like this she wishes she's a smoker, to make her feel better. Fags were all you could taste when you were eating in the Beefeater anyway, so why not. The only things she has in her pockets are fluff and a leftover Locket. Normal people had purses and cash, so why doesn't she even have 10p for a phone call?

Climbing over the crash barriers at the roundabout in her skirt wasn't dignified, but at least she was off the carriageway and into the backways of the retail and leisure park. Not much to look at under a white afternoon sky. The new boxes of the multiplex, the bowling place and Garfunkel's that could just as easily be used as incarceration centres. Meant for darkness and people too relieved to have finished work to worry about how much they were spending.

Home in her flat, Sarah sits on her settee with a pile of shopping catalogues and the Yellow Pages and waits for the TV to warm up. The cheque she'd written for the recovery men was going to bounce but she'd talk to Dad and start getting the bus to work. She wasn't going to cook tonight. Domino's took cheques. Better than her effort at something that looked like dinner, the Smash, Turkey Drummers and Beans combo.

245

The picture on the screen thickens and spreads in a mud of colour, the fuzz makes shapes, things, faces. And there is tonight's feast of entertainment, Through the Keyhole *starring Gross Loydman.*

*

No good will come from looking for a simple coherence of meaning in *Jordan*. Paddy's songwriting train has always been in motion, he's not stopped to assemble a philosophy on anything, and we've only had glimpses into carriages as they speed past, leaving just impressions of light and hope and oddness. He was suspicious of the written word being over-analysed. It had certainly done religion no good, as he pointed out in his most unashamedly literary set of lyrics on *I Trawl the Megahertz* (2003): "Like centuries of scholars poring over Jesus' words / Anything that doesn't fit my narrow interpretation I will carelessly discard". Meanings were changeable, and the idea that people were interested enough to look for a meaning was enough.

And yet *Jordan* still feels like a concept album. In his conversation with the Japanese novelist Banana Yoshimoto in 2000, Paddy hinted at why that might be. "Earlier you mentioned that when you're writing you imagine a single space. When I'm making an album, it's a similar kind of feeling. I'm looking for something original for those songs, some world of sound that exists for those songs only." So each of the Sprout albums could be said to contain its own aural universe—and none more so than *Jordan*. The songs occupy the same starlit cosmos; and with that sound and feel comes a bunch of common sympathies and ideas, if not nailed-on

meanings. There's the obvious four-part structure: beginning
with everyday life and preoccupations; then the Elvis songs;
the love medley; finishing with God, the Devil and Death.
But they all belong to a cosmos where there's a powerful feeling of immanence—a flowing, circular spirit. Maybe that's
to do with God, maybe it's not. Maybe it's something more
transcendent and elemental that's closer to the idea of Tao,
the natural flow through all things that's physically visible in
the movement of water, in the grain of wood, the shifting of
sands, the "force that through the green fuse drives the
flower",[31] and flows through us in our response to what we
see and experience. The flow is essentially good, deaf to
God's trumpeting of "thou shalt nots": "This is where a
kinder bugle blows / This is where you'll wake / To find the
River Jordan flows." A cosmos soaked in blue. Running with
blue waters and the slow, spiralling circulation of a blue
aether. Which is why the album begins in the big blue of the
ocean and the underwater city of Atlantis. We're all looking
for something in that aether, kind of hopelessly, looking for
our own versions of a lost mythical city. The blueness is always there (whatever you read into it, and even if you don't
notice or don't care): "Blue as skies and blue as heavens /
Watching over Galilee and Rome / Blue as water, Jordan's
waters / Blue as dawn, and dawn will take you home". And
when night falls on *Jordan*, it's never quite a descent into
darkness, the light is always there in that star-filled "gorgeous
night". Everywhere, a frail and tenuous enchantment, like a
lost fifth element we all live with, there to be called on to
summon some kind of wonder and belief into our dried-up,

---

[31] Beautifully put by Dylan Thomas in his poem.

over-rationalised civilisation: "Is there one spell can bring / The once and future king?" Because it's also a cosmos we're partly making for ourselves through our choices: "We ask for any wrong we've done / The years ahead forgive us / We ask for any good we've done / That all of it outlive us". In his next album, Paddy would go further with the metaphor and build his own house in the spirit of *Jordan* that was on the side of a mountain, a house where he could always be happy inside his own head: *Andromeda Heights* (1997).[32]

The flow includes the natural circle of life and death. In other words, a cycle of comebacks. 'Comeback' was a keyword to the album, Paddy explained. The most obvious model, deep-rooted in his psyche, would have been Jesus and his resurrection, but he chooses Elvis instead, an all-too-human icon of our twentieth century.[33] A return to life doesn't have to mean resurrection from the grave or getting the band back together for another shot at the charts, it could just be a kind of awakening—in the way that Elvis found consolation through gospel music. Death, in itself, was a preoccupation for Paddy. "Death is an element which deeply pervades my music, although I don't make direct references to it," he claimed in a 1986 interview. "The music I like from other composers is the kind which has this same intensity of feeling." Paddy's dad, Tommy, had died in March 1989, immediately turning the idea of death from a concept into something real and present and doing its work around him. As

---

[32] Paddy was drawn to places of safety, like the one described on *I Trawl*: "The farm where the crippled horses heal / The woods where autumn is reversed / And the longing for bliss in the arms / Of some beloved from the past."

[33] 'Meet the New Mozart' was meant to be on there too, about "Mozart coming back as Neil Tennant and making a pile of money".

Cathal had noted in 2022, "The existence of death seems like such a glammy toy when you're 25. Now, not so much." But death isn't an ominous threat in the *Jordan* universe, just part of the furniture of a transcendent realm: "There is a door we all walk through / And on the other side, I'll meet you." A reunion: another comeback.

> There are links between songs [said Paddy]. The idea of having your time again and doing things properly in coming back, a common regret that people have. No-one likes to think they wasted their life. Life didn't work out the way they wanted, they wish it had gone another way—that's a common thought. A few of the songs contain that… the devil across the divide of hell from heaven, saying to Michael the Archangel, can you do something to help me make a comeback, can God change his mind?

One of the most memorable lines, "Death is a small price for heaven", mixes the idea of the afterlife with pop-love and sexual desire. The atmosphere inside *Jordan*'s blue world is haunted by ghosts from the past and the present, by nostalgia, by what's come and gone. Paddy was sensitive to those feelings of Gothic-romance, irresistibly, as a source of inspiration. Like when he would visit his old seminary at Ushaw. "There's now a tree growing through a window upstairs where the dormitory was. Most places when the ruination thing sets in, it's more dramatic and it doesn't look like it did. But this place looks like it did… but as if J.G. Ballard had got

249

his hands on it. And I'll go back as if I'm trying to tune in to some ghostly thing, very poetic, as if you incorporate something of how things were."

Both time and space are conflated in the album's cosmos. So Elvis can be alive on his back in the American desert with the rattlesnakes one minute, living on the Moon the next, and yet still go a-wandering along the banks of the Jordan. Jesse James and King Arthur are his compatriots—along with God and the Devil from the deepest abyss of time. Paddy had liked to introduce celebrities into his lyrics, from Bobby Fischer to Steve McQueen, country singer Faron Young, Marvin Gaye ('When the Angels'), Hayley Mills ('Goodbye Lucille #1') and George Gershwin ('Hallelujah'). It was "old-fashioned showmanship". In *Jordan*, though, there was an evolution towards explaining ideas in a more novelistic kind of way.

> I suppose now I have greater fondness for using characters to tell a story. Which isn't to say they're not about me, or not personal… They're still personal but instead of doing it in the first person singular, 'I do this', 'I think that', the ideas are transmitted in stories about Elvis Presley or Jesse James… An idea close to the author's heart, but he does it through his characters. I like that as a style of writing. That's a new preoccupation.

A novelist's approach was the way—maybe the only way—to get closer to understanding any truth in what was a mess of contradictions, feelings and reactions at the heart of every-day experience. Which explains why the album isn't much about Elvis, he's just one character helping to tell a bigger story. Elvis and his music was no big deal in itself. "We romanticise the songs he did in the '50s but if you listen to them now, they're nothing, just bits of fluff without his presence," clarified Paddy. Elvis appeared in his imagination like a character for a novel, or in this case, a screenplay for a movie where the camera finds Elvis lying on his bed in a grand old hotel suite, the curtains shut. He's hiding from the world, from the "crap" that was being written about him in "quick cash-in paperbacks". He's thinking about his past in the room's darkness. Scenes appear before him, regret after regret. A single light appears in his memory, a lucid blue light from the gospel music he'd been making at one time, somehow that was something better, the music he'd made with the Jordanaires vocal quartet. If only he'd made more, and been content with that feeling more often.

There was an intention to tell a story over the course of *Jordan*. "I planned the running order very carefully too, to get a definite effect." The beginning is Paddy Joe walking the streets, grounded in his everyday distractions. It's not mundane because there are constant choices to be made. Most of all that means appreciating what matters in the flow of things that can quickly run away from you: "quit looking for all the Holy Grails in the world" (like the Hollywood myths of perfect lives), "the world's your cherry / But tomorrow? Maybe not"; "the loveliness of youth" is fleeting (on 'Wild Horses'); and don't take love too lightly and think there's someone better around the next corner, your vanity could well feel painful later (as recounted on 'We Let the

Stars Go').[34] If anyone needed a reminder of how time was passing, the Millennium was coming and you might as well go out and party. Good things are easily corrupted, by people like Mister 'Machine Gun Ibiza'. The track was made from Saturday night booze-ups and their disco noise and swagger, and from a particular night out with Dave Brewis in a pub in the town of Stanley near Durham. They were having their usual conversation about bands and fantasy records they should have made; Dave suggested a Jimi Hendrix album called *Machine Gun*, then started talking about something else. All Paddy heard was 'Machine Gun Ibiza' and the dude with a ready smile, rolled-up jacket sleeves and dubious intentions was born.[35] Paddy was making pop music, and while the cosmos of *Jordan* has soulful depths, it's always balanced by humour. The daft figure of Machine Gun Ibiza; Paddy's fond mickey-taking of the Elvis persona, "If I'd taken all that medication / Man, I'd a rattled like one of my li'l girl's toys"; how you used to be able to summon God with any old burning bush and "he'd pull up a chair"; the chats with an apologetic Satan. Humour is there inside the intelligence of it, the tone and mood throughout.

Next, the Elvis suite: we see how legends have regrets too. Two of the Elvis songs are about the singer himself; the two Jesse James tracks were written for Elvis to perform.

---

[34] "I wrote 'We Let the Stars Go' in August 1988 – the day Michael Jackson played Leeds. I had tickets but I gave them away because I love Michael Jackson and I thought it would spoil the dream. And I'm glad I did 'cos I I wrote this."

[35] "I thought, what a great idea for a song! Dave immediately said: 'I can see the video – it'll be a Fuzz-face pedal on a robot, walking into this disco with a machine gun, and mowing down all these people dancing to these poxy records!' So it's the portrait of this imaginary, but legendary star…"

> I asked myself, "What would he like to sing?" And it seemed to me he would like to sing— in his late Vegas period—about American things. There's a song 'American Trilogy', Presley sings 'Glory glory hallelujah'… I thought, "Give him a subject that he can identify with: bad boy, outlaw, who has come a long way from the cradle, his hometown, ended up long way from where he belonged"… on stage in Vegas he must have thought at times, 'How the hell did I get here?'

There's not a lot of bell-bottomed glitz to the Elvis section; it's tinged instead with melancholy, with the great man wondering what could have been—if he'd reached the river in time and not become a rock 'n' roll icon of decay and early death. Which is why the mood of a scene from the film *Blade Runner 2049*, set in a fallen, ghost-town version of Las Vegas, with Elvis performing as a hologram, reminded Paddy so much of his own album.

Is love all we need? The ABBA medley that follows (as per 'All Boys Believe Anything') is a set of love songs partly inspired by the tensions and final crack-up of the Swedish pop band. A clutch of complicated, grown-up love songs that burst the pop bubble with its spiky perspectives and insights ("I think you like being unhappy"). Each one insists on the need to face up to the complexity of love, the gamut of emotions involved, how innocence and cynicism, sincerity and pretence, happiness and misery, hope and despair, can follow each other so closely. So much is hidden behind the expected gestures and routine phrases, and who can be sure what any of it means, or whether we really know what we feel? Paddy was an admirer of Sondheim's 'Every Day a Little Death' and the lyrics that portray the petty humiliations of love: "He assumes I lose my reason, and I do / Men are stupid, men are vain / Love's disgusting, love's insane". Paddy never shies away from the psychological tangles: "There's something very romantic about saying all these things like 'I'm going to be hard-headed about this, not going to make all those mistakes, not going to hope for all those things lovers hope for', but secretly I want them to come true [he said of 'All the World Loves Lovers']." Maybe more than icy reserve, an unassuming simplicity—like that of the young girl 'Paris Smith'—can be hard to take, because you know it's going to be eventually soured or destroyed one way or another.[36] Love is seen as an awful thing (in the original sense of the word, a source of both wonder and fear), and the legally binding contract of marriage isn't much to look forward to ("I really don't know how people can make that big leap and get married," said Paddy at the time).[37] But by looking love straight in the eyes, by being sensitive to all of its fugitive moods and implications of longing and loss, the songs are more deeply romantic than any 'I love you baby' sentiment. And they come freighted with an ache of nostalgia, an ache that maybe only a new thirty-something

---

[36] Paddy wrote 'Paris Smith' because Wendy was sick of her "common" surname and planned to give her children more glamorous names like 'Rock' and 'Paris'. It's another example of wanting to write pop songs that no-one else would think of, in this case about someone giving advice to a young girl.

[37] He learnt to dance the Wedding March in 1997.

could feel so acutely, because the passing of romantic youth is so recent and yet suddenly so far away. "All those nights I dreamt of you / I wonder where they've gone?"

It was a joke among the Sprouts that by the third verse of any of Paddy's songs, God would surely have made an appearance. Religion had a prominent place in his lexicon of references (flaming in letters of gold), from his childhood, and now in his Leadgate home, and the view from his window, as well as the manners and kindliness of home. He couldn't avoid it. Especially not if he wanted to be honest about his personal vision of things. But he also knew exactly what the pitfalls were. "I'm not a spokesperson for Catholic rock, a new-wave Cliff Richard… there is nothing worse than a preacher in song form. You have to put all sides, reveal the unpleasant side of following a religious discipline, the smugness, the club atmosphere." He knew the smell of anything 'worthy' in his music would kill the mood. "You can scare people, push them away, a little as if you wrote a song about body odour." It wasn't like he was sure what he believed anyway.[38] In an interview with Nicky Campbell for Radio 1 in 1992, Paddy suggested he probably did believe in God, but that nothing was certain. A more appropriate question, he said, might be to ask ourselves "Does he believe in you?" The mention of 'God' and 'Jesus' was an instant invitation to be written off, because you'd dropped to your knees and submitted to superstition; whereas for Paddy the idea of God was only one element, a token, within a bigger view and

---

[38] Paddy would often be asked in crass media interviews why it was important to put a cross on the bottom of Brussel sprouts before cooking them. The devil in him wanted to respond with "'Because they remind me of my saviour!'… which would have frozen the atmosphere in the studio as well as horrified my mother! What are you supposed to say?"

a bigger flow of emotions—the flow that runs through
Jordan. Paddy wanted to avoid a narrowness of thought. It's a
thirst for some kind of spirituality, for a goodness rooted in
wisdom and not dogma, and it doesn't matter what the
source of spirituality happens to be. Music, books, nature. As
Elvis says: "Hand me any cup you find that's lyin' spare".

A song like 'One of the Broken' points to the possibility of a humanistic version of religion, where acts of kindness are more important than ritual worship; where truth
comes from appreciating different perspectives, even those of
the Devil; where God is something as simple as the aether
itself: "Above the noise, behind the glare / I know you're
listening out there – somewhere"; and music is all the proof
needed of that kind of universal grace—the simpler and
more rooted the music the better: "If there ain't a heaven
that holds you tonight / They never sang doo-wop in Harlem." Religious characters were also another way of telling
stories. "The Devil versus God raises a whole bunch of issues," said Paddy. "Can an all-merciful God forgive his arch
enemy, can God exist if there isn't a Devil? Isn't it just a
strange notion and good subject for a song, to have God sing:
'Don't sing me any hymns of praise, look after the people
around you, don't write me any fancy psalms.' Whether you
believe in God or not—I think that's a warm notion to have
for people. I think it tells you something about the way we
should treat each other."

He wouldn't get away with talking about God for
long, allusively or not. Sony pushed back against the lyrics on
Let's Change the World with Music. They "got queasy about it"
according to Thomas, and that was what led to the break-

down in the relationship between Paddy and his major distributor.

*

According to the earthly record of things, *Jordan* reached number seven in the UK's mainstream album charts and was nominated for the Brit Award for Album of the Year (won by George Michael and *Listen Without Prejudice Vol. 1*). Critics were mostly won over by *Jordan*'s big pop smorgasbord. "It's the ludicrous moments here that lend the record durability. Dare I say it? A major, complex work," said the *Spin* magazine review. "Romantic, groovy, heart-breaking, side-splitting, homely, bizarre and all shades of in between," declared Stuart Maconie in the *NME*. He also saw there'd been an evolution in approach: "a conscious movement away from the clotted textures and alienating cleverness of *Swoon* to a more simple beauty: a warmer, more human impulse… Prefab Sprout are that rarest of things: a group who have actually got better." There was a quality to *Jordan* that set it apart from standard pop: "a certain incidental beauty that could never be contrived," suggested Paul Lester of *Melody Maker*. A distillation of essences. "Paddy's genius is his ability to take those few breathtaking seconds from your favourite record— the thrilling intro or swoonsome chorus that you play over and over—and construct whole songs of them… there are numerous instances of Paddy's ability to sustain freak moments over three or four sublime minutes." He was "a Shakespeare in a world of cheap novels," argued George Berger in *Sounds*.

Paddy would have taken particular pleasure from the comparison made by *Rolling Stone*: "If Brian Wilson at the height of his creative powers had spent a year in the studio working up a concept album about love, God and Elvis, the result might have sounded like *Jordan: The Comeback*." As it turned out, the album did less well in Wilson's homeland. It was too eccentric to fit into any commercial category and too obscure for radio. Even in the UK, not everyone could see beyond the surfaces of cleverness to the swell of vision and emotions involved. *The Guardian* wilted, saying "nothing [Prefab Sprout] ever do appears to spring from impulse. It's always a pastiche, an echo or a gesture, as if McAloon has studied music from books and old movies and set about turning his discoveries into a crossword... It's skilful, but it's a little like sitting in an examination." Morrissey didn't try. "I heard that new Prefab Sprout album the other day. It was bombarded with critical acclaim. And I literally fell into a coma. It was absolutely lifeless."[39]

Whatever the response from the critics, the rewards were never going to be quite in proportion with such a prolonged physical, psychological and emotional effort. Making *Jordan* had almost given him a heart attack. Sony had invested big and they wanted their money back and more—a debt the band was still paying off fifteen years or more later. *Jordan* had turned out to be a "beautiful folly" according to Paddy himself. A monument of creation that might be appreciated for decades to come. "I thought, if I never get to

---

[39] Morrissey later apologised for being so critical of *Jordan* — he'd met Paddy and liked him—but still thought he was right about the album's failings. By comparison he thought *Swoon* was "reasonably priceless".

make a record again, at least this is something I can be proud of." It was the *Jordan* debt that meant there needed to be a greatest hits album in 1992—and a *Jordan* tour starting in the October of 1990. Paddy let Neil take charge as the tour's Musical Director. He recruited friends to the live band, Jess Bailey (keyboards), Paul Harvey (guitar) and Karlos Edwards (percussion/voice), "to flesh out the sound and give us more sonic options. They were all consummate musicians that I had already worked with, so I knew I could trust them and they did a fantastic job. To make things less of a grind for Paddy (and his voice), I rehearsed the band for a couple of weeks before he came in to join us." Neil also put together the set list in a way "that flowed", "including segueing songs together and extending endings to songs like 'Jordan' because they sounded so dramatic with the extra musicians." There were plans for both recording dates in Paris for a live album, and a US tour, neither of which happened.

> For me that tour was the best we ever sounded. I know that Paddy hated hearing recordings of concerts, which is a shame because when you are on tour and travelling long distances by bus, listening to the recording of the previous night's concert together is a very enjoyable way to pass the time, but Paddy couldn't bear it. I found it quite odd because technically his singing was fantastic live. But he always saw the record as being the ultimate version, so "what's the point of playing it badly live?"

The *Jordan* tour was the end to Wendy's involvement with the band.[40] [41] [42] There would be no more Thomas either.[43] And Paddy would have an ever-diminishing involvement with the music industry, as if *Jordan* had been his last concession to pop. Just as Dave and Harriet had done, he built his own studio, like an eyrie on the side of a mountain: a nest of old keyboards and recording devices, remote from the machinations and media of the world below. "I hate being in places connected to the mechanism of the music industry," he confessed in 1997. "Even the thought that my name appears in business magazines alongside Michael Bolton or Mariah Carey makes me sick. Messages in press releases: 'Prefab Sprout are recording the tracks for their new album in such-and-such a studio. It is produced by so-and-so. The engineer is so-and-so. The record company has great expectations and will place advertisements in such-and-

---

[40] Martin has been a lecturer at Newcastle College, sharing his knowledge and experience of the music business, on everything from composition, performance and arrangements to production and promotion. One of his HND students, now Dr Matthew Rowan, described Martin as a "natural educator… with the talent to converse at length on compositional topics ranging from the dissonant atonality of the Second Viennese School to the warm closed-harmonies of the Beach Boys… At times, a glimpse of Martin's personal approach to composing would shine through, particularly in his observations that displayed (coveted) lateral thinking   Joni Mitchell's 'big hands' at the piano, for example." His solo tours playing his brother's songs in 2023/24 were very warmly received.

[41] Wendy initially worked as a tutor in the Alexander Technique (a posture therapy to improve health), and was married in 2000. She went on to a career in arts management and is now the Director of Contemporary Music at a major arts venue in Gateshead.

[42] After a long career of touring and recording, Neil set up his own recording studio, minimoon, in France in 2002 where he continues to live and work.

[43] Since *Jordan*, Paddy has mostly worked with the Scottish producer Calum Malcolm (who was the producer for one of Paddy's favourite bands, The Blue Nile), which has allowed Paddy to keep the process more local and small-scale. Rumours suggest Thomas has found his own lack of involvement hard to understand.

such.' I wanted to disappear completely from these magazines, and the only way was simply to make the record myself." The need for detachment from the system, 'the thing', had always been there from the beginning. Interviewed in 1984 for an article given the title 'From Brussels with Love', Paddy said: "There is a little part of me that's not attached to it in any way, which would love to just get married and sit at home."

A shared love for classical music brought Paddy together with Vicki (an eighteenth and early nineteenth-century fan—the Baroque, Mozart etc—while he was still more early twentieth century, Debussy, Ravel, Alban Berg, Stravinsky). They had a baby in 1996 while they were engaged but not yet living together. Paddy would drive up the north-east coast to visit until they were married in 1997, the year he turned 40. The family then settled together: Vicki and Paddy and their three daughters, Georgia, Cecilia and Grace, in the McAloon home in Leadgate. His mum lived with them until she fell ill and moved into the nearby St Mary's Convent in 2011.

Paddy installed lots of lamps in his room so he could dabble with painting and hang the canvasses on his studio walls. "There is no artistry in this, I'm amusing myself. When I started I did it to make my wife laugh and make my children laugh, so they have kind of sporting themes to them. Like tennis players. But they're really bad! I'm not being modest, they're just not good." And he also took on the cooking duties: "It's my job. Tomatoes with chilli and pasta is a classic. It tastes pretty good because I don't have a big repertoire, I just use tinned or frozen things." Through all of these years, from 1993 onwards, Paddy had to endure a series of well-documented health issues. Ménière's disease (a condition of the inner ear which can lead to tinnitus, a loss of balance and deafness), and two detached retinas ("I started to see the world through these huge raindrops, like you're in a car where the windscreen wipers don't work", requiring the need for metallic buckles to hold them in place and a collection of spectacles he can use for different purposes). He's been through it all with good-natured, self-deprecating grace.

Married life has meant being even more able to be Mr Quixote. "My wife says it doesn't matter where I am because I live in my head, and she's right. This hotel is nice [where he was being interviewed], but it could just as easily be a Premier Inn." Paddy keeps on with his work, composing on a two-octave Yamaha keyboard in hour-and-a-half sessions to spare his bad ear and avoid dizziness. He still prefers the charms of clapped-out tech.

> I use an Atari 1040STE with a four-megabyte chip inside it. You can only get them second hand now, reconditioned, they've gone. It's extremely, extremely unreliable. I have a hard drive attached to it which when I switch it on sometimes doesn't connect with the computer, it just doesn't. So the first 20 minutes of any morning are me switching this on and off, on and off, and then when it fires up it works. And then sometimes I will lose things from it.

Thomas has encouraged Paddy to take advantage of the self-publishing platforms. "I try to talk him into a digital approach and I felt that with the fan base that Prefab Sprout has and the musical proclivities that Paddy has, he could just put stuff out, considering the quality of stuff coming out of his home studio. You can see it on *Let's Change the World with Music*, there's nothing shabby about the production that he does at home." But something about this doesn't sit right with Paddy. "From the very beginning," Thomas suggests, "Paddy had a point of view that an album was something where you go into a studio with a producer, backed by a real record label… they have a release date and they put it out… put it in the shops. Then one day you walk down the High Street and in WHSmith's there's a big poster of the band, you go inside and you look where you are in the charts."

There could have been an unexpected break-through—a Prefab Sprout musical—when Spike Lee and his brother Cinqué got in touch in 2016 about Cinqué's film script *Chasing Invisible Starlight*, based around Paddy's songs.[44] "It was madness," said Keith. "We met up, the four of us, in a place in Soho, then I went over just to see Spike in New York, and they came over to London again. We walked along the South Bank together, with people coming up to take photos of Spike. Even though the songs were already chosen, most of them from *Jordan*, Paddy went away and wrote a whole set of new songs, a whole album full."[45] There was a

---

[44] *Chasing Invisible Starlight* was published as an illustrated short story. It's a Disneyesque tale of a trainee stork learning his trade of delivering babies to expectant parents, a coming-of-age story used to frame insights into forgotten moments in human history.

[45] In a box in Paddy's garage is a whole film of footage made for Spike and Cinqué of Paddy playing each of the *Chasing* songs with an explanation of what they are about.

disagreement between the brothers about whether the film should be animated (the expensive option) or feature actors wearing masks; Spike got wrapped up in making *Da 5 Bloods* (2020), and like so many film ideas, the project was left on the shelf.[46]

Paddy continues to be a familiar figure in the local area, the elegant *flâneur* with a healthy appetite. "The last time I saw Paddy," said Keith, "was one morning when I was going out for breakfast with my mum in central Newcastle. He was having a burger and a beer, trying to be inconspicuous—except he was wearing a purple suit and carrying a cane."

*

Each of the five albums contains tell-tale signs of an unfashionable sincerity that was out of place in a culture of easy cynicism. The Sprouts have been an extreme case. Those beautiful, beautiful songs pushed them into the spotlight and yet the beauty of the songs was beside the point. The image of the Sprouts, the delicacy of the music, the gentle delivery, was a kind of heresy, and increasingly so in a land that had bought into Britpop's roughhouse cool. You could put Paddy on a motorbike, give him stubble and sunglasses, and it made no difference. He was still seen as being about as sexy as an RE student passing round the fruit punch at a party. And we need to acknowledge the disgrace of this. How immature and grisly a world must be to feel uncomfortable in the pres-

---

[46] It's not impossible   Keith, Paddy and Spike are still in touch by text.

ence of goodness and good-humoured decency. "My desert island poem," he once said, "would probably be 'He Wishes for the Cloths of Heaven' by William Yeats. I love the lines, 'I have spread my dreams under your feet / Tread softly because you tread on my dreams.'"

Rejecting authority was easy. It was happening everywhere in the late Eighties and early Nineties. The mindset of the modern consumer was taking over, free and elastic, untroubled by values and principles. A mind not so much interested in questions of reality, of what might be the work of God or the Devil. Expected to be self-interested first of all; happy in its personal, double-quilted truth.

Paddy and Cathal were brothers in this. Both of them rebel angels expelled from Heaven for their beliefs.

4.

"You will go from place to place, leave, then leaving never ends."

The Apartments, *drift*, 1992

B y the Nineties, Britain knew Heaven really was a place on Earth. There were reminders every week-day lunchtime and late afternoon from sunny, sub-urban Ramsay Street, where the boys were good-natured hunks and the girls wore dungarees and could fix your car; a place of no worries that was casual and classless. Any evening you wanted, in a warm apricot twilight, the barbecue would be lit and a cold beer cracked open.

Australians themselves knew *Neighbours* was just an-other crappy soap opera, in the same way they knew Fosters was an *ersatz* product they didn't much want to drink. But nothing was going to spoil the Brits' version of what Aus-tralian life was like: an Elysium of easy freedoms where you could live outdoors in sloppy T-shirts and shorts; drop into each other's homes whenever you wanted; be forever swimming and playing sports (or at least look like you might be). Somewhere as simple as sunshine, because a blue collar job was as good as any other, and no-one took themselves too seriously. Australia was proof that life was much simpler than the stuffed shirts had made it out to be. In one Brit-pleasing Fosters ad from the period, Paul Hogan turns up at a fancy wine-tasting party. He can't believe what he's seeing. They're spitting the wine out? He's just glad he's brought his cans of the Amber Nectar to share round: "Looks like I did the right thing too, 'cos that stuff looks about as popular as a rattlesnake in a lucky dip."

Unlike the traditional soaps, *Coronation Street* and *EastEnders*, the easy sunlit mood of Ramsay Street was for everyone, including the university students, who had the time to watch once or even twice a day, and become addicted to its corny charm. Almost 20 million people in Britain tuned in to watch the wedding of Scott and Charlene in November 1988. Fans wanted souvenirs of the happy day and made a hit of the song played during the ceremony, 'Suddenly' by Aussie rocker Angry Anderson, as well as 'Especially for You', the duet by TV's new prince and princess, Jason Donovan and Kylie Minogue.[1] When the cast turned up for the Royal Variety Performance they were exposed to the full weirdness of the British phenomenon. Their minibus was mobbed by Scott and Charlene wannabes (along with some Mikes and Plain Jane Superbrains), who rocked the vehicle

---

[1] Their TV profile made young stars like Kylie and Jason a shoo-in for pop careers. Even co-stars like Stefan Dennis (who could forget 'Don't It Make You Feel Good') and Craig McLachlan ('Mona') were given their chance.

off its wheels and started a mass sing-along. By 1991, *Neighbours* was the country's most watched TV programme, leading to more dreams of emigration, and a whole generation who were speaking differently, adopting the Australian rising inflection at the end of every sentence to signal a cool, careless enthusiasm, and talk about 'tinnies', 'barbies' and 'dags'.[2]

So the latest episode of *Neighbours* is over, and we've been left feeling deflated. There's no barbecue to look forward to, no popping round for a large sherry with Helen, just another evening at home with the magnolia walls and oatmeal carpets; sitting on a futon with the TV and a muted shine of laminated wood flooring. The brassy character of Eighties' homes and their jumble of old and new furniture has gone. The glass-topped tables and chintz, the bathroom carpet smelling of Harpic and wee, have been bleached into something more neutral for a new decade, into something clean and serene; the kind of blank spaces that were waiting for the arrival of IKEA and a regular cycle of decorating and replaceable looks. There are unfussy displays of money about the place. A TV in the kitchen. A microwave. Two telephones, one of them hooked to an answering machine. A hi-fi stack in the living room. William Morris curtains and brass fixtures. The instant credit and container shiploads of cheaper products on their way from the Far East have been the fuel to power a cycle of higher expectations and assump-

---

[2] It wasn't just Britain. The Australian tourist board's "Come and Say G'day" campaign in the US (with Paul Hogan promising to "slip an extra shrimp on the barbie" just for you), along with the film *Crocodile Dundee* (1986), have been credited with turning Australia into the most desirable tourist destination among Americans in the Eighties and Nineties.

tions about living standards. We were going to keep on getting better stuff, loads of it.

When being a premium consumer was so important to identity, marketing became a louder voice, a more influential guide and prescription. Marketing was busy making must-haves and celebrities everywhere (because celebrities are brands that sell). The art world had its package of Young British Artists like Damien Hirst, Tracey Emin and Marcus Harvey. As critic Craig Brown was quick to point out, there was as much business as 'art' involved: "Hirst is, in any real sense, far closer to an entrepreneur than to an artist, little separates him from, say, Sir Bernard Matthews of Turkey Roasts, a man who has also, incidentally, glimpsed the profit to be found in corpses."[3] Comedy was the new rock 'n roll. The stars of stand-up, with their bowl-cuts and studiedly unshaven personas, were selling out big concert venues. The impetus of marketing meant choices were suddenly easier to make, and, slowly and surely, there became fewer of them. You didn't have to go and watch the local football team when big clubs like Man United were available on the telly (Sky had bought up the Premier League and FA Cup matches). Or stand in a queue for the cinema (blockbuster movies could be picked up cheap from the High Street or a corner shop). Or go out anywhere on a week night, now that TV had been reinvented (with imported zeitgeist shows like *Twin Peaks* and *Thirtysomething*—a model of what grown-up lives should be like, with their brilliant careers, great sex, and basketball hoops in the office). Or fetch a newspaper and bother

---

[3] A reference to Hirst's most hyped work, the carcass of a tiger shark preserved in formaldehyde, 'The Physical Impossibility of Death in the Mind of Someone Living' (1991).

to find out what was really happening in the world outside. A major global event like the invasion of Kuwait and the Gulf War was played out on TV as a kind of sanitised entertainment, about as authentic as *Neighbours*. Operation Desert Storm turned into a TV event worth staying up for, to watch the superiority of liberal democracy in action; the cross-hair precision, the satisfying mushroom puff of Iraqi stone and dust and whatever else. In his book *The Gulf War Did Not Take Place* (1991), the French cultural theorist Jean Baudrillard argued the Gulf War hadn't happened in any traditional sense. It was a TV-mediated, hyperreality game (used to hide crimes against the Iraqi population). The language used was being carefully managed by the military: there were 'surgical' strikes, 'smart' bombs, 'laying down a carpet' (of lethal explosives), and for the first time, the idea of 'collateral damage' (dead or mutilated civilians). Even the output of mainstream TV and radio was kept tidy and on-message. The BBC removed anything with wartime connotations from its schedules, like *'Allo 'Allo!*, *M*A*S*H* and *Carry on Up the Khyber*. Its DJs weren't allowed to play the Fugees' 'Killing Me Softly', Edwin Starr's 'War', Tears for Fears' 'Everybody Wants to Rule the World' or Blondie's 'Atomic'. Not even 'Waterloo' or 'Walk Like an Egyptian'.

Meanwhile, both the commercial and cultural currency of music was in decline. Dance music had become the new pop. It was ideal as a product, because it was easy to manufacture (did you really want to build up calluses and learn acoustic guitar, or be a DJ?), there were no shortages of supply (four track samplers and PCs were becoming cheap), and dance was both more disposable and perfect for feelgood radio. But dance anthems didn't necessarily work as a sound-track to people's lives in the same way, and the audience for chart music was growing ever smaller (grandmothers didn't buy Kriss Kross). Rock itself had become a minor part of youth culture; and there was a widening divide between 'in-die' bands on major label subsidiaries and those happy to belong to an unworldly sub-culture. From a US perspective, nothing 'alternative' was happening, it was just a hiatus be-fore the grunge of Nirvana, Pearl Jam and Sonic Youth—and even then the scene was not so much the sign of a counter-culture as an example of how businesses could bene-fit commercially from positioning their products as anti-commercial. Industry commentators have suggested the early Nineties represented a peak in terms of artists thinking primarily about shifting units, and that often meant morph-ing themselves into dance (by at least adding the 'Funky Drummer' sample or a House piano line). They had to do something. Sales of singles had collapsed to half that of 1979, people had lost interest in the charts and everyone ex-pected *Top of the Pops*, which had been a weekly event in the schedules since 1964, to be cancelled.

Tonight we'll get up from the settee, leave our warm can of Heineken on the nest of tables and go into town. It's Friday night and all the twenty-somethings are out. We park the Ford Escort outside Safeway, check the sun-roof's shut (in case some joker tries to post their leftover pizza through it) and take in the look and feel of the town centre streets. There's an early evening buzz around, no threat of boy racers yet, nothing manic, just the gentle fever that comes with the beginning of the weekend, when there's no need to be punctual, switched on or polite about anything. The clocks are unstuck and running free.

It's a different planet to the early Eighties, when pub and social clubs were the venue for a night out for anyone and everyone. Before market segmentation. The lush variety of regional British breweries with their own ways of doing things, their mish-mash of one-off, characterful pubs and 'living' cask beers—made from the local water, individual hop varieties and flavours of malts—has disappeared. By 1990, the six big drinks firms had taken control of more than half of all pubs in the UK and 75% of all the beer being brewed, meaning a shrinking of the offer to standardised, pasteurised fizzy drinks. The decade saw the end of the local traditions established over hundreds of years by Bristol's Courage brewery (operating since 1702), Morrell's in Oxford (1782), WH Brakspear in Henley-on-Thames (1799), Castle Eden (Hartlepool, 1826), Ruddles (Oakham, 1857), and Mitchells & Butler (Lancaster, 1871). Street corner pubs were closing at the highest rates ever seen: 21 every week in 1989, 25 a week in 1991.

We pass a young couple heading for Deep Pan Pizza. You can tell they've been together a while because they're looking comfortable with themselves (and kind of round). It's their usual place to go on a Friday evening and they're look-ing forward to the 'all you can eat' deal. He wants to get in quickly and get his first lager in, holding open the door im-patiently; she's taking a critical look at the state of his train-ers and getting ready to tell him what a mess he is. Next door is the new bar, Valentino's, which has filled the old Lloyd's Bank with mirrored mosaic walls and red neon stripes that are targeted to the pre-club market. Customers can't move, the girls in black dresses, smoking with the sleek, half-open eyes of cats, are wedged in with the blokes dressed in Concept Man chic. They can't hear anything over a Jive Bunny mega-mix, so there's shouting and drinking and dispassionate looks instead.[4] A gang of lads give it up and try the Rose. They're old school-mates: Dave, the telesales bloke who's been suffering over his targets all week; Geoff the earnest estate agent; and the blushing customer services assistant Chris. They're different, now they're out in their paisley shirts, chinos and suede shoes, ready for clubbing. They've got their pulling pants on and a couple of lagers down they're gleaming, ready with a smile and a sneer for whatever comes along on their long ride of pubs, the club and their early morning appointment with the meat and onion stink of the kebab shop.

The glow of streetlights, the closed-up offices and department stores, the thud-thud rhythm from a passing car, they're part of the same fantasy island of a Friday. Even the medieval church is lit up like an ancient pleasure palace; the traffic lights are nodding through the colours. Even the taint of carbon monoxide and drizzle in the air can't change the party feel tonight. We're following in the lads footsteps as they shove and jostle and take the piss, and see them pretend they're not seeing the ladies go past, the confident bustle of lashes and handbags, a clatter of heels. Foot soldiers from the opposing side.

---

[4] An accepted tactic for increasing profits in chain pubs at the time was to turn them into 'high volume vertical drinking establishments'—there's nowhere to sit, you can't hear anyone speaking or even put your drink down, so you drink faster and more.

273

If we stay out long enough in the streets, pace around until the pubs start closing we'll be able to watch the change in mood. How the night sky becomes an orange dome over town. A crowd sunk in alcohol queues outside Bazooka's. Smart and hollow and soggy in their little worlds that are getting smaller and smaller, shrunken down to eyes and teeth and hairdos and flesh. Poisoned, they'll be entering a series of rooms that get progressively hotter and darker and noisier and make less and less sense. They'll be pelted by the organised assault of Chicago House, some silvery Luther Vandross, followed by a squealing, bippity acid track. Then, from nowhere, a Sixties medley of Lulu and 'Hi Ho Silver Lining'. Later, the music turns out to be just endless noise and a pounding beat, the drinks are only more liquid. And what they're feeling might be elation, it might be nothing at all; they're horny or sick or passing out. Another lager, another JD and coke, another pill, and the night's on a knife edge.

"Pop music is about drugs," wrote John Robb in his review of the Nineties. "Drugs are part of human nature. Altered states: blow yer mind. Just go somewhere else. That's the appeal. From the boring suburban afternoons to the escape from shitty hi-rise inner cities, they are an escape route." Was it that simple or that attractive though? Maybe it was often closer to the scene described by Cathal where people were "queuing for drugs that make them dead for a second or two". The music wasn't enough, the dancing wasn't enough, not even the potential for love and/or sex. Not really a glad celebration anymore but another little death. We'd been modernised to the point where being human was the smaller part of us, clotted instead with manufactured needs and doubts and ways to react; an itch inside that demanded escape, and escape from ourselves as much as anything else. Whatever the impression might have been of people in the streets, filling up the pubs and clubs with chat and hugs and back-slapping, this was a less sociable and more competitive night out, whether it was competition over who was shagging who, the race to find 'the one', or competition between the sexes.

Any man flicking through one of the bestselling women's magazines like *More* would know he was in trouble, from the regular 'Position of the Week' column to the questions raised by the features and quizzes. Like the one on 'Sexercise, the Fun Way to Fitness'. 'The Joys of Being Single'. 'My Orgasm Face'. 'Does Your Boyfriend Know Where Your Erogenous Zones are?'. 'How Does His Penis Compare?' Throughout the previous decade, young women had been increasing their earnings and spending power, and the media and the culture as a whole had responded. So the rise of the new 'lads'—the *Loaded* and *FHM* readers who loved beer and football, living in the same dirty jeans for weeks and farting—was more a case of men trying to cope with that challenge. Educated, often unathletic men, who found themselves intimidated by successful, promiscuous women. You don't care about love? No. You know what, nor do I. Insecurity made the lads' bullish sexism and adolescent humour feel okay, especially when it was hidden inside yet more layers of irony. The pressure and disillusion was being bottled. Between 1950 and 1998 the rate of suicide among men under 45 doubled (and fell among women) in the UK.

The early Nineties was, and remains, the worst recorded period for male suicide.

We're not going to bother about getting into Bazooka's, we've seen it all before. We end up instead in a place in a back street away from the town centre with a copper-topped bar and café-style tables and chairs. There's a bitter glamour to its quiet obscurity that matches our mood. The barman hovers by the optics, stone-faced, and waits for an order. What should we have now? We've had that pint of shandy with The Sundays, the first taste of which brought back so many memories, sweet and sad. Then something that looked like a Guinness from a distance but was a lot weirder and stronger, a pint of Kahlua with a Baileys top. Followed by Prefab Sprout's brandy cocktail, the kind of drink Brian Wilson might have dreamt up after a day at the Radiant Radish, a concoction resembling the pinks and greys of the sinking Californian sun with added kiwi and pineapple slices. Now it's time for something short and dry. Maybe with a drop of water to bring out the flavour.

*

The title of the first Apartments album, *the evening visits… and stays for years* (1985) was a signpost to a night-time realm that was separate from routines of work and responsibility; one populated by streets of cheap rented rooms and bars and late night music; seen far off, it looks better, alluring, like a sparkle of lights in the velvet darkness.

If that was your place, your nightly adventure, the return to reality was hard to take, when you found yourself with another hangover. Morning light. Letters about overdue bills on the table and a sink full of dishes. Full of no coffee. The only compensation being that you knew the evening would come again. The dull, fussy demands of adulthood would recede in the wake of drinks and talk and laughter, the warm waves of attention and the eyes of attractive people; the sweet unrest of new love affairs and fall-outs and jealousy, the drinks, the cigarettes. The evening was the only place with any salt or spirit, making it hard to leave and even harder to forget.

This is the place that Peter Milton Walsh's *drift* album came from. "I can still see and hear that world at times—its nights and drinks and careless laughter, the records that are playing, high heels upon a wooden floor," he said. His haunting memory of somewhere that didn't exist anymore, that wasn't on any maps. Like the lost domain of *Le Grand Meaulnes*,[5] a world of lost youth and lost love—but one that was messed-up, when relationships had been burnt down to the filter: "Years of licking honey from a thorn will wear you down, kids—so the ashtray no longer sees its cigarettes." Those years lived on in *drift*. Not as a record of hedonism but a palette of bitter moods, not dissimilar to a Miles Davis trumpet solo from a Fifties' ballad; solemn but with unexpectedly subtle and delicious emotional colour.

For Peter, that escape into the other-land of evening was bound up with the practise of songwriting. "It's that beautiful lapse of thinking, forgetting about yourself, that is

---

[5] Alain-Fournier's classic novel from 1913 about the end of youth. Wandering in the French countryside as a 17-year-old, Meaulnes stumbles upon an old estate where he ends up spending a magical evening and falling in love. He and the narrator spend the rest of the book trying to find the estate and the girl he'd met.

promised by both the creative and the sensual life. That's the rainbow's end we're always after. Always." But the appeal was also in feeling and describing particular kinds of emotion, not to shut them out. Emotions that were affecting enough to want to live outside some of the more usual grooves of security. "I still read poetry, buy poetry books, because I think it's important that there's such a thing as a poet in the world, because there's nothing in it for poets," he explained. "There's no glamour, there's no money, but they're doing it simply because this is what they must do, so I like that idea, they have to." He's been drawn to examples of troubled intensity and fatalism, a piquancy of experience— like that recounted by Malcolm Lowry in *Under the Volcano* (1947) ("I deeply love [that book]… it's within my bloodstream") and by the characters of European New Wave cinema. *La Notte* [Night] (1961) in particular. "In the morning, I'm like the Antonioni movies, I'm a little sad, I haven't the courage to start the day," the lead actress Monica Vitti once said. "In the evenings, I'm happier, more alive." Not an empty aesthetic experiment, but part of his psyche. One of the reasons for living.

> I am trying to make something beautiful… I lean on beauty all the time and when I'm at the bottom of nowhere I will lean on something that means something to me. It'll be a song or a book, movie, whatever, but I'll lean on it. It's not going to change the world, it's not activism or any of the necessary acts of resistance. It's not like that but it is some-

thing for people's spiritual lives. And I do
know from my own experience if your spiritual life is in trouble you don't have any life
at all.

In a photo of Peter from November 1978 he's standing around with an early version of the Go-Betweens:
Robert Forster, Grant McLennan, and Tim Mustapha on
drums, after recording the song 'The Sound of Rain'. It's
summertime in Brisbane. Peter's the cool one among the
geeks, the junior sophisticate with his big hair and shades. "I
thought I was a bit like the local Dylan, the *Highway 61*
Dylan. The guy apart, a bit vicious and arrogant." For the
small-town boys of Brisbane, Walsh was a fascinating mystery. "He was flamboyant," said Robert, "like someone out
of a novel, and we liked him. He was enormously funny, very
quick-witted, very sharp-tongued." To begin with though,
none of the charm washed with the Go-Betweens' future
drummer Lindy Morrison: "Peter was very confident, small
and thin, well dressed, with a very studied hairstyle and
sunglasses." "Peter and I had a number of altercations at the
start because he made the mistake of calling me 'darling' at
one point and I very quickly said, 'Don't you 'darling' me'."
Always on the move during the Eighties and Nineties, Peter
remained a man of myth and legend among his friends and
associates. "He was ghostly," according to Robert. "A correspondent through letters, someone you saw for a night only to
then vanish." Much of the mystery feels deliberate. As if
Peter was consciously creating himself in line with his tastes,
like the post-war American culture found in the classic Billy
Wilder films, in the Burt Bacharach and Hal David music,

Johnny Mercer and Harold Arlen's 'One for My Baby'; John
Cheever's booze-sodden short stories; the journalism of
Martha Gellhorn. And over time he became like a character
from an American novel of the early Sixties, standing at the
bar in a grey herringbone suit with a whisky tumbler resting
in his hand.

> I used to believe that a change of towns, a
> change of rivers might change your luck. I
> started carrying a dime and three picks in my
> coin pocket—every single day, for luck—after
> I moved to New York. I'd walk past the for-
> tune teller's on St Mark's Place and think I
> don't need you. I believe in 'threes'… With
> that dime in my pocket, I still feel like an al-
> bum of songs might just turn up with the
> next rain.

A gambler playing for high stakes in the big city, the Donald
Draper of indie.[6] Peter was restless. He needs the feel of a
proscenium arch over his days and nights, and like French
poet Baudelaire, he believed we should always be drunk
("That is the be-all and end-all, the only choice there is. To
no longer feel the horrible burden of Time, which racks your
shoulders and bows you downwards to the earth, you must
make yourself ceaselessly drunk. But drunk on what? Wine,
poetry or virtue, whichever you prefer; only, get drunk.")[7]

---

[6] The hard-drinking, womanising advertising creative of the TV drama *Mad Men*, set in
New York in the Sixties.

[7] One of Baudelaire's *Poems in Prose*, 'Trinck!', in a translation here by Francis Scarfe.

280

Peter had been drunk on his own cocktail of the Great American Songbook, the Velvet Underground, and the music of Maurice Ravel or Erik Satie as it mingled with the mood of a Sunday morning (and sometimes maybe just a bottle of Courvoisier). It's not been a pose he's dropped as soon as the journalist and photographer have left the room. Fame and money in themselves haven't mattered so much as being (romantically) drunk. "I led an invisible life for such a long time. I was sort of quite at ease in the shadows, and when I do come into the light of some attention, obviously it's good, but it doesn't bother me if it disappears. My identity is not tied up with sort of some sort of acclaim," he told *Rolling Stone* in 2020. He's not felt the sting of ambition. A friend once even felt the need to warn him about his future:

> he poked his finger in my chest and he said, 'you don't do the work, you're like the grasshopper who sang through the summer and then the winter comes and you won't have done the work'. This was from someone who was doing 200 shows a year or something like that, because at the time that was exactly what you had to do... I would love to find a way to blame somebody or something for things not happening but it all comes down to me! Look, it's a casino life anyway, being a musician, that's the nature of it.

Peter preferred to give himself up to chance, driven by a search for sensations and experiences. "I wanted to never be spoiled by success; I have lived up to at least that one ambition. I know I could have used a little more ambition, but a 'career' seemed to take a lot more stability than I thought I had. Me moving in and out of people's lives, everything temporary, for a long time I felt it was always like that. I seemed to drift, and couldn't find one feeling that could be relied upon from one minute to the next."

A smooth and civilised character with the neat, serious features of a TV soap hero—but not bullet-proof. Peter was a vulnerable man, according to the Go-Betweens' Amanda Brown, "by nature shy and quick to loneliness". Being a rolling stone was romantic and exciting but it came with those brick-wall moments of realisation, when you had to remember the account books and the existence of the void. Like the time in 1989 when Peter decided to leave England, and his latest girlfriend and circle of night-time friends, and go home to Australia. "I found myself at my parents' house, in Brisbane, in the town where I grew up. One evening I was sitting out on the steps at the front of the house. My parents had gone to bed. I realised that compared to where they were at my age, I had almost nothing in the world." And this is where the essential quality of The Apartments' music comes from, this tension between the inside and the outside. As he explained in 1993, when *drift* was released: "You realise you have only the songs—no home, no children. Ultimately, I don't really care if things work out well for me on the outside. I know that within there is something that still goes on, and that is the songs." The emotion of it is there in Peter's voice, a brass-like vibrato, a scrunched twang of Queensland; sometimes seeming to run on the power of quaver. A curiously in-the-moment way of singing, as if nothing has yet been written, we don't know—and he doesn't know—how things are going to work out.

Having the defences of a cool persona and a detachment from worldly things, a teeming inner life. It can feel like it's enough. But however well-founded, none of that wisdom and none of the consolations and distractions mean anything in the face of tragedy. In 1997, Peter's two-year-old son Riley was diagnosed with a rare condition affecting his immune system; he died a few months before his fourth birthday. The music stopped and Peter disappeared.

*

Drinking her morning coffee, Sarah's reading the newspaper like a grown-up, like she knows what a Liberal Democrat is, or could afford anything advertised in there, like the holidays to Florida and the cars with sunroofs.

On to the best bit, the classifieds. She folds the paper in half to make it easier to read and hold a biro:

"N/S professional for large, sunny room—£50 pw."

Professional? What does that really mean. And does it count if you try to blow the smoke out the window? Probably better not ask.

"Lovely studio annexe attached to main house with views to garden. Would suit single lady professional. Use of outdoor spa bath by arrangement. £350 pcm."

No thanks, pervo.

"Large room in fun shared house. £45 pw. No DHSS. No pets."

Yeah. But you get loads of fun-loving psychopaths. Probably make you sit down together and watch Beadle's About.

"Handsome blue-eyed blonde, 25, looking for fun."

None of that. Concentrate.

"Roomy two-bed first-floor flat with park views. Two minutes walk from station. Professional couples only. £420 pcm (bills included)."

Sounds nice. But at that price it would have to be with Fraser, like they were a real couple. And then only if she still had a job.

Remember the Performance Review meeting.

"How are things going?"

Her line manager had that focused, concerned look on his face which they must have spent years practising.

"Oh. And why is that?" they said.

Curious, straight face.

"What do you think you could do to change that situation?"

Suddenly alert face.

"I see. And why is that?"

Confused but know they have to stick with it anyway face.

The secrets of business leadership are contained in an expensive-looking box, lacquered and with a gold trim, but it's still basically empty. Keep the mystery close to your chest boys.

*

Peter Milton Walsh was born in 1956 in Sydney, but grew up in Brisbane, the state capital of Queensland.[8] The 'Deep North' as it was sometimes called, because of the oppressive summer heat, the slow crawl of time as the cicadas buzz and click, the moths flapping around the lamps on the rows of wooden porches in scenes that were so reminiscent of the American South. The same ominous sense of torpor, of beliefs and attitudes not able to move on. Outsiders unwelcome. "The Brisbane in which I grew up was a small town, almost like a country town, and was very slow, and was very hot. The cops were insane. There was a corrupt government, and the cops were supported by that government." Peter lived with his family—he had an older sister—on one of the many suburban streets of wooden houses. His father Jack Milton Walsh would be away driving his truck. There'd be just sports and old British repeats on TV. Left to play out in the street to the sound of the cicadas. A phone ringing somewhere. People arguing, guys in vests with moustaches drinking beer. A small dusty world made bigger and brighter by the radio.

> I grew up in the Sixties so it was a golden age
> for beautiful, huge melody. You could hear it
> and you could chase songs because you could
> guarantee it would turn up on the next sta-
> tion. I remember doing that with a song

---

[8] Peter had been known by his full name, Peter Milton Walsh, since Year 11 roll calls when, to distinguish him from the other Peter Walsh in his class (Peter Graham Walsh), teachers used their middle names. The name stuck. 'Milton' was passed down from his grandfather, Thomas Milton Walsh, a train driver, through his father, Jack Milton Walsh.

called 'It's Not Easy' by an Australian artist
called Normie Rowe, and I would just chase
the song across the three top 40 radio stations, trying to hear it.[9]

There wasn't much spare money around and Peter's collection of a few books and LPs were treasure. His mum let him
have some of her Frank Sinatra and Dean Martin albums,
he'd borrow vinyl from friends at high school (fingerpickin'
things like *Young Brigham* by Ramblin Jack Elliott (1968), Gordon Lightfoot's *The Way I Feel* (1966) and Graham Gould-
man's 'No Milk Today' (1968), and ask for the occasional
greatest hits collection as presents (Petula Clark, Sandie
Shaw, the Hollies, Manfred Mann, Henry Mancini) and over
the course of the long hot evenings, take the time to steep
himself in the romance of them.

> They were sacred objects. I would listen to
> them for weeks, months. You'd always end up
> spending so much time with an album that
> you knew its world, every detail of the cover
> and photos and credits and liner notes en-
> tirely, the sleeve, the artwork. You had
> drenched yourself in it. An album was a
> world. There was a strong sense of ritual and
> ceremony in putting an album on the
> turntable.

---

[9] Norman Rowe was a teen idol before being conscripted into Vietnam. 'It's Not Easy'
was released in 1966, a song originally written by Barry Mann and Cynthia Weil for the
Righteous Brothers (and you can tell); the recording featured an orchestra that included
Jimmy Page and John-Paul Jones, pre-Led Zeppelin.

In the early Seventies he fell hardest for the songs of Dusty Springfield, Scott Walker and Bob Dylan—but the first LP he bought with his own money was by the French composer Satie.[10] Growing up in the back streets of Brisbane, he was thirsty for style. Peter had heard just a scrap of Satie's music playing in the background of a Sunday night TV pro-gramme, *Weekend Magazine*. The connection he felt with its dream-like reverie, the shock of recognition and sympathy, made him write to the Australian Broadcasting Corporation (ABC) to find out what the music could be.[11] It was an exten-sion of his interest in French culture that would come to en-compass the music of Debussy, Serge Gainsbourg, Françoise Hardy and the existentialist works of Albert Camus such as *L'Étranger* (1942). By that time, Peter could also play acoustic guitar. His cousin had taught him during a holiday trip up from Sydney when he was 13, along with a repertoire that included songs by The Seekers and Peter, Paul and Mary.[12] With the money saved up from his Saturday morning job at a supermarket, he bought his own guitar.

Brisbane was a place made for dreaming. Being young and stuck inside behind slatted shutters, the wider world beyond could take on a starry mystique. And outside

---

[10] The eccentric outsider Erik Satie liked to walk the streets of Montmartre dressed as a priest or in one of his velvet suits; he wrote short musical pieces with titles like 'Flabby Preludes for a Dog' and 'Desiccated Embryos'; with musical directions such as 'Play like a nightingale with toothache'. His friend Ravel once called him a "complete lunatic".

[11] Satie's 'Gymnopédies No.3', the version orchestrated by Claude Debussy. The first record Peter bought was by the Royal Philharmonic Orchestra, *Entremont Conducts Satie* (1971) with Debussy's orchestrations of Gymnopédies number one and three. Peter used a phrase from the piece for the opening and mid-section of 'End of Some Fear'.

[12] '*A Soalin*'' and '*Sinnerman*'.

287

the door was an isolated, rural city that nurtured a lust for travel. Peter started out on his life of farewells by leaving home when he was 17, living on "cigarettes and rice crackers", doing some travelling (to England, Italy and Morocco), cultivating habits in drink and drugs and girls. He'd come back and spend a while working in the post office to raise funds, imagining himself as one of the cool, romantic losers, like Camus's Meursault or Charles Bukowski. He eventually returned around five years later and fell into the arms of the Brisbane music scene. "It was a golden time," said John Willsteed, another of the city's legendary musicians.[13]

> Everyone was in a band. When I look back at the stuff we made, the cassettes, the posters and fanzines, it was a really special period in our cultural history. The Labour government of the early Seventies had introduced a bunch of stuff, free university study, free medical care, and the dole money was enough to live on. Housing, food and booze were cheap.

Brisbane wasn't big enough to be divided into tribes so there was a single, hotchpotch community. "We'd all turn up at

---

[13] John played bass and guitar on the Go-Betweens' *16 Lovers Lane* album. In 1978, he'd dropped out of uni where he'd been studying architecture, and played with Lindy Morrison in the band Zero before going on to play guitar and bass with a number of Australian bands and working on media projects as a sound editor and musician. He's now retired from his job as a lecturer in music at the Queensland University of Technology and continues to play with Brisbane band Halfway. John had been playing bass for 15 years before *drift*. "I've been lucky to play—as an embellisher—with so many great songwriters. Everyone should know about the Walsh catalogue, he's found a fabulous niche. I've only had a few chances to play live with Peter, the last time was in Pig City in Brisbane in 2010s, but I'm always ready!"

gigs together, hippies, skinheads, punks and the postpunk kids. The quality of that scene has proven itself, you see people from those years now and the friendships are still strong."[14]

In 1978, Peter got talking with Robert Forster and Grant McLennan of the Go-Betweens.

> I'd liked the Go-Betweens from the first time I saw them play two songs: 'Karen' and 'Eight Pictures'. I heard in them some of the same records I'd soaked up [the Velvet Underground, the Monkees, Bob Dylan, Creedence Clearwater Revival]. I would deal with a very different world with my own band yet what I liked most about them, and the world of their songs, was the immaculate innocence. A childlike world, radiant with hope. Huge, huge hope. Daydream believers. In the howling chaos that seemed to be my life at the time, there was nobody like that. I'm not sure there ever had been.

Grant once said that the Go-Betweens were day and Peter was night: similar post-punk indie sounds, emanating from two different kinds of soul. "We had very different worldviews," said Peter. "They often wrote about where they wanted to go, while I wrote about where I had been." It was hearing the Go-Betweens play live that convinced Peter he

---

[14] A time and place celebrated in a book of photographs by Paul O'Brien, *Nowhere Fast: Brisbane's Punk and Post-punk Scene 1978-1982*, alongside essays from John Willsteed and Robert Forster.

could write better songs than them, songs about actual experience rather than dreams (of going to New York, being in the movies, having a girlfriend). As Lindy put it: "Robert and Grant were kids, they lived in books and movies."

Mostly on the basis that he had a similar amp and guitar sound to Tom Verlaine of Television, Peter was hired to play on 'The Sound of Rain' and 'I Wanna Be Today', but when the deal with Beserkley Records and the promised recordings and trip to England fell through, the Go-Betweens decided to return to their three-piece format. They all stayed close friends and had fun taking potshots at each other: Grant's song 'Don't Let Him Come Back' versus Peter's lines "I've seen the choirboys dancing cheek to cheek / I could sell it all, talk about the world, but talk's so cheap." Or so it seemed. "Since I had been in The Go-Betweens for almost five minutes, people assumed the line 'I've seen the choirboys' was about Robert and Grant. In fact, the line came to me while watching a late night movie, *Top Hat*, with Fred Astaire and Ginger Rogers dancing to Irving Berlin's *Cheek to Cheek*. Now, Robert may well have been a Fred Astaire figure but really—did anybody think Grant was Ginger?"

Peter had a formula for The Apartments right from their inception: "arrogant lead singer/guitarist, friend from high school on bass, drug buddy on guitar. Three-part harmonies. Throw in a stranger who turned up out of nowhere to the first rehearsal and could really play drums." Robert and Grant would be at the early gigs, "two silhouettes, one tall, somebody shorter beside him", and help Peter release the first Apartments EP, *the return of the hypnotist*, through their

Able Label in 1979. It was Grant who provided his film buff's nod of approval to the band name: "Billy Wilder—the cynical and the romantic," he told Peter, "that's perfect for you!" *The Apartment* (1960) had been a scandal in the year of its release, because of its depiction of the sleazy double-lives of management that went hidden behind the confident handshakes and tailored suits. Apple-pie America didn't want to know about the casual affairs and attempted suicide. It was a melancholic film that wondered whether innocent love was even possible. Jack Lemmon's character is a corporate drone whose only social capital is his apartment, and the film's romance is restricted to the black and white cinematography of rainy, night-time streets. There's not the obvious happy ending that audiences would have been expecting from a rom-com, only an ambiguous suggestion of hope as Shirley MacLaine sticks around for another game of cards. "'Shut up and deal' is my all-time favourite declaration of love, movie-wise," noted Peter.

The Go-Betweens, the Saints, the Triffids and Nick Cave's Birthday Party headed for London to be close to the home of post-punk—and an industry that would fund it. Rather than stay in Brisbane where there were family and friends (and his new band), Peter left instead for New York and a different class of adventure in 1982. A rollercoaster without rails. He didn't want to be part of the stagnancy that he'd seen among Brisbane's heroin users, a kind of rock purgatory filled with a cast of lotus-eaters never able to keep a beat. "If you turn up for a rehearsal and somebody's stoned, that's fabulous if you're stoned, but if you're not stoned it's just gruesome. You're rigid with boredom, looking at pinned eyes."[15]

*

Saul Leiter's old photographs of New York in the snow capture the city with its back turned. And in a rueful, reflective mood. They're pictures of a real town where people walk through the black slush with bags of groceries and worry about being passed over for promotion and the price of shoes. Above them, in the austere winter mists, are still the towering miracles of Art Deco architecture from a mythical past of airships and radio stars and hot jazz. The only colour comes from the red bloom of stop lights, an umbrella or a dirty yellow taxi crawling by. Leiter's photographs come charged with a feeling of ambivalence, recalling the moments when you're never so alone or so alive—a reminder of what's important or could be important in the raging nothingness. Frozen heartache.[16]

This was the kind of plangent, real-life drama our Australian romantic was looking for. His budget didn't allow for anything more than seedier views from downtown anyway. "I was living in an illegal basement beneath the Joe Junior diner on the corner of East 16th and Third Avenue.

---

[15] Peter depicted the heroin mood in 'Sunset Hotel': "The Sunset Hotel is covered in Spanish moss [trailing shaggy growths, often found in Queensland] / Go and hide there cause so much has changed / Are you keeping a score? / Can't stay clear / Still a child / It's like a long holiday".

[16] Besides the photos, Peter liked this line from Saul Leiter: "In order to build a career and to be successful, one has to be determined. One has to be ambitious. I much prefer to drink coffee, listen to music and to paint when I feel like it."

The basement had no fresh air except via the elevator shaft. It was like a dungeon or a ship, heat pipes running across ceiling ticked and clanged like clocks. Steel girders, prefab walls and a concrete floor." Then he found an apartment building in the Alphabet City area, near the corner of Avenue C and East 11th Street. "Most of the people in my building were Puerto Rican. Spanish would float up and down the stairwell at all hours. Some of the kids, some parents too, used to sleep up on that rooftop on hot summer nights. I never did. Waking when the sun came up did not really agree with me." He had moved to the Avenue C apartment when The Colors broke up—a New York band that had had some financial support from Clem Burke of Blondie—broke up. Peter had joined the band at the invitation of another Brisbane export, the mop-topped Robert Vickers. Peter was meant to replace songwriter and lead guitarist, Paul Sass, who'd left the band. The dream suddenly looked to be on a plate: he was going to live in Jack Lemmon's New York and his nights would be spent in silky black and white.[17] But leaving town hadn't been easy. It had meant selling his guitar amp to buy a one-way ticket. And burning some bridges: "my girlfriend from Brisbane accompanied me to the airport with three of her girl friends, and they were all crying. I had been drinking, and wasn't exactly sure what I was getting myself into—but I *was* going to New York."…"At times I felt I had escaped from a burning house—but everything I loved had been left inside." So it was a bruised Walsh who'd ar-

---

[17] Robert Vickers joined the Go-Betweens when he moved to London in 1983 and played bass on *Spring Hill Fair* (1984), *Liberty Belle and the Black Diamond Express* (1986) and *Tallulah* (1987). He was part of touring bands with Lloyd Cole and Yo La Tengo in the Nineties and stayed in New York, to work as a publicist and set up his own PR company.

rived in New York, someone who'd found a fresh relevance in the work of playwright Tennessee Williams. "I felt an affinity with those writers like him who'd come to the city from slow, hot towns of the South that seemed so much like my childhood town. I was a slave to luck in New York, as many are, and often it was strangers who were kind who'd kept me going." Managed by Hilly Kristell, owner of the famous cavern of grunge CBGB's, and produced by Clem Burke, the Colors and their bubblegum punk were expected to make it big like the Ramones. It didn't happen and the band folded not long after Peter's arrival. The band's sudden demise opened the way for Peter to experience sides of New York life he would write about for the single, 'All You Wanted'.

> New York was inspirational to me, having to survive there, get by, all of this gave me access to a vast range of experiences that would never have been available to me had I just stuck with the band. That said, experience is usually just a word that people give to their mistakes. Sometimes you live so much in the present—and in New York I lived ecstatically in the present tense—you never think you will have a past.

The blurry, ramshackle nights suited him fine, the trips in and out of the Lucky Strike bar and enjoying a "river of vodka". Making friends and losing friends. "I would go to parties on rooftops across the city. I knew people who had fallen from rooftops and lived. Had a friend who, having spilled her last spoonful of hope, jumped from the rooftop of her mother's apartment up in the East 60s. Rooftops, like songs, are worlds, and they have all of life in them; the air at twilight there is sometimes full of ghosts." He was in New York for less than two years, just long enough for the city to become familiar but also keep its magic, like a brief love affair that stays in the memory as a perfect thing. The image used for the cover of The Apartments first LP, *the evening visits…* was a photograph from that time. "I shot it around 3am from the roof of the first apartment I lived in there. Looking across to the East River. Rooftops, a water tower, the steeple of St Ann's church in the distance."

There was another invitation, this time from Ed Kuepper, who was putting together a new version of his band Laughing Clowns in London.[18] Would Peter freelance for a year, make a record with them and then tour Europe and Australia as their bass player? Peter sublet his apartment, expecting to return to his life there later. He never did.

London was a very different proposition to New York, because somewhere there, amid the low skylines of smoking chimneys, mossy-green roofs and TV aerials, was an Oz-town of shared gigs, squats and drugs. British immigration rules meant Australians under the age of 26 were granted a waiver to live in the country for two years, as long as they had a family connection. The growth of indie labels, the alternative music press and roster of live venues meant there were scraps of money tumbling out of the walls every-

---

[18] Ed was an early hero of the Brisbane scene. He'd started his proto-punk group the Saints in 1973 and moved to London in 1977 in the wake of being signed by EMI (while always trying to keep a distance from the punk subculture). Laughing Clowns, a more experimental fusion of rock and jazz, was his project from 1979.

where. So many familiar faces had ended up in the city, trying to get a foothold in the home of New Wave and post-punk music that Peter wouldn't be able to turn a corner without bumping into someone from the Go-Betweens, or Nick Cave and his gang, or David McComb and his Triffids, and be whisked away for another night of hard drinking. If they'd not already played together on the same bill in Brisbane or Melbourne, they would surely have hung out before in the cool bars and cafés around the Darlinghurst district of Sydney.[19]

Victor Van Vugt, the future production and mixing legend, lived in the thick of London's Oz-town. He was a 16 year-old planning on a film studies course in Melbourne when the first enquiries about production work started coming in. Victor had got himself involved with fixing up the sound systems at local venues while he was playing in a high school band (because the alternative rock bands struggled to get sound engineers to help them out). "I was a kid on their side, I was enthusiastic." One of those bands, the Moodists (fronted by Dave Graney), wanted Victor involved with recording the single 'Gone Dead', and one thing could easily lead to another in those days. *NME* journalist Barney Hoskyns was often out on the tiles with the Australians in London and had ended up back in Nick Cave's bedsit with the Moodists' single on the turntable. Hoskyns made 'Gone Dead' his Record of the Week (even though it wasn't even available for sale in Britain) and that was big news. It was the first time an Australian indie band had received that level of

---

[19] The period celebrated by Robert Forster on 'Darlinghurst Nights' on *Oceans Apart* (2005).

attention and more groups wanted a splash of Van Vugt on their material. The Moodists got a record deal in England and Victor went with them as their sound mixer in October 1983. "The Birthday Party had been the trailblazers. You had to go to England if wanted to do anything, there was a kind of wonderment around it. I still wanted to do the film studies course but my lecturer said 'take the year off and come back, make some money and tour Europe'." That was the last advice they'd give Victor, who was soon lost to the dirty fog of band life. "I was in with 'the Brisbane squat'. We'd meet with the others in pubs, go to gigs together, and it was another big thing to meet up at someone's place over a chilli con carne. There was no money for going to restaurants. It was a supportive scene, even though there might be petty competition and a lot of bad jokes about each other."[20] Not everyone was enjoying the squalor. Being a fucked-up Bohemian gets progressively less appealing as the weather gets colder and damper. In the case of the Birthday Party there were self-destructive gigs and an armageddon of drug-taking, a kind of musical psychosis. "They starved and hated it. But I loved it. I was 19 and from a middle-class background where the attitude was that you couldn't make a living from a hobby like music. And there I was in London, and I could do stuff." There were tours around Europe, piggy-backing as support for better known English bands, not because there was much money in it, but there was a reliable supply of hot food and beer instead. London had changed since the Seventies, there wasn't the excitement around punk

---

[20] For a true picture of that time, Victor recommends the *Mutiny in Heaven* (2023) documentary on the Birthday Party. "I cried all the way through. That was my life."

and post-punk many of the Australians had been expecting, the industry was closing in around the more commercial prospects. "Bands like the Birthday Party reacted to that by becoming even more aggressive," said Victor. "England meant a mix of emotions. It was important to just be there, in that bigger world, but all of us were taken out of our safety zone, with a feeling of being shit-kicked in a big pond." There was an angry fusion going on, according to the theory of Apartments drummer Nick Allum: the Australians in London tended to adopt an exaggerated, hyper-charged version of European culture, leading to avant garde, art rock, noir and New Wave expressionist styles—both as a way to distance themselves from traditional Australian music, and to shove themselves back in the faces of European audiences as a better alternative.

Peter had left behind his life in New York and arrived in London as a penniless freelance on the edges of the Australian set, running around in his own night-time world of bars and parties. His London years would be torrid times of romance, despair and "Richard Burton daydrinking" (so not just any old boozing, but an urbane, studiedly reckless, nonstop drinking).[21] It was when some of the songs of *drift* were written, and also the stage when he and The Apartments would begin to get serious recognition. He got himself together to play bass for Laughing Clowns' tours of England, Europe and Australia and the recording of the *Law of Nature* album. The first London show was at the University of Lon-

---

[21] The iconic Welsh actor Richard Burton was famous for drinking three bottles of vodka a day. A surgeon operating on his spine found it to be coated with crystals of alcohol.

don Union where The Smiths were supporting. But it could sometimes feel like the circles of daily life were growing smaller and more colourless. "When I lived in London, particularly in winter, the sky was a relentless grey that seemed about three feet above your head," said Peter. "I found the winter particularly hard and gloomy." Lindy Morrison saw it happen: "Peter wrote all the time, sometimes gave concerts. He may have been unhappy."

For Laughing Clowns' Australian tour, he returned home and recorded 'All You Wanted' in 1984, but with London still on his mind. A cassette of material was sent to the only big label he knew of "not precisely paying attention to the business side of the music world." As we so often did in *Like Magic*, we've needed to rely on the taste of Rough Trade's Geoff Travis. Through a friend in a record shop with a telex machine, Geoff got in touch to offer an album deal that included air fares, wages and a place to stay for six months. Geoff had found Peter a place to live with Gina Birch of the Raincoats (an experimental, feminist post-punk band) in Gloucester Terrace, Paddington, a street famous for its stucco Georgian mansions with flaky Doric porches. "It was an incredible opportunity and Rough Trade seemed the ideal label, with The Smiths, Aztec Camera, Microdisney. I didn't hesitate; the songs for the album had already been written."

There was a rush to get *the evening visits…* LP recorded and in the shops in time for a British tour supporting Tracey Thorn and Ben Watt's Everything But the Girl in the

October of 1985.[22] Peter had lined up Victor to produce the album and they worked together at a studio in Brixton under the railway arches, before moving for the mixing to a basement in Harrow Road, the Addis Ababa studio best known for reggae.[23] "Peter was really into Scott Walker and Alex Chilton," said Victor, "which was great for me because it meant an introduction to lots of non-rock instruments and a more interesting way of making records." But the budget of £3,000 wasn't ever going to deliver the Sixties grandeur that Peter had in mind. "I felt I didn't record the songs as I heard them in my head… I wanted something like Dusty Springfield's *It Was Easier to Hurt Him* or something off *Scott 3*, and I failed," admitted Peter. "The producer was wonderful, a miracle worker. But the studio was very much an 80s studio—a broken down place in Brixton called 'Cold Storage' because it had once been an industrial freezer." Peter invited new friend Ben Watt to the studio and he added some extra guitar textures to the recording of 'Mr Somewhere'. Even more importantly for the Apartment's frontman, it led to a few months of free accommodation in genteel Hampstead. "He was the perfect guest," said Ben, "courteous, polite, always full of stories to tell. Me and Tracey were going on tour and Peter occupied the apartment for us. He fed the kittens,

---

[22] One of the members of the audience on the Glasgow Barrowlands leg of the tour was John Douglas of the Trashcan Sinatras. At the end of the night he found a copy of the new *evening visits* LP which had been left lying on the toilet floor. John took the LP home and found himself playing it constantly. He's loved The Apartments ever since. Peter and John are in touch on Facebook. "I'd love us to do something together," said John.

[23] Lee Scratch Perry, Sly and Robbie, Aswad, Soul II Soul etc, all used Addis Ababa.

he wrote."[24] The flat included keyboards and the tech Peter needed to record some electro-pop, inspired by what he was hearing (and loving) from the Pet Shop Boys.[25]

Nick, Jürgen and Peter. London, April 1986. Courtesy of Jeremy Hayes.

Peter needed to find a keyboard player for the Everything But the Girl tour and recording new material. Louise Elliott, who'd played tenor sax and flute with the Saints and the Laughing Clowns, recommended someone with whom she'd been teaching jazz improv at a Community Music scheme in East London. This was Nick Allum, freshly arrived from his time at the Berklee College of Music. A minor mix-up. Nick was, of course, an expert drummer, but Louise had only seen him playing piano because the musical

[24] "I was always very good with kittens. They were strangers who were kind to me," said Peter.

[25] Ben suggested Peter should offer the songs to Kylie Minogue. Rough Trade toyed with the idea of releasing the electro-pop album but finally opted out.

director of Community Music was renowned free jazz drummer John Stevens, and he'd be the one to play drums during teaching and performance events. It was only when Nick got a chance to sit at the drum kit—during a sound-check at Hammersmith Odeon, on the final night of the tour with EBTG—that Peter discovered what Nick could do. Nick was on the drums from then on.

It was with Nick and his schoolfriend Jürgen Hobbs that work on the songs for *drift* began.

> Peter used to come to my Dad's, where I was living, and we'd rehearse in the front room with the piano and drums. We'd sit around drinking coffee and talking, waiting for Jürgen to finish at the hardware shop where he was working and arrive with his bass. Peter was interested in all the ideas I'd learnt about harmony at Berklee, and would get to know my Dad well on those afternoons. He got me into country music, things like Charlie Rich and Glenn Campbell, music I'd not heard before… He was a singular chap, like Cathal, in that he knew so much culture. Books, films, music. I'd not met anyone like him before then. I'd go round to his flat in Hackney, teach him how to play Bridge. Lindy [Morrison] would come round and play too. Harry

Enfield[26] and Charlie Higson[27] lived nearby
and were part of that same circle.

The first elements of 'On Every Corner' were put together
at Nick's home, with Nick coming up with the signature piano hook; as well as the first version of 'Could I Hide Here?
(A Little While)'; and an experiment in a new kind of vocal.
"It was in our front room that Peter first started using a softer
whisper for singing. We'd been trying to record a demo of
'The Shyest Time' on my tape recorder, but he had a sore
throat. I suggested he try a lower octave and it kind of became his thing."

The evenings were Londonesque, with their burning
traffic, wet pavements and raddled old glory. A city as solid
and reticent as its Victorian train stations and crescents of
villas and porticos. Twenty thousand streets with their lime
trees, department stores and novelty outlets and sex shops,
ingrained with a history of soot and quiet respectability. In
the damp moonlight there were districts that came tailored
and velvet-coated with money; the hotels had a doorman
and carpeted steps; there were the gated gardens with their
iron-spiked railings, mulberry trees, lilacs and rhododen-
drons; the hushed private member's clubs inlaid with polished oak and mahogany; the exclusive squares where the
Bentleys with tinted windows would arrive. And in the very
same street or outside the next Tube station were the places

---

[26] Starting to be known in those years for his appearances on Channel 4 shows, playing
characters like Stavros, the kebab shop owner, Essex boy Loadsamoney, and lesser
known Geordie, Buggerallmoney.

[27] A writer of material for Harry who went on to be a writer/performer in *The Fast
Show* (1994-2000).

behind the moon. Tower blocks. Shit jobs. The sad pubs
where the regulars were waiting for the end of the world to
come. A Spar or Happy Shopper on the corner for fags and
a packet of something for tea.

On his nights out, Peter would have seen it all as one
London, as cliffs and valleys of lit windows. A hum of possibility would hang over the river and the city's unimpressive
skyline, featuring only one skyscraper, the NatWest Tower,
and the protruding stalk of the British Telecom Tower was
still a landmark. London had brought so many people together and made so many stories. Made love happen and not
happen in a cold and arbitrary procession. With jealousy following in its wake, spite and revenge. But still, on any night
there was always the chance of a once in a lifetime story—
happening sweetly, extravagantly—with the appearance of a
West End Girl from somewhere, thinks Peter. He's waiting in
the living room of someone's flat, drinking cheap brandy
and listening to the stereo; a glass smeared with scarlet lip-
stick on the coffee table; looking out the window at the glow
of the lights, somehow made warmer by their contrast with
the cold of the weather and the guarded manner of the
people. A London kind of glow, a golden caramel, suggestive
of comfort and firesides, roast beef and Toby jugs. He'd
been thinking about another girlfriend, one that would have
worked out better, wondering where she was. Out there in
the darkness of the streets, she was a face upstairs on a bus,
running her fingers through her hair and absorbed by the
reflection she saw.

The good years turned bad. It started with what
could have been Peter's breakthrough, the chance for one of

his songs to be on a soundtrack for a John Hughes film *Some Kind of Wonderful* (1987).[28] Bands like Simple Minds ('Don't You Forget about Me' and *The Breakfast Club* (1985)) and the Psychedelic Furs ('Pretty in Pink' (1986)) had demonstrated what a Hughes soundtrack could do for a career. 'The Shyest Time' had been due to be released as a single before Hughes' musical supervisor, Tarquin Gotch, came across it, thinking it was a fitting comment on the teenage years. The title had actually come from a *Time* article on divorce the Peter had come across while on a night ferry to Amsterdam in December 1985: "About those who had been lucky, whose lives had been renewed and refreshed by divorce. And about those whose lives had been ruined as well. That interested me. One woman said after her divorce, her self-confidence just jumped off a cliff. 'It was the shyest time of my life'. That was her take on the post-divorce world."

> Stephen Hague, who'd worked with New Order and the Pet Shop Boys, remixed it [explained Peter]. What happened then was that they claimed they owned the recording—which they didn't—but they did own the remix. It took more than two years and £5,000 in lawyers bills to get that fixed. Two years when everything for The Apartments

---

[28] 'The Shyest Time' had been due to be released as a single before Hughes' musical supervisor, Tarquin Gotch, came across it, thinking it was a fitting comment on the teenage years. The title had actually come from a *Time* article on divorce the Peter had come across while on a night ferry to Amsterdam in December 1985: "About those who had been lucky, whose lives had been renewed and refreshed by divorce. And about those whose lives had been ruined as well. That interested me. One woman said after her divorce, her self-confidence just jumped off a cliff. 'It was the shyest time of my life'. That was her take on the post-divorce world."

was just frozen, because we couldn't release
it, and the various labels that were chasing
the band said they wouldn't move on anything until there were no lawyers making
threats.

At the same time there were arguments with Rough Trade,
as the label was putting everything into looking after The
Smiths. By the end of 1988, Peter had also lost his guitar ("I
left my black 1961 Fender Stratocaster, my first electric guitar and one I loved, in the back of a car in East London one
night in 1988—and it was stolen. I took this as a sign that for
me, in England, the fair was over.")[29]

The wandering life can sound romantic, but it's often
moving on castor wheels of misery. "It took me some time to
understand that the melancholy side of my songs might have
been connected to the situations I was in," Peter confessed,
"once things began going badly, I felt I could not move on,
could not go back."[30]

By 1989, Peter was back in Australia again with
plans to do nothing other than look for work. He worked in a
downtown restaurant and ended up selling his other

---

[29] It was Nick's car. "I was working as a sound engineer at the Bass Clef in Hoxton
Square. I came straight from an Apartments rehearsal to work, and left the gear in my
car while I did the soundcheck, planning to get the stuff out after that. I feel bad to this
day. it was a black and white Strat. Sounded amazing."

[30] As another way of explaining himself, Peter has pointed to lines from Anton Chek-
hov's 'The Story of an Unknown Man': "Why are we worn out? Why do we, who start
out so passionate, brave, noble, believing, become totally bankrupt by the age of thirty
or thirty-five? Why is it that one is extinguished by consumption, another puts a bullet
in his head, a third seeks oblivion in vodka, cards, a fourth, in order to stifle fear and
anguish, cynically tramples underfoot the portrait of his pure, beautiful youth? Why is it
that, once fallen, we do not try to rise, and, having lost one thing, we do not seek another?"

favourite guitar, a white semi-acoustic Maton (which he described as "a poor man's version of Gretsch Country Gentleman") that he'd lent to Grant McLennan for the 'Was There Anything I Could Do' video shoot. Even in Brisbane and Sydney, Peter carried his exile with him.

*

Cathal's favourite records were made by people who'd reached the point of giving up, and *drift* would certainly fit into that category, as an unlikely return to recording for someone who'd had a skinful of the industry and, like Paddy, much preferred writing songs to the pressure of studios and quizzical engineers. But there was a bunch of London and Sydney songs with possibilities, many of them influenced by listening to Bob Dylan's *Blood on the Tracks* (1975) and the *Velvet Underground* (1969) album. Friends like Ed Kuepper and Greg Atkinson were telling him they shouldn't be left unheard.

It was Greg who made the introduction to Paul McKercher, the producer/engineer for one of ABC's youth network radio stations, triple j.

> I had been recording and mixing several bands every week [said Paul], from local indie artists [Hard-Ons, Hellmann, Glide, Dazy Chains, Bondi Cigars] to world-conquering touring acts [Faith No More, Throwing Muses, Violent Femmes, Mudhoney etc]. I guess he knew I could run a recording studio and had a feel for the aesthetic of the

time where making art of consequence took
primacy over considerations of its commerci-
ality. It struck me that Peter's poetic nature
and his sensitive view of the world and the
people in it were as easy and natural to him
as putting one foot in front of the other. I
liked him immediately, he was kind, charming and waggish with a great love of art in all
its forms.

They worked on the album together in ABC's Studio 227,
the home of triple j's weekly 'Live at the Wireless'. The band
were a crucial part of the formula for *drift*, because of Peter's
often improvised approach to recording. He wanted the im-
mediacy (and fatalism) of first and second takes. Something
was going to be added and something lost. He never liked
rehearsing, according to Nick. "He'd just say 'oh yeah, let's
go with that'. It was more about getting the right people
around him and seeing what happened. Peter's an artist
rather than a technical musician—he'll sing the songs differently each time, there'll be improvisations and embellish-
ments on choruses, which means he's relying on the band to
take care of business." Throughout the course of the recording, Paul saw the acceptance of imperfection.

I believed then, as now, that with musicians
who believe in the artistic worth of the songs
and who can play parts that serve those
songs, you put them in a room together, make
the sound clear and inviting, have an atmo-

> sphere of honesty, generosity, enthusiasm and
> shared commitment to the art something
> magical happens. The result is unpredictable,
> un-divinable but full of tension, risk, emo-
> tional power and, hopefully, beauty.

So the painterly contributions of the band members on *drift* were critical, including those from Greg on guitar and backing vocals. "At least three songs would never have sounded the way they do without Greg's guitar playing," said Peter. "'The Goodbye Train', 'Nothing Stops It' and 'What's Left Of Your Nerve'." Greg had grown up in a suburb of Brisbane, close to Ed Kuepper and Robert Vickers, in the flood plains of Oxley Creek. He'd been in the Ups and Downs with his brother Darren during the Eighties, a cult band that percolated influences like REM, The Cure and Echo & the Bunnymen through the blue skies of an Australian sensibility. Greg brought the song 'Mad Cow' with him ("a song I wrote about my father's loss, due in large part to alcoholism when I was 17… I'd played it to Peter the first time we met.")

On drums there was Mark Dawson, who'd been working with Ed Kuepper and the Jackson Code. And on bass, John Willsteed. He'd been one of those happy staying put.

> Life in Brisbane could be really hard, it was
> Deadsville. Younger people would be perse-
> cuted by the police, especially punks, musi-
> cians. Police would bust into gigs as a regular
> thing, steal money, arrest people—and there

was no alternative entertainment industry to slot into, it was DIY. My attitude and a lot of other people's, though, was different from those keen to get out. I was happy to wallow in it, sit around and put my feet up, full of heroin and gin and tonics. I loved consuming culture and making stuff.

After Peter's early Brisbane years, he and John met up briefly in London when he was touring with the Go-Betweens in 1988, and not again until 1992 when Peter turned up with some cassettes of songs (acoustic guitar and vocals) for a proposed album. It had been a different kind of year for John, who'd decided to quit drinking just the month before ("to open up and test my capacity to deal with stuff, people, life, without drinking"). "I wasn't an avid fan, I really didn't know any of [The Apartments] other material, just as I hadn't when I joined the Go-Betweens. But I really liked Peter, we were friends—and old friends with his wife Katy— I liked hanging around with him."[31]

It was an 'after work' project, made at night. The band would meet at ABC's Studio 227 around seven and keep playing until they were happy with what they'd captured. It was a large space for a four-piece to occupy, with its high ceilings and a Steinway grand piano. In terms of the tech it was Paul's "dream setup of SSL console, Neve channels, Pultec cq, 1970's URIE compressors, a Studer 24-track

---

[31] Other musicians involved in the sessions included backing vocalists Carolyn Polley (with Greg's post-Ups and Downs band, Big Heavy Stuff), and Clare Kenny (who'd toured playing bass with Aztec Camera and Sinead O'Connor etc, as well as on the Orange Juice track 'What Presence?!').

tape machine with an enviable collection of vintage mics to capture the performances"—and he knew the room and its reverb feel from all the live recordings for triple j. There might be days or even weeks in-between the evening sessions, undertaken gradually over the course of those Australian winter nights, until the record was completed in September 1992. The songs on *drift* were essentially recorded 'live' in one or two takes, partly because of the lack of time and budget, but mostly as a way of keeping the emotion and instinctive quality of performances intact, un-diluted by over-recording, repeated takes and overdubs. Without being given a formal brief, Paul had picked up on the vibe Peter was looking for: the pensive drama of Scott Walker. "I gathered that the music should have a sense of grandeur, despite us not having an orchestra, an epic sweep, a clarion emotional resonance and reverb, lots of it." The big performance room meant distance and separation from the control room, which was reached by a set of stairs, but Peter's affable relationship with Paul made it work.

> Peter was genuinely interested in my opinions which, for a young producer, was a huge boost for me [said Paul]. Micromanagement and nervous scrutiny were more what I was used to from less assured artists. Emotional content always held primacy over nit-picky detail—an important lesson at the time—and when he sang, he committed to the performance completely, as though nothing else mattered.

"Peter is definite about what he wants, but at the same time he lets people do their business, what they do well," said John. And that could lead to the occasional anomaly. "I remember sitting with just the two of us working out the bass lines; and I look back now and they were jaunty, playful on a couple of tracks. When Peter played later, years later, he did them differently, and that's how I should have done them in the first place." The songs they played could be intense and angsty—but the evenings in 227 were good times. There was mucking about and teasing; the bonhomie among a group of musicians enjoying each other's company added fluency and honesty. They could let rip. "There's a big sound on the record, thunderous sometimes," added John. "It sounds like a proper band, sitting down and getting ten songs done in one go." The album's closer, 'What's Left of Your Nerve' has been picked out by those involved as an example of the live chemistry: "the energy shifts that build to a kind of beautiful mania by the outro," said Paul, "the white-hot fire of Mark Dawson's drum take, the dreamy counter melodies of Greg's guitar, John's exquisite note choice, the clawing tension of Peter's vocal delivery make for a song of searing emotional power—perhaps this is why the record has stood the test of time, sounding unlike so much of the music from that period of the early Nineties when it was recorded." The string accompaniments were added later by a quartet led by Kathy Wemyss (John's landlady at the time).[32] "The strings, those lovely strings, tie things together beautifully," he said, "they

---

[32] Kathy's musical education (in singing, guitar and trumpet) came from being part of a Salvation Army family and attending the Conservatorium, but she also went on to play with Sydney post-punk bands like Wet Taxis, Kings of the World and the Jackson Code (and played live with Midnight Oil).

really dig into the album, in ways that remind me of the
Jimmy Webb album with Richard Harris, *The Yard Went on
Forever* (1968), the little interludes that lead into songs. I've
always loved that."

The finished album has the feel of a funfair closed
down at the end of summer; where the innocence and excitement of holiday rides is now only a memory, there as a
palimpsest; a funfair venue that's changed instead into a
backdrop for the more adult and complicated pleasures of
drink and flirting and sex.[33] The dark funfair feel of the album cover was provided by the vividly atmospheric photography of Daniel Frasnay. You can smell the sweetness of
cheap perfume mixed with smoke and sweat in his black and
white images, taken from Peter's copy of the book *Nights in
Paris* (1958). He'd had a copy "lying around since 1977, possibly waiting for my moment". Born into a gypsy family,
Frasnay chronicled the Paris of fishnet stockings and artfully
placed feathers as the official photographer of the Cabaret
Lido, a club with an indoor beach on the Champs-Elysees.
He was a familiar character hanging round the hottest clubs
and strip shows of Pigalle and the Left Bank for more than
forty years. Another of Frasnay's books of photographs was
called, simply enough, *Les Girls*. But it wasn't just the sparkle
and sequins of the shows he caught inside his camera, but
the woozy-headed customers living through those night-time
moments, experiencing disappointment and longing as much
as anything else; the desolation of a lonely club. And this
works perfectly for *drift*, from the moody still life of the cover

---

[33] It seems only natural that the stripped down, more intimate follow-up to *drift* should
be called *fête foraine* (1996).

(a wine tap and candle—maybe a drunk's eye view from resting on the counter?), to the young dancers and empty chairs next to a carousel. The pictures are tinted with a sulky, end-of-the-night blue, a nod to the Blue Note designs of Reid Miles.[34]

A new indie label based in the small town of Nagambie in Victoria, Torn & Frayed, took a chance on releasing *drift*.[35] Reportedly, sales in Australia amounted to around 200 copies.[36] In France, the album was received very differently. There it was in context. The dry rasp of its indie sound and emotional aesthetic made glorious sense. The release by New Rose sold more than 25,000 copies initially.[37] Since Peter's discovery of Satie, aspects of French culture

---

[34] Miles Reid's covers for John Coltrane's *Blue Train (1958)*, Freddie Hubbard's *blue spirits (1966)* and Wayne Shorter's *Night Dreamer (1964)* were an obvious source. Another influence was the designer Saul Bass, who created the classic movie posters for *Rear Window* (1954), *Vertigo* (1958), *Bonjour Tristesse* (1958) and *The Shining* (1980). The logpile photo of Peter in the inside cover was taken by Ed Kuepper's wife, Jude. The original CD artwork was put together by Peter's brother-in-law and re-worked by Pascal Blua for the re-issued LP.

[35] Torn & Frayed had started out with releases from Townes Van Zandt, collections of Tom Waits' early material and the Dirty Three's eponymous first LP. The label shut down in 2017.

[36] That doesn't mean Peter wasn't influential among Australian bands. "Peter was a great signal or anchor point for me," wrote Dave Graney of The Moodists in his memoir. "I learned poise and attitude from him. He encouraged me in areas where he'd seen I'd said or suggested something in a casual way that stayed with him. It can be powerful when somebody you respect and admire cheers you on or points out a quality in your work or general shape in the world that you weren't aware of. They give you the direction to accentuate some sort of limp or speech impediment if it's working for you. You take heed of advice from players you rate. Peter had this rare pop sensibility amongst a bunch of people obsessed with post-punk self-righteousness and striving for authenticity. He had his own brew he'd cooked up himself... He took risks by just walking away."

[37] New Rose grew out of a Paris record shop in 1980 to become the largest indie label in Europe. Patrick Mathè and Louis Thèvenot championed post-punk bands, including many 'alternative' American artists who couldn't find a label at home, such as Alex Chilton, Roky Erickson and Elliott Murphy. New Rose closed in 1994, morphing into Last Call Records.

had been assimilated into his way of seeing and writing, and become more of an instinct than just plain interest or sympathy. An instinct that meant he chose to drive around Brisbane in a Peugeot 203. It was normal in France to take an interest in art, photography, jazz, poetry, with no need to be conscious of striking an intellectual pose. And that way of seeing, that taste, affected so many other aspects of French life, in the look of a Parisian park or street or room, the way people dressed, because matters of style were meant to be taken seriously. When it came to creating one of the first posters for an Apartments gig in 1979, Peter used a Christian Dior advert for Les Rythmiques cosmetics created by the great style-maker in hair, make-up, clothes and photography, Serge Lutens. "I saw the ad in *Vogue* magazine—elegant, French, rhythmic: what's not to love, steal, imitate?". *the evening visits* LP and the first gigs in Paris and the university city of Tours in 1986 had led to a cultish French following which included the *Inrockuptibles* journalists Gilles Tordjman ("Pronouncing [Peter's] name was like entering a discreet, lively freemasonry"); and Jean-Daniel Beauvallet: "[*the evening visits…*] was love at first sight… like [we] were discovering Joy Division, Scott Walker, the Byrds or the Velvet Underground."

For Peter, being in Paris was like finding himself in a piece of fiction, a screenplay imagined by Godard, Agnés Varda or Jacques Demy.

[T]he car skips off a Périphérique exit and then there we are, in that unforgettable Haussmann landscape—five-story sandstone buildings, broad boulevards filled with

December light, chestnut trees lining the
road. The countless bridges that cross the
Seine are spread out before us beneath a
beautiful sky. We are back in Paris. As always,
it feels grand. Saturday afternoon in Paris—a
recording session with the band, a French
radio studio built in the Sixties, driving down
Avenue du Président Kennedy beside the
Seine—all of this makes it suddenly feel like
some kind of destiny is at play.[38]

"Paris has seemed to work on me like a spell," he wrote in
2018. "Rounding a corner in the Montmartre fog, lost, looking for a street where Jean-Pierre Melville had shot *Bob le
Flambeur* and suddenly finding myself instead on Rue Cortot,
where Satie had written the 'Gymnopédies' when he was just
23. The first morning I went walking, just around the corner
I found a plaque: Paul Verlaine lived here. Another marked
James Joyce's house, Hemingway's." The more sober sensibility of French music fans also helped. "In Australia in the
Eighties," recalled Victor, "music was played in huge beer
barns, you had to scream and have simple songs to get
heard." Peter didn't want to an Australian career for that
very reason. "If you play hard enough for people who drink
and yell at you to hear you, then it's okay. But I didn't want
to do that, I like to play softly, I didn't want to force myself to
do anything else just to fit into the mould."

---

[38] He was in Paris to record the *Seven Songs* mini-album in 2012, issued for Record Store
Day.

'Mr Somewhere' felt to me, at the time, like a manifesto—"*the hardest words are spoken softly...*" The New York I lived in when writing it, had of course changed from the Television/Ramones/Talking Heads etc New York of the 70s and was now very much in thrall to local noise bands like Sonic Youth, Swans and passing-through-town screamers like Hank Rollins' Black Flag. The Birthday Party were also a noise band, and screaming when they passed through as well. These were all great bands and there was plenty to be screaming about, but I felt not just that these acts would paint themselves into a corner but that I wanted no place in a screaming world, not that there was a place for me in it anyway. To be fair, would Sufjan Stevens or Bon Iver or Joanna Newsom ever have been heard above the boisterous and talkative Australian pub rock crowd? Not even Jeff Buckley taking it down to a whisper could get people to shut up in Sydney music venues.

But why were the French, more than any other nationality, so spellbound by The Apartments? Maybe because Peter has never been a purveyor of obvious pop, indie or otherwise. He's not done fast food. The bittersweet mix of emotions, the subtlety of his searching melodies—so well suited to a slowed-down French *chansons* feel and the addition of horns and strings—make for a more grown-up offering.

So in France, the release of *drift* was an event, if only for the indie-literate. "The announcement of a new Apartments album had somewhat the same symbolic weight as if we announced the release of an unreleased Beatles album," said Tordjman. "*drift* is a masterpiece. As if Peter Walsh couldn't do anything else. As if this sick music, of weak complexion, constantly on the verge of cachexia, were only the painful face of a somewhat celestial glory… The voice is more assured, but no less anguished. It is that, as Rilke said, 'by dint of living with your questions, you end up finding answers' and that, traveler of all abysses—alcohol and self-hatred composing a tasty cocktail—Peter Walsh could only rise to the surface. *drift* is a masterpiece because all the melodies it contains seem to have been discovered rather than composed: scattered nuggets strewn across an Australian backroad." Along with radio airplay from France's John Peel, Bernard Lenoir, it was a feature article by Emmanuel Tellier in *Les Inrockuptibles* that sold the idea of The Apartments to a bigger audience.

There's a little Australian flame, one that has been burning in The Apartments fan since that day in 1984 when the notes of 'All You Wanted' rang out for the first time [wrote Tellier]. It was, along with the Smiths' 'Hand in Glove' and the Pale Fountains' *Pacific Street* album, one of the first real shocks of light… *drift* isn't any happier, just less stuffy. It's another album of tears and dust, which oozes and hurts. Ten songs more cried than sung,

comatose, lonely, desperate. Even 'On Every
Corner', almost cheerful, drowns in the
mist… Eight years have passed and Walsh
creates a masterpiece again.

Apartments fans, French or otherwise, knew they had something special. As Pierre Lemarchand wrote in 2015: "if those songs were heard only in the underground, passed between people like a secret without the kind of public attention others got, well, they still found the listeners who needed them. They became songs that someone loved. When people get them, they really get them. When they fall for them, they fall hard."

*

There's a strange postcard pinned on the bedroom wall that Adrian had never noticed before. They'd spent a whole year in that house and no-one had seen it, mentioned it, called it weird.

A sun-faded postcard of Disney's Bambi. Right above the mantelpiece in one of the bedrooms, the bedroom he'd shared with Monkey. How had they not seen it? A big-eyed, brown-striped cartoon Bambi.

Now he's wondering whose hands had pinned it there, how many years ago? Could have been early Eighties. The dump they'd lived in looked like it had been a student place—undecorated, uncared for, unimproved—for decades.

It wasn't yet the end of the summer term but Monkey had already taken most of his stuff away and gone back home to do some evening shifts of telesales and see his girlfriend. So there was just Monkey's bed with its smeggy forget-me-not duvet left behind as a reminder. A beer bottle collection and a copy of Jane Austen's Sense and Sensibility. *A note pinned to the mantelpiece with one of the 'rules' Monkey had made up when he first moved in. 'NO WANKING'. More of the room was visible than ever before, making it look exposed and odd. A dusty carpet and darker shapes on the wallpaper where the light hadn't reached for so long. Monkey was coming back in the week, then he was done, he said.*

The age of Cilla and laughing at the Kevins and Traceys before going out was now over. Rather than sit in the empty living room with all its noisy memories, Adrian has taken the TV into the bedroom, shut the curtains against the evening sun and watched the Ruth Rendell mystery from his bed. He knew that across town, the Union would be randy with first and second years and their cheesy grins. None of the old crowd anymore. They'd been scattered by the winds of summer. Reduced to a bunch of addresses he could write to, numbers to call sometime (Karen's too, though he can't remember her face anymore, just bits. The streak of black pencil in the corner of each eye that gave her a look of Oriental beauty. There was still always the danger he'd walk past her in the street).

Left in the house with Bambi. Why couldn't things ever stay the same? Like it had for Dad. He'd be home watching Casualty. *Sarah would be doing the ironing in her flat. Mum in a restaurant, complaining about the wine and getting Tony to send it back.*

The whole summer had gone and curdled around him.

*

As teenagers we became used to being told what we should be doing each day, where we had to go. Suddenly—in those days of finishing education, starting work, leaving home— there was nothing more to know, other than that we were free. It was a time when anyone could discover, all at once, that they were solitary.

The same prescription of the culture, that happiness would come with love, still applied as much as ever, but the nature of that game for twenty-somethings had changed. For the average teenager, love was a choice, a pursuit that could be taken up—with all its crystal aches and jags and longing—and then put down again. A time of accidents, when there was no need for sense or logic, only the impossible-seeming happiness that came with being one of two. They could take a chance, see what might happen and enjoy the pain of uncertainty, even the woes of rejection, and decide to try again or just forget. It was kind of romantic either way. Twenty-something relationships came with a burden of implications, a weight of security and insecurity, winning and defeat. First love, with its aspect of bright perfection, couldn't come again; it belonged where it would always stay from now on, behind a pane of glass. Only a few years on but a universe away. Suddenly older. And love wasn't something to 'fall' into anymore, there was knowledge and negotiation first—and a quickened sense of time passing as we saw friends change, turn into couples, set up home, get engaged.

That's too simple a description though, like it was just snakes and ladders. There was no reason why someone couldn't prefer the single life. A sense of lonely isolation, even one of rejection, could come with its own attractive poignancy, making life more interesting and affecting; a way to avoid the closing of doors and possibilities. Preferring the bittersweetness. A space to stand apart, trying to read the meaning of vapour trails in the sky.

Growing up itself doesn't change. But there was a different flavour and intensity to the experience in the early Nineties—because of the decades that had preceded it. After all, what was expected to happen to people's psyche and their expectations of each other after so many years of messaging that proclaimed the importance of the good consumer? Because you're worth it. Just do it. More impatience, more vanity, more self-obsession; analysis over instinct; an awareness of the market value of individuals, their looks, their wealth. And rather than an escape into something real and romantic, the relationship game became wrapped round more tightly with conventions and expectations.

Paddy knew how the system worked, as he sang on *Jordan*: "All the world loves people in love… Love whatever the price". Ideas of value and 'price' were the problem. Asked about his 'HATES' by the *NME* in 1983, Paddy included "Being an ineligible bachelor" along with "Being poor". And no-one could be trusted anyway. "I think my viewpoint is really intensely romantic," he said, "but it's romantic in a sense that it's the romance of hopelessness… It's a kind of 'I wish that things were that way or that things could be that way.' Everybody makes promises. Everybody vows this and vows that, and to let it all down is a completely chilling experience." In 'You're a Rose', Cathal wrote a brilliant commentary on the modern dating game. "This is Mister Blank, calling gorgeous…" he sings down the phone to his latest dear one, his new rose: "Were you sleeping? Do you hate me?" allowing some unspoken truths to break through alongside the clichés, "I miss your smile, your laugh, your snore, your fond contempt, your faithful rage", until he gets tired of playing and truth is all that's left: "You don't mind deceiving lovers / You ignore the stinking air".[39] Power and deceit were everywhere in Cathal's London, and were a brutalising and corrupting force.

> Pork-eyes, he will stroke your long hair tenderly in all the waterfront bars
> Where the wine and hollow talk-of-men will muffle things that really, really are
> And you'll go back to your room with him on your healthy sandalled feet
> To come out minutes later, bleeding, torn above, torn underneath.

The Trashcans' routine was one of pub piss-ups and trying to impress the girls by cruising around the empty town centre in their "Ford Spectacular", followed by the lonely return to their rented room. Any youthful idea of romance had long been replaced with feelings of confusion: "We know where our love lies / Through the catacombs we roam… Our love becomes this useless box of tricks"; a haunting kind of confusion: "I don't remember what you said or did / That made you so attractive / The perfect reminder"; and they prefer to laugh at themselves and their place in the market: "One at a time please ladies / No need to rush now". As we've seen, there were no love stories on *Reading, Writing and Arithmetic* and that was followed by a slide into resignation on *Blind* (1992); like this from the song 'Love': "This is my life and it's

---

[39] It's well worth watching the video of 'You're a Rose' to see Cathal treating his date to a Wall's Viennetta.

all very well / But never never never again… Just love yourself like no one else".

    Romance and alcohol work well together—probably
too well. As Peter has said: "The association of romantic
music and alcohol is dangerous." No liquor, no *drift*.

> A river of alcohol runs through these songs,
> with all its rapids and turns. It rushes when
> things are new and happy in exactly the same
> way it rushes when they come to an end. The
> river turns when hopes are high and every-
> body wins and rushes on again when the
> same hopes are exhausted or lost. Whether
> people are trying to be good or if they're bad
> for each other, the rattle of ice in a glass is in
> every scene, there for every seduction, every
> argument and every declaration… Drinking,
> they think, is the only way to live but it's
> really the only way they know to jack up the
> drama of their lives.

And the drinks have kept on coming at the student union in
Bristol, the London pubs, Paddy's drinks cabinet—acting as
inspiration and consolation, a warming of memory. Maybe
it's the secret to being creative, said the Trashcans' guitarist
Paul Livingston. "People drink a lot in Scotland. Being drunk
or stoned or tired takes you out of yourself, which is always
the best way to write. As the late Captain [Beefheart] said,
'If your brain is part of the process, you're missing it.'" And
so we find the Ayrshire lads with their "Guinness elbows"

resting on the table, drinking themselves "lame", getting a "little wrecked", seeing life through a bottle: "Pull the cork on us, there is no tomorrow".

Alcohol is the emotion potion. It works most of all on the cerebellum area of the brain, where things like memories and emotions are regulated, and encourages the release of the feelgood chemicals serotonin and endorphins. So there's a lovely haze. Confidence grows as inhibitions are forgotten and it's easier to make decisions (although they're more likely to be bad ones). Talk spills out easy and any old how. The problem is that the brain keeps wanting that fix of lovely, runaway feelings, to dispel ordinary feelings of anxiety. The drinking generates a cycle of need, stronger emotions, more tears and nostalgia, regret, and a craving for the release it will bring. Difficult romances, booze and songwriting form a wonderful triangle, but it's also a trap of illusion and disillusion, where alcohol ends up being the only relationship anyone needs: a one night stand, the reliable standby, the insistent partner who can't be let down.[40] Raymond Chandler put it better. "Alcohol is like love. The first kiss is magic, the second is intimate, the third is routine. After that you take the girl's clothes off."

*

The lyrics to *drift* are a diary account of having lived deep within that cursed circle of alcohol and love. Velvety nights. Sulphur yellow mornings. A poetry of lost time, full of

---

[40] *Viva Dead Ponies* was Cathal's last album as a heavy drinker, and includes the grim warning of 'Chemical Cosh': if you want a population to be weak and compliant, it argues, get them smashed on drink and drugs.

shrugs and bitter smiles, which recognises the disenchantment that comes from fulfilling a desire. There's an honesty
to the lyrics that could only come from someone looking
back, from the distance of maturity. It's a different Peter
from the young man who wrote the songs on *the evening visits…*, who was still playing the game with a hope and confidence that's reflected in abstract language and distracted
ideas. The moody stories are happening in a rock 'n' roll
elsewhere, and only enter the music as an amorphous shine.
By contrast, *drift* is obsessive film noir about transience and
emptiness where the lyrics are concrete and about particular
people and their fate.

> This is just what happens, as you're swept in
> the whirlpool of your early twenties, racking
> up trouble, taking on every experience you
> can. And I also loved songs that packed a lot
> of living into them. Leonard Cohen at 'four
> o'clock in the afternoon not feeling like very
> much', Billie Holiday saying 'I get along
> without you very well, of course I do… except
> when soft rains fall'… I liked Sinatra more
> when he started losing, when he was at the
> bottom of nowhere with all the hope beaten
> out of him. After Ava had left him to a last-
> ing loneliness, he was still a skinny singer in a
> dark suit but it would be a while before he felt
> like being Mr Ring-a-Ding-Ding.

The screenplay takes place in a city of rented apartments—not somewhere to stop and live in, but emblematic of emptiness, of the packing and unpacking of suitcases. "I had a simple story to tell, a set of characters who drifted in and out of not just the songs but each other's lives. My address book from around that time was a mess, crowded with crossed-out names and numbers." The lyrics are about people looking and not finding, or finding what could be both "beautiful and dangerous". The original title for the album was *Someone To Ride Down With:* "What comes with love is a kind of chaos and what comes with that chaos tests and proves and makes that love feel real. For many men, that chaos is when love begins to fail. For me it's when love begins."

The atmosphere can sometimes take on a swamp-like feel of stasis, repetition and misty *deja vu*. "Nothing here was new. None of the drama, none of the situations. The stories are the oldest stories, like the one where two people took something that had been worth something once and ran it into the ground… The people here would always drink, they would always move, they would always want. They still believed that a change of towns or a change of rivers might be enough, that other might change them too." There was something else in there, a mystery that needed to be remembered and understood. Because there'd always been happiness mixed in there too. The times when he'd let the stars go. Maybe something significant had been left hidden in the details of what happened.

> Did they say goodbye on the street? In the half-light of Paddington Station as a line of carriages disappears through a wreath of

fog… last looks, last kisses blown from a train
window. Who walked through the departure
gate in tears? Who stayed behind, a letter
that might have been an explanation kept in
a pocket, never given and never sent?

Peter had been left with lots of questions from the whirl of
years. Like the line "I left something back there, in the gut-
ters and smoke… My baby face vanished", which he forgot
to include in the lyrics booklet: "Did I forget to insert it or
did I deliberately exclude it? I do not know." He'd been left
to work with scraps of memory that were evaporating with
time. As per one of the notes he'd written and forgotten
about: "Happiness written in white ink on white pages".[41]
The lyrics on *drift* act as a way of breaking the spell for good,
by bringing some perspective to a muddled chamber of
memories. A way to let go.

Up until a certain point in your life, if you
think back to times you shared, days that
have your friends in them, you believe that
they still exist somewhere. That they're still
available to you. That we are all just in different places on the ferris wheel and that when
it comes round again, you will see them
again. That you'll take up where you left off.
And it's true, the wheel does come round
again—but sometimes, the carriage is empty.

---

[41] A quote from French essayist and novelist Henry de Montherlant. Now a controver-
sial figure because of his anti-feminist ideas.

The album's landscape is expressionist. Backstreets exist in black and white, obscured by shadows and rain and blooms of smoke like billows of messy, only half-understood feelings. Peter once said that Jacques Tourneur, director of the film noir classic *Out of the Past* (1947), could have made a film out of the material on *drift*.[42] The lyrics describe "streets in the mist / in the strung-out world of old memory"; "those days that blur the stones of loving her / scenes that flicker in your head"; places that are somewhere and nowhere: "the Neverland that's your address". Impersonal streets and empty station platforms where lives have detached. After midnight, time seems to collapse, "the night is long everywhere", but darkness isn't an escape or cover. Another world comes to life, one where feelings weigh heavier, people move in and out of the light (The Apartments' striped darkness sound). As Peter explained: "The characters… tend to live by night. They don't really have any great ability or talent for the daylight world, and count down the hours until the evening begins." Night is a stage set with a back projection of lights and traffic, made for moments of possible romance. Not plain black but luminous with silken grey shades and starlight, or the "four-cat moon through the Judas trees": a ghost of light seen through a mass of heart-shaped leaves and pink blossom. The songs emerge from heightened moments of awareness, at that instant when a light turns out in

---

[42] Tourneur moved from France to make a string of Hollywood B-movies like *Cat People* (1942) and *I Walked with a Zombie* (1943). He was known for the dark, misty streets of his films — created by shining lots of lights into empty spaces and then getting the actors to puff on their fags. The cinematographer on *Out of the Past* was Nicolas Musuraca. Robert Mitchum, who played Jeff Bailey in the film, said the budget was "so small that the lighting was done with cigarettes."

the flat above, doors slam, and a couple appears in the street below.

Peter draws on a store of language from the grifters of American *noir* (the "crummy" rooms, "jackknifed and all washed up in vaudeville… liquor rushes, losing tricks", "you go and hold down any job / a world of bills, a run of jacks"). But in the end the songs' approach is closer to the observational and impressionistic style of European cinema than Hollywood's more linear and contrived stories.

It was the larger world outside (and not Peter) that took revenge on anyone who thought they can stay young or live solely in a lovelorn stupor. They'd been given plenty of warnings over the years: "Lonesomeness was sent to warn you both / on every corner", but still they end up clinging to easy delusions and hopeless superstition, the "spell where everything will work", "the cheap illusions / maybe a hundred towns ago / [when] they had a hundred kinds of hope". They might try again somewhere else, look for somewhere they can stay a little longer and use as a sanctuary: "hurry, hurry, hurry", "you packed your whole life in the back of a car", "move, move, move" and then "drift like a lost kite". But it's the same wherever the lost romantics go, "all the tickets go nowhere now / heaven's hidden, hidden, it disappeared". A dry-eyed fatalism goes with them, until they start believing no relationships could ever be good for them: "we're bad for each other sweetheart / that's part of the deal", "whoever loved you, you'd just wreck". There's self-pity: "you milk your drama for all it's worth / like you're the only one who's ever been this hurt". And a dust of nostalgia: "what magic is there left in town? what magic?"

It's a personal story, at least to begin with. "When I was younger, I was very good at this game which consists of disappearing, leaving," said Peter. "When you're young, it's easy to do. You believe in the big tomorrow, then you wake one morning and find you have nothing to show for the years spent on the run." It was a story that, in the telling, drained part of him away. "Someone wrote these songs [on *drift*], someone who resembled me. Where is he now? He has gone away. Songs use you up. Use your life up." The characters are set in motion and go their own way, the ordinary clowns and losers, and make new connections with listeners who see something of themselves or at least recognise the mood involved. "They come to life from out of a constellation of conversations, memories, lines. The characters may have made the same mistakes, had the same experiences, been in the same situations a lot of us have." Peter could easily be assumed to be an adventurer. But as would happen with anyone who feels the poignancy and pain of the end of youth, he's looking for a home and security.

*

French fans fetched Peter back. In 2009, Emmanuel Tellier of *Les Inrockuptibles* talked to him about doing some acoustic concerts in Paris, Clermont-Ferrand, Chignon and Villeurbanne (near Lyon); and the affection he experienced there, from both the established and a new generation of fans, along with the idea of a return to the City of Light, was the start of a new chapter for The Apartments. The album of songs for Riley, *No Song, No Spell, No Madrigal*, arrived in 2015 after a crowdfunding campaign by French label Microcul-

331

tures, and was received with fitting reverence. Reviewer Matthieu Dufour wrote:

> A well-kept secret, impeccable but delicate and graceful music: polished, golden and melancholy compositions, rare and precious songs. Music with magical powers (consoling sadness, bringing tears in moments of joy, a love time machine, a black hole in which it was finally allowed to be oneself, to accept one's mistakes past, one's weaknesses, even sometimes questioning God). A balm for sensitive skin and loose hearts. He is one of those rare artists whose work has an extra soul that is difficult to explain, this ability to touch the heart, to never leave a stone unturned.

Another reviewer, Jérôme Florio, pointed to another way of understanding the "extra soul" of The Apartments: via a poem by the French surrealist Louis Aragon, 'There is no happy love' (1944).

> by the time we learn to live it's already too
> late
> let our hearts cry in unison at night
> how much unhappiness it takes for the least
> song

> how many regrets to pay for a thrill
> how many tears for a guitar melody
> there is no happy love

While Peter may have wanted to get off the ride that *drift* described, it doesn't mean those experiences were ever a mistake, a matter of false steps. The same stings of loneliness and regret were the source of an unusually acute emotional response. Being alone could mean being free from the dust of convention and complacency, and turn sensitivity into a source of stoic acceptance and strength. Like the song 'Nothing Stops It' (with that special use of the impersonal 'it'), which recognises that it's really not one person or situation that is our problem; we're subject to a much larger flow of currents over which we have no control, that will keep on bringing change. In other words, that's life. "I have a weakness for songs that find a way to make sadness bearable and beautiful," Peter explained. As one of his French literary heroes, Blaise Cendrars, once argued: "Only a soul full of despair can ever attain serenity and, to be in despair, you must have loved a good deal and still love the world."

There's a margin between the darkness and the light where grim realism accompanied by a spirit of romance works endlessly well together, beauty-wise.

5.

"Here's to all of us. I know you are worried."

Trashcan Sinatras, *I've Seen Everything* (May 1993)

*H*ungover and blue. The reality that remains after last night is made of strange aches and bruises. The room was spinning, we remember that, but did we fall on the floor or did the floor fall on us?

We're back among the places we've come to know by heart. The kettle's started to wobble and steam, the cat's nuzzling against our legs. With all the ups and downs of doing our own thing, getting used to the rules of work, washing clothes and paying bills, we can't feel anything but glad to be somewhere that feels like home. Especially when the alternative is the spare room with the parents, our tail between our legs.

The glamour of any new place doesn't last long though. It will soon take on the look of sadness that comes with everyday things, because we've been there through too many nothing-to-do Sundays and Monday work mornings; looking at the same white skies and watery sunshine, the sprawl of rooftops into town, the multi-storey car park and blocks of council offices. Washing lines and pigeons. We've come home each evening to the same four walls, the friendly hum of the fridge; the cupboard door that's stayed open (kindly, just for us); the view onto next door's satellite dish, stained a pale orange by the last of the day's sun. The breadcrumbs are there, the Marmite jar. And in those quiet moments we'd be thinking of the people and places we've not seen for a while, the episodes of romance that now belong to an unreachable past. Because it's getting obvious what's missing from this new place of independence.

We've taken a long walk out of the town centre and gone deep into the post-industrial scrubland of Kilmarnock to find Shabby Road, the studio home of the twenty-somethings of the Trashcan Sinatras (established 1989).[1] It's a big town of arterial roads meant for lorries to make their way from one factory depot to the next, cursing their daily descent into the hell of the one-way system. A town made from a landscape of clouds and urban bric-a-brac: ribbon roads lined with council houses, supermarkets, tyre replacement shops and leftover Victorian monuments. The factory making Axminster carpets is still one of Killie's biggest em-

---

[1] A play on 'Abbey Road' that also seemed to fit with the backstreet spirit of the band name.

ployers, along with the Johnnie Walker distillery.[2] Saxone's shoes and Massey Ferguson have gone. So it might not be the glory days of the Seventies, when the town was a paragon of modern industrial Scotland, but there's bustle enough around the King Street shops and the precinct, there are still shoppers and their kids sitting round the Robert Burns statue with their cans and pies.

We've walked our way south along the main road towards the A71 and reached Glencairn Square, next to the traffic lights and the turn-offs for the industrial estate. A Square with a lozenge of grass and a tree, next to the Howard Arms. Across the junction is the band's favourite drinking hole, the Tudorbethan landmark of the Hunting Lodge. Here there's a sign for the Shabby Road studio in the upstairs window above Walter Duff TV Repairs, the Ayrshire Hospice Charity Shop and Ka Poo Chinese.[3] It's a single Victorian construction of reddish-brown sandstone with some fine details that have been left over from a past age of affection for design; a frontage with a back-to-back chimney (like two duelling gentlemen), a number of sills and grooves and mouldings, and on one side, a leaf quatrefoil pattern—for good luck—placed into the bricks. There are some nicely-crafted ironwork railings round the back. But from trembling next to the main road for so long, 1 Glencairn Square isn't what it once was, it has weathered,

---

[2] Diageo closed the historic Johnnie Walker factory in Kilmarnock in 2012. BMK Carpets shut down in 2005.

[3] In 2024 the shops were occupied by Marmaris Kebab House and Oriental Taste (with an empty place in-between). Opposite is a Lidl supermarket.

blanched and blackened with the traffic's dust and dirty breaths of carbon monoxide.

The band members decided to set up home in Shabby Road with the advance paid by Go! Discs for their first album. They took over what had been Sirocco Studios, a well-known facility in the region, used by Roddy Frame, The Bluebells and Del Amitri, as well as many of the traditional waltz bands. Lead singer Frank Reader already knew the place—he'd been the "tea boy", learning how to be a sound engineer under the wing of producer Clark Sorley—and they got a good price as the leaseholder didn't want to see the property split into flats.[4] For the new band it meant they could get themselves together for the promised album, a place where they could spend as much time as they wanted; and with eight rehearsal rooms to rent out, a way to generate other income to pay the bills. They could record at home, out of the way of the industry's watchful gaze.

Here it is. A scruffy back entrance up a flight of steps to the first floor door. There's a poster for 'Obscurity Knocks' as soon as we get inside, so we know we're in the right place. A pump and clatter of drums comes from somewhere. The rehearsal room doors are mostly closed, but we can stick our head into one of them: a high ceiling and the original sash windows, corniced edgings and plenty of light. The carpet's a bit dirty. The odd plectrum, amp lead and ashtray has been left lying around, a stray piece of A4 with indecipherable scribbles. We can see there's not a lot of cor-

---

[4] They worked together on LP recordings by Andy Stewart (of 'Donald, where's your troosers?' fame), Anne Lorne Gillies (a singer and TV personality known for supporting Gaelic music), Alistair MacDonald (folk singer) and John Carmichael (hero of traditional Scottish music who led the house band for TV series *Thingummyjig*). Clark was kept on at Shabby Road in a consultancy role.

porate gloss in Shabby Road, just some hasty paint jobs to cover up the damp patches caused by the leaky roof. It's an old building that's kept its funky old building smell; but kind of comforting in its own way.

It's a family business. Frank's younger sister Richeal is the Saturday girl who replies to the fan mail and handles the room bookings; and Edna—the number-one-maker Eddi Reader—the miraculous voice of Fairground Attraction, makes appearances in the studio like gentle, unassuming royalty. We keep looking for who might be around from the Trashcans, but for the moment there's only Angela: Shabby's 24-track mixing desk. So we go down and try the other door, there's more stairs, and this time we reach the studio office and the smiling face of the office boss Nanette, who sorts us out.[5]

"Kitchen."

A pair of ice-blue eyes are following us as we leave, making us look up: the eyes of Sinatra himself, his face framed on the wall in a place of honour, next to the band's treasured 'Wee Stinker' crossword T-shirt. Frank Sinatra was the best kind of hero for the Scots. A blue collar guy who was classy but not fancy; he could hold his drink and be straight about how he was feeling. He'd seen a few things; been through four marriages, punched a nosy gossip columnist in the face, and made a few useful connections with organised crime. When Sinatra made his last ever performance in Britain at Ibrox Stadium in Glasgow in 1990, there were tears shed

---

[5] John Douglas tells the story of how one intrepid member of a band using the rehearsal rooms had been desperate to get to the Shabby Road kitchen (and its bottle of whisky). They got up into the attic and then tried to creep through to the other side before falling right through the ceiling plaster.

both by the audience and Sinatra himself. Only he could keep that weepy, heart-on-sleeve stuff masculine.

One of Shabby Road's cats escorts us along the little hallway to the real nerve centre of things, where the fridge and the kettle are, next to the room where you could go for a kip.[6] The lads look kind of guilty, as if they need to live up to their status as an indie band, start being rock and roll or at least strum at a guitar. Instead they're playing a game of cards. Would we like a coffee while we're here? They take turns sniffing the milk and decide we'd prefer it black. Frank, a slight figure with glasses and scarecrow hair, boils the kettle. Rhythm guitarist John Douglas washes a Killie FC mug. They've run out of biscuits so lead guitar Paul Livingston finds a bag of prawn cocktail crisps and passes it round. A tall youngster with seriously imposing eyebrows. John's younger brother Stephen, they explain, is next door setting up his drum kit so he can try out the acoustics in the hallway, along with bass player George McDaid.

So, down to business. We want them to tell us about *I've Seen Everything*. What made it different to their first album? More inventive and musically rich. And where does a bunch of lads in Kilmarnock get that kind of romance from anyway? Blank faces. An album called *I've Seen Everything*? The awkwardness breaks into hoots of laughter.

"Mebbe you got the wrong band?"

Holy shit. We're too early. Maybe they've not even started writing the songs for the album yet. Let's make our excuses

---

[6] If you lived in the Kilmarnock area and wanted a cat-sitter, by the way, Frank was your man.

and leave. Our mistake. You know—we did have lots too much to drink last night.

*

For a small town in the west of Scotland, unemployment in the Eighties was set in for the duration, something you had to get used to, like the patter of rain on the windowpanes. So there was no shortage of young people out of work, going through one government scheme or another and persuaded to join projects that would keep them off the streets. One of the schemes produced the Trashcan Sinatras: not another bluesy pub rock band from the production line, but music with its very own bittersweet sound. The Scots West Coast Delta Blues. A melting sympathy for a cold sky. Bloke poetry. Night-walking lyricism. Optimism in a pac-a-mac.

In 1986, Frank and his pal Davy Hughes joined a three month arts scheme so they could keep their dole money, with a fiver a week extra for their travel to the community centre and at the end of their stint they decided to put on a show. Davy knew the chords to 'The Lady is a Tramp', Frank sang along and the two others, without any instruments to play, smacked some spoons against rubbish bins. Coming up with a band name was easy enough after that—what did it matter? They could always change it later.

The soul of the music came from Irvine, one of the new towns built to help deal with the overcrowding in Glasgow in the Sixties along with East Kilbride and Cumbernauld.[7] A coastal town eight miles to the west of Kilmarnock, the original Irvine was an ancient sea-village and the town centre was mostly Georgian. The surrounding mass of council housing, though, could look less attractive. "It's basically a big horrible new town," said Paul in 1990. "It's boring! We've got to stay here really because our mums live here and we all still live at home."[8] Moving families out of Glasgow could sometimes export problems with them, and Irvine's acres of grey estates and high rise flats included colourful characters. Bikers, heavy metal fans, drugheads and alcoholics. Going into town could be an adventure in itself. It might be your turn to be noticed by one of the hard faces looking for fun and trouble, because they wanted a swig of your Irn-Bru, they didn't like your football shirt or the way you'd looked at them—"gadz, lookit that arsepiece"—and maybe you'd get chased down the street, maybe caught and given a slap or a kick as a reminder of who they were.[9] "It was a divided town, there always seemed to be two sides," said John. "The old Irvine families on one side and the influx of newcomers on the other. Then you had the Irish Catholics and the Scottish Protestants. All of it was background noise mostly—there'd be fights—but I wasn't subjected to anything physical myself."

---

[7] East Kilbride and Cumbernauld are names with a deeply romantic resonance for fans of Aztec Camera and Bill Forsyth's film *Gregory's Girl* (1981). What was it about those seemingly soulless new towns that led to such magic?

[8] 'Freetime' on *Weightlifting* (2004) is a song about Irvine, about having lots of that free time, but also a sense of wasted time and small and ever decreasing circles, and the need to make the most of the sparse moments of west coast delta sunshine.

[9] And not so different from any other British town of the time. Irvine has gentrified, like so many others. "Irvine (the harbour area in particular) is seen as a trendy place for all your social media influencers these days," says Craig McAllister, author of *The Perfect Reminder*.

The band members grew up in the Castlepark and Bourtreehill estates on the outskirts of town, in working-class families where earning a living meant having a trade or making stuff for one of the big employers. Doing something real. Frank and John's families were typical in that they'd moved to Irvine following the collapse of the Clyde shipbuilding industry, looking for work with local industries like ICI and Massey Ferguson. When there was work to be had, Frank's dad was a welder, his mum was a cleaner. For John's dad there were periods on the dole.

John said he was "a bit distracted" as a boy, he'd always liked to find poetry in the mundane, an alternative and a protection against the greyness of days: appreciating what's there, noticing the spirit and character of places and how they could be transformed by moods of weather and light into something more than just background scenery. "We lived on the edge of town, looking out over rolling hills. What I remember most from being a boy is the woods and the countryside," said John. Being close to those "stickleback waters" of 'Orange Fell'. And if there was one ingredient that could change the feel of anything, the meaning of the moment, it was music. Like the way *Top of the Pops* could make Thursday evenings momentous—the living room turned into a portal for space-age dreams, with the silvery glint of a drum-kit, the red and orange moons and starbursts of the spotlights, the impossible outfits of dancing girls. Even if it was only Showaddywaddy up there, the fancy dress Teddy Boys from Leicester stepping side-to-side in close formation, even those cheeky geezers were on another planet. "It must have been the early Seventies when I saw *Help!*

and *Yellow Submarine* on TV. Must have been a Beatles season or something. And I was hypnotised by it—these things that the smiling people made. I'd not got any notion I could ever make music myself, it was something to be lost in." His parents had their 'stereogram', a solid piece of furniture with a lid to hide the mechanics away, and their only records were

Cake-era John. Courtesy of Ross Mackenzie.

Ravel's *Boléro*, a Clancy Brothers LP of Irish folk/drinking songs, and a couple of singles: The Rolling Stones' '19th Nervous Breakdown', and, unforgettably, David Bowie's 'The Laughing Gnome'. Eventually John get his hands on his older brother's collection of Bob Dylan, Genesis, Thin Lizzy and Led Zeppelin.

Music was never going to be a respectable trade in itself, there were no apprenticeships or long-term security there. At 19, John headed off for London, living in bedsits and doing jobs in restaurants.

> When we were in secondary school it was the usual thing to expect to go and work for ICI, but by the fifth year everything had changed under Thatcher [the number of unemployed people in Scotland doubled between 1981 and 1983]. There was very little work, only the YTS schemes where you'd spend three months in a factory knowing there wasn't going to be a job at the end, just another three months somewhere else. I had a circle of friends who did manage to get jobs through their family, they'd go into Ayr and Glasgow to the gigs and clubs and I felt left behind. I wasn't the most social person then, it was all about what other people were doing. The ground had been swept away and left everything unpredictable, so I flung myself into the deep end of life to see what would happen in London. I didn't worry, didn't think about explaining why I was going or Mum and Dad would miss me. I just went.

Back at home, Frank had got lucky. Big sister Edna had already fought the battles over not getting a real job. "She would have to argue with my mum and dad about living a life as a busker on her way to France. She is an adventurous person, much more so than me. But when it came time for me—when I was wanting to do music and to give up my job, and my mum and dad were quite happy to let me have a shot at it because my sister had earned a gold record on the wall."

Turning into a new town helped Irvine become part of a music scene. The Irvine Development Corporation had funded the construction of the largest indoor hall in Europe, the Magnum Leisure Centre close to Irvine beach in 1976. Part swimming pool, part ice rink, cinema, sports hall and major gig venue, the Magnum was a national tourist attraction.[10] "Unbelievably, big-name bands would play Glasgow *and* Irvine on the same tour," recalled the writer Craig McAllister.[11]

> Thin Lizzy played the Apollo one night and the Magnum the next (Phil Lynott had his afro trimmed at George's at Irvine Cross). The Jam[12]—you shoulda seen the line of Vespas and Lambrettas buzzing down Bank Street and on to the Magnum! The Human League. Spandau Ballet. Madness. The Clash. The Smiths… they all played in Irvine. I grew up thinking that it was perfectly normal behaviour to leave the swimming, hair dripping wet, and, with superior knowledge of the warren-like corridors in the Magnum's underbelly, stand stage-side and

---

[10] The Magnum was demolished in 2017.

[11] plainorpan.com

[12] 1981 – £4 for a standing ticket.

watch UB40 with my pals until we were spotted and told to leave.

In Irvine, the young Trashcans—not being into Iron Maiden or the usual chart music—were the outsiders. And that meant being part of another fraternity, if only the kind that no-one would bother mentioning or even notice. They were lads with no great future lined up, no easy pathway to an apprenticeship or accountancy qualifications, a two-bed semi and kids. Maybe not on the radar as the most fanciable; not smooth posers; not the loudest jokers either. They could blend into the background of any boozer, supping their pints and smoking, hogging the jukebox—they were the outsiders who were into reading books and making music fanzines as well as beer and football, who wanted to leave home but were stuck in-between, spending nights on mates' floors.

"When I got back from London," said John, "there was suddenly this new scene in Irvine of creative, likeminded people. And by then I'd lost my shyness. We'd been too young for punk but got into the post-punk from '78 to '83, listening to John Peel and spending our pocket money on records by Joy Division, the Fall, Teardrop Explodes. Not so bluesy. Bands that had regional voices, and the new melodic guitar of people like Roddy Frame, Johnny Marr, Paul Weller and Will Sergeant [of Echo & the Bunnymen]." There wasn't going to be the chance to take a music HND let alone attend a Conservatoire. And there was no local student circuit they could plug into either. "You'd go over to Strathclyde Uni, but it was four or five pounds just to get there, then the gigs were heavily policed and you'd have to be signed in by a student. It was too much of a risk." So the education institutions of choice were Walker's record shop and the town's pubs and clubs, the Crown on the High Street, the Turf, the Ship Inn, the Volunteer Rooms, the Grange Hotel, the Redburn Centre, the King's (with its Attic venue upstairs, bands on a Friday, disco on a Saturday) and the Ingledene in Saltcoats.[13] "We went to the 'safe houses', the places where it was safe to look a bit different, to be wearing an unusual jacket or T-shirt without there being trouble." Craig McAllister saw the range of night-life first-hand.

> When we started braving the pubs as 15- or
> 16-year-olds, we'd try and fail to get into the
> grown-up Argyle and its downstairs
> 'nightclub' Amandas—a sort of big hair 'n
> suit sleeves rolled up to just below the elbows
> joint that played wall-to-wall Wet Wet Wet
> and PWL [Pete Waterman's stable of artists
> like Kylie, Jason and Rick Astley]. It was full
> of posing guys with Grolsch bottle tops on
> their Docs who eyed up the girls from our
> year at school who'd somehow done them-
> selves up to look at least 22. Every wee town
> had a place like this, but if you were into gui-
> tary music and wanted to hear it played at
> volume, it really wasn't for you. You had to
> seek out other likeminded folk in corners of

---

[13] Craig recounts the story of how the Attic turned down a gig by the Happy Mondays in 1988 because they didn't want to pay the £250 demanded.

pubs less-ventured. They were out there
somewhere. Not in The Burns though. The
Burns always seemed to have a fight on the
go just outside the front door, so that was to
be avoided.

Bit by bit, the Trashcans came together with a plan, on those
fuzzy nights in the kinds of places where making music suddenly seemed possible and however scratchy and dog-eared
the scene might look, there was a practical mechanics and a
ritual for making something out of nothing.[14] The first song
the band wrote together, naturally enough, was called
'Drunken Chorus'. The common ground between them was
Sixties' pop, The Beatles, Bacharach and David, Dusty
Springfield—mixed up with the punk spirit of Johnny Rotten
and the ingenious guitar patterns of The Smiths.[15]

By now there were a load of Ayrshire bands playing
anywhere they could plug in an amp, often sharing equipment and band members. The Stogbags. Surf Nazis. The
Hodads. Mary White Aryans. Stuffed into the corners of
pubs and dreary hotels or up on the block stage of draughty
community centres, set up for karate lessons and the local am
-dram run of *Jack and the Beanstalk*. The Trashcans turned
their amps up to eleven and dished out a noise that was the
only way to get the drinkers' attention. Some of their own

---

[14] The original band members were Frank on bass with Davy Hughes (from the Galloping Gunshot Boys) on guitar and vocals, George McDaid (guitar) and Paul Forde
(drums)—but not for long.

[15] Frank himself pointed to more eccentric influences: Richard Harris's work with
Jimmy Webb, along with albums by Dory Previn and Harper's Bizarre—all of which
are interesting pointers to the risk-taking side of the Trashcans.

songs, but then crowd-pleasers from The Clash, The Stooges, and a Velvet Underground number for the Goths hanging round the back with their pints of snakebite and black. Full of the kind of courage that only booze can give you, Frank would lose himself in the energy of songs like

Cake-era Frank. Courtesy of Ross Mackenzie.

Motörhead's 'Ace of Spades', dropping onto his knees, white with sweat, and writhe around in the muck and fag ash of the floor. Frank was the constant factor in the band, with the determination and the intensity to make the Trashcans happen, but also the member with the least confidence. In the early years he was never sure about this voice, he didn't like the sound of it, whether it was howling The Cult's 'Love Removal Machine' (*"bay-be baybe baybe baybe bay-bee"*), or singing something softer from their own repertoire. And that made those live performances in front of disinterested punters a battle between nerves and desire. A torture made possible by being among friends, the friends who knew Frank's voice was an essential part of their Delta Blues. As John said, Frank was a good example of how hard it was for someone Scottish and working-class to blow their own trumpet. At the same time, Frank was a fighter, he knew how to face up to lukewarm audiences and deal with the hecklers. "You're a knob," a wag called out one night. "Hey—that's Mister Knob to you," responded Frank.

The first time John was invited along by Frank to play for the Trashcans the venue was a tea room, where he was asked to strum the chords to the Velvet's 'Sweet Jane'. "I didn't get a guitar until I was 19," said John. "I would check out different gigs at night [in London] and spend all of my money on records. That eventually inspired me to buy a guitar. I quickly learned some chords and I became very interested in writing songs rather than becoming a guitar virtuoso." Besides trying out his own material he'd been helping out local Irvine legends, the Galloping Gunshot Boys, with their drum machine.

The arrival of Paul in 1987 altered the band's assessment of themselves, and the real work began. "It was strictly an amateurish affair until Paul joined… He was a mean guitar player," according to John. "We thought, fuck who's this?" Paul sounded like the next Frame-o. He'd been taking lessons since he was eight years-old from a "really cool teacher at school", learning to play Harry Chapman and Simon & Garfunkel songs and playing in a school group that went out to old people's homes. But his guitar heroes were Judas Priest, Iron Maiden, Black Sabbath, Led Zeppelin. "I was really into Robert Fripp [of King Crimson], but as time went on I realised Heavy Metal just wasn't cool and I found Johnny Marr of the Smiths." Paul was in a local band, the Shock Club, when he went over to Castlepark Community Centre to see the Trashcans play: "Someone had said they were a jazzy band, and I thought that sounded terrible." But the chemistry between Paul and the rest of the band was already there in a raw form, somehow, in their shared affinity for the possibilities of melody that became stronger and more binding as more songs were written—falling out of the Irvine aether.

*

With his job at Sirocco, Frank knew about making demos and the ways of record labels. Sending a cassette tape to Andy Macdonald, the boss at Go! Discs, led to a meeting in London, some good chats and gigs opening up for Stephen Duffy's Lilac Time in Edinburgh and Dundee. A deal was eventually sealed by 'Obscurity Knocks': proof that the Trashcans could write hooks, a whole giddy procession of them in a single song. The timing was just right—a year later and it's unlikely the Trashcans would have been picked up by a label so easily, and they wouldn't have received the money for Shabby Road. In 1987 it was still possible for raw talent (or "clueless teenagers" as John later put it) to be taken seriously. There was money for taking risks on indie as long as there was also a glimmer of chart potential, and to some ears, the Trashcans were a prettier Smiths or Stone Roses (especially with the involvement of the Roses' producer John Leckie with the first album, *Cake*). Even with such an unfinished band, Andy had recognised a core quality that was

more important than being able to follow a commercial formula: they meant it.

> I look for pure artists who are driven to ex-
> press something that they feel deeply, and I
> try to create an environment where they can
> really do that. As a songwriter, the moment
> you get a commercial reward, you start writ-
> ing to someone else's pace; it gets a little bit
> out of shape. I think if you want your artists
> to make really lasting work, you've got to al-
> low them to (a) empty all that emotion out
> into their work, and then (b) live life again, to
> gain more experience and [feel] the emotions
> that come from that. Essentially, music is an
> emotional language that connects people,
> and we all do well to remember that.[16]

Not everyone in the local scene was pleased for them.
"There were two camps in Irvine," said Craig. "One camp
would never say so outright, but they were a bit green-eyed
over the Trashcans getting signed—'second-rate Smiths', 'it
should've been us,' and all of that—and another camp who
delighted in seeing local musicians – their pals—'making it'.
I loved the fact that the Trashcans had landed a record deal.
It was obvious they were gifted, lyrically as well as musically,
and it showed that bands from our neck of the woods could

---

[16] Go! Discs was set up in 1983 by the former press officer at one the original punk
labels, Stiff Records. Andy Macdonald's first signing was Billy Bragg, followed by The
Housemartins, The La's and Paul Weller. He resigned when the label was taken over by
PolyGram.

prick the ears of the tastemakers and hip-shakers in London." The Trashcans got to spend almost three years assembling the ten songs of *Cake* at Shabby Road[17]. Which explains the cream-layered sound that resulted, the added strings, keyboards and piano that comes with free studio time.[18] There could be just one more thing, one more dusting of atmosphere. The album was quietly well-received when it was released in June 1990. The melodies were obviously a treat, the lyrics were playful and clever (if maybe a bit self-consciously so). But *Cake* was like a supreme version of an indie guitar music that was now considered old hat. Where was the snag-tooth guitar and crunchy dance beat? The album eventually found its audience in the US where college radio stations were still nostalgic about indie's golden era, The Smiths, REM and Echo and the Bunnymen. *Cake* was a natural accompaniment, and sold five times more copies in the US than the UK.[19] Leaving the studio for the bigger promotional gigs for the album exposed their lack of experience when it came to dealing with the oddness and unreality of being a recognisable band with ads in the *NME*. They were "twitchy as a bunch of four year-olds on the first night of their school nativity play…" reported *Record Mirror*. "But their honey-dripping, Aztec Camera-influenced pop oozes maturity and confidence far exceeding their tender

---

[17] There were sessions in other studios — Wessex in North London (where *Never Mind the Bollocks, Here's the Sex Pistols* was recorded), and Eden in West London, where producer/engineer Roger Béchirian had worked with Elvis Costello, Squeeze, Nick Lowe and the Undertones.

[18] The contributors included Frank's old boss from Sirocco, Clark Sorley on piano.

[19] *Cake* reached 74 in the UK top 40 album chart, 131 in the US Billboard top 200. The vinyl re-issue of *Cake* by Last Night in Glasgow finally entered the UK top 44 in 2023.

years… conjuring up pictures of a broken-hearted bloke staying in bed forever rather than facing the big, bad world outside. The bashful Trash Cans share their heartaches in half a dozen golden tunes, before disappearing with as little ceremony as humanly possible." The touring included spending most of the month of October travelling round the UK as the support act for the Sprouts and *Jordan*.[20] It took a visit from their new A&R man, Cathal Smyth—better-known as Chas Smash of Madness—who'd been sent up by Go! Discs to persuade the Trashcans to go on a US tour at the end of the year. All the fuss didn't seem right for a little Ayrshire band. They took the flight, but kept on saying "no" to the stretch limos, the meet-and-greets with bigwigs and distributors, as well as the circuit of TV and radio appear-ances. Meanwhile, something clicked in the US—whether it had been just a matter of time or the sight of big American crowds getting excited about the shivering opening chords to 'Obscurity Knocks'—but the band found its way to play, its own persona. Other hyped British bands had never really "connected" live before, said the *Los Angeles Times* (singling out The Sundays as one example), following the Trashcan's night at Club Lingerie on Sunset Boulevard.

Lead singer Frank Read [sic], a skinny kid who looks like he could be Michelle

---

[20] The Trashcans never got to meet Paddy. At one point during their soundcheck a door at the back of the stage opened and they saw a silhouette of a man in his hat and overcoat. Paddy stood and listened for a while before the door slowly closed again. But when he sang 'Hey Manhattan' on tour, Paddy would change the lyrics to give his sup-port band a nod: "Hey Manhattan—here I am! Call me star-struck Uncle Sam / Strolling Fifth Avenue / Just to think, the Trashcans have been here too."

Shocked's younger brother, is a natural. It was hard to pick out many words through his burr, but with spontaneous-seeming movements and gestures he illustrated the emotions of the songs—mostly tender, wistful and wondering—creating drama without dramatics. He was communicating with the members of the audience, not just performing for them.

As a debut, for all its moments of greatness, *Cake* hadn't turned out the way the Trashcans wanted. "*Cake* had not been universally well received by any stretch of the imagination, and you tend to focus on the negatives," admitted Frank. "It wasn't good enough. Not what we'd set out to make. It was just so piecemeal with too many versions of songs and a lot of debate about what we were using in the studio. We felt we can't do that again." Whisked away from the Attic in Irvine by an influx of record label money, they didn't necessarily know who they were, or where they fitted inside the indie guitar scene anymore. So *Cake* is sometimes tainted by its eagerness to please, by a perky pop sound. The reviews kept talking about them as a bit Smiths, a bit Aztec Camera, but also influenced by the Go! Discs mould of the La's and the Beautiful South. Consequently, the period leading up to the making of *I've Seen Everything* was messy—and the doubts were affecting the songwriting: "We had five new songs and only two were worthy of being B-sides at best." They had no manager to fight their corner. And Frank was conscious of his sister's problems with her record label and their insistence that she stick to a formula (just do a 'Perfect

#2'). The band photo on the inner sleeve of *Cake* was a tell-tale sign of that moment in time: a generic image of blow-dried, consumer-friendly indie.

The West Coast Delta Blues was always there, only straightened up and temporarily tidy for its first outing. Not rock music or pop music or traditional indie either. More civilised and musical than the Postcard bands, and tinged with a romanticism that would have been out of place on anything by Morrissey or Paul Heaton. Where did that golden-grey sunlight sound come from? Maybe the beach at Irvine Bay. An unglamorous stretch of wet sand and pebble beach next to the harbour car park and the Pilot House, a four storey tower block built in 1906 for signalling to ships. On warm evenings after the pub, the lads would retreat to the open stretch of sands away from town centre hassle, gather driftwood and make fires. They'd talk music, football and girls and watch the fading light over the Isle of Arran and its mountains, the "sleeping giant" in the sea. With no neighbours to bother they could shout and bawl and sing. The bay was a place with a spirit that seems to come through in the songs. An airy, bracing feel. A surprising softness to cold waters. Guitars like the silvered movements of the sea, the surfaces lifting and crimping in gentle rhythms, wrinkling and breaking. Or sometimes thicker, like the sound of the tide dumping itself onto the shore and moving through the shingle. A sense of reflection in the music that's evocative of irresistible, hypnotising views across the sea. Because they are songs infused with coastal skies, the sight of passing islands of clouds and distant cliffs and hills tinted with a bloom of orange; and as the hours pass, there are the more subtle and obscure colours of sunset, where the blue turns pale with the green of evening.

As Pete Paphides wrote, even from a journalist's swivel chair in the fluorescence of a London office it was possible to sense the "graphite ganache rainclouds" and "a sweet melancholy spray". The Trashcans were able to "alchemise the ineffable magic of silent nights in small towns into not just lyrics but music too", because they weren't just any old group of lads sharing out cans on the beach, but that fraternity of outsiders able to see the poetry. Not really poetry in any formal, literary sense, but the spirit of things and the sensations they can lead to. Patterns of feelings that seem to come together and have a single thread between them. A kind of truth that no microscope could ever see or algorithm ever imitate.

*

Sarah puts on a record.

Her old bedroom at 112 Simpson, with its sun-faded zig-zag curtains, is full of boxes of pet food so the door won't open ("My office and my HQ," Dad had said to her with a wink. "You could be my secretary. I'm in a recession-proof industry you know. You can't starve Tiddles."). So she's ended up moving into Adrian's room instead.

Adrian's vinyl collection was still on a bookshelf next to his Roy of the Rovers *annuals. She'd been hoping to find a porn mag hidden in there too, or a 12-inch of Johnny Hates Jazz. The records weren't organised in alphabetical order either, more by type—there was a big lump of Eighties stuff she'd not heard for a while, with their scuffed and broken corners and their smell of old cardboard.*

Sarah feels like a kid, lying on the bed because there's nowhere else to go. In a world that's shrunk. But it makes her feel safe to be there. A quietness and sense of time passing slowly she'd not known since she'd been a teenager. Like the feeling she'd have at the beginning of the long school holiday, thinking about all the TV she'd watch, the picnics, the trip away to a caravan, going to the social club and drinking cokes and eating crisps. But this was now. Her bags of stuff in a corner were still there in the corner ready for the next place to live. The crockery she'd collected for years before she'd moved out, her interview suit on a hangar. Her life in Safeway bags.

The record was jangling, the singer warbling low. They took the music seriously in those days didn't they. Like they thought they were Albert Camus or something, sitting in a café next to a rainy window, making up art.

Funny what playing old records made you remember. A holiday when they'd gone to Wales when it was still the four of them. They'd been stuck in a caravan playing Monopoly all afternoon because Adrian wouldn't go to the beach and no-one wanted to visit the museum. It was so boring, and she'd decided there and then she'd never have holidays like that when she was older, not like that, not with family. She told them exactly that, out loud, and not in her head. They'd had fish and chips without her, the Welsh fish and chips with the curry sauce on, and made her sit in the tiny room on her own. She could still picture the bunk bed, the puzzle book and tin of travel sweets in powder they'd bought her for the holiday. On her lap next to the blond hairs of her knees.

The past hadn't seemed to matter much before.

*

The five albums are an expression of ordinary voices, and how something can be made from nothing. Folk music from bedsit-land, about the struggle to make money out of the system, to be recognised and heard; with dreams and desires that come from behind the moon. In the past, it would have been possible to talk about them as a product of working-class culture (with no music degrees, connections or funding from wealthy parents to ease the way to stardom, just the songs). But by 1990 there was beginning to be no such thing as a working-class culture in Britain.[21] The sense of identity among the working-classes had been a vivid force in society as recently as the Sixties and Seventies. 'Common' people might not have had much money, but they had other currency, their own kinds of jobs and streets to live in, the frowzy pubs where they'd drink together, their chats over cups of sugary tea, their own kind of values and humour and lingo, their healthy, bred-in-the-bone scepticism (rather than cynicism), when it came to royalty, big business and the nobs, who were more likely to be the subject of music hall songs and jokes than unthinking reverence. But as we've seen, that shared culture had been disintegrated by the drive towards standardisation. Most of all, people needed to be consumers—competing consumers that would be economic players believing themselves to be free and classless. Housing was one example. If you wanted a home, you needed to forget about belonging to a local community and take your chances with the market. More than 1.5 million council houses had been sold off by 1990, and the estimated number

---

[21] Most obviously in England, but also in Scotland, Wales and Northern Ireland in spite of their areas of stronger community and family bonds.

of homeless in Britain had surged to around 500,000.[22] If you had nothing to spend, then really you had nothing to say, even nothing worthwhile to think or do. In the new knowledge economy, people without specific skills and qualifications had only a low value. But unemployment had stopped being such a dangerous political issue, even when levels climbed back up to 9.7% (higher than in the year of nationwide riots in 1981). Trade Unions were weak and out of fashion, representing only around a third of the nation's workforce. Self-employment had grown by 57% over the course of the Eighties, as a consequence of the push for proactive enterprise over dependency on settled jobs. But for low-to-middle-income entrepreneurs that only meant chronic insecurity as the banks became tougher on loans and repayments during the period of boom and bust.

The traditional working-class institution of the local pub—the neighbourhood centre, canteen, cabaret, market stall, clinic and front room all rolled into one—wasn't making enough money to satisfy business owners and investors. Between 1990 and 1992, the National Licensed Victuallers Association lost around half of its 15,000 members and was dissolved. Even fish and chips, the cheap staple of the British working classes for a century, had officially become a 'luxury food' and made subject to VAT. Anything 'uneconomic', whatever was too small or out of step with market conditions, whether that was a grocer's shop, a traditional manufacturer, a café, theatre, library, school, a burger van or a bingo or whist night, was being replaced by whatever was

---

[22] Or 'cashed in'. The great sell-off meant a one-time bonus for the Treasury of around £20 billion.

found to be more financially viable, and that meant many changes to the British way of life.

The takeover of land and property rights by the wealthy has been a gradual process over modern times, propelled by ideas of 'progress', from the Eighteenth and Nineteenth century Enclosure Acts that allowed landowners to claim ownership of 'common' land for agriculture, to the more recent boom in 'gentrification' and 'urban re-development'. The early Nineties was a golden age of publicly-funded development corporations and regeneration schemes that transformed the grunge of inner cities—the derelict factories and dirty canals—into attractive, waterside residential areas with cycle paths and grassy tree-lined avenues. A shoo-in opportunity for property developers to become very rich. But re-development for who? The existing residents themselves were priced out, unable to afford rents or even the kinds of prices charged by the local boutique cafés, bars and comedy clubs. The most fortunate would sell their property and end up in an anonymous suburb with a costly commute to their low-paid job. The least fortunate had to stick around as an increasingly alien life form.

What had also been happening, insidiously, over the course of the century, had been the enclosure of culture. There'd been an end to anything that was independent and identifiably working-class. Beliefs and attitudes had been subsumed within a classless culture dominated by big business and its stakeholders. As a way of limiting the risk of cultural trespassing, the working-class poor were kept in their place and vilified throughout the Nineties. There were the first references to 'chavs' and reinforcement in tabloid newspapers, piece-by-piece, of the myth of a low-income population that was work-shy and sponging. A land of single mothers and errant fathers. Stupid people. Drunk. Violent. Racist. The working-class poor had nothing to offer anymore, no principles or politics, and were really just after money like everyone else—a mindset epitomised by Harry Enfield's *nouveau riche* plasterer Loadsamoney: "Shut your mairf and look at my wad!" (who also once said: "That Mrs Thatcher, she's done a lot of good for this country… Mind you—I wouldn't shag it.") Working-class protest had evaporated from the mainstream culture and turned a fashionable classless pose, proletarian and matey. No working-class culture meant a shortage of independent thinking outside of liberal middle-class norms (where, naturally, careers and consumption came first), with nowhere for lower-income people to work out their own truth and beliefs, express what was real, what mattered and what didn't; along with the removal of their sense of control, agency and responsibility. An identity replaced by cheap shopping, a bottle of Lambrusco and *Blind Date*. There was a new sense of hopelessness, especially among the white working-classes that lacked any other cultural identity or community to be part of. Inner-city GP and social commentator Theodore Dalrymple observed in the Nineties how "having worked in several countries of the so-called Third World, and having travelled extensively through all the continents, [he was] convinced that the poverty of spirit to be found in any English slum is the worst to be found anywhere."

The rise of middle-class culture is very recent and there are relatively few British people whose psyche doesn't contain a working-class foundation, who wouldn't feel a twinge of sympathy for those lives spent in small homes, packed tightly with emotion, the nights of chippy teas. Think about the TV sitcom *Only Fools and Horses*. The further that working-class world receded into the distance, the more affection the nation seemed to have for Del and Rodney Trotter. When it first aired in 1981, it looked like a Seventies relic to an audience caught up in the mood of aspiration, swooning over *To the Manor Born* and *Brideshead Revisited*. By the Nineties, *Only Fools* had become the most popular TV programme of the era, not only because it was funny—there were other, sharper comedies around—but because it was charged with nostalgia for a lost way of life, depicting how working-class ways were bumping up against a new and improved modern world (Del Boy with his executive raincoat and Filofax, having a go at Trivial Pursuit).

Unusually for such a long-running sitcom, every word of *Only Fools* was written by one person, John Sullivan. He'd grown up in Balham, the son of an Irish father who'd worked as a plumber, and hung round with the market stallholders of Peckham. Mum did occasional shifts as a charlady. John himself became a second-hand car salesman and scenery shifter at the BBC before trying his hand at scriptwriting. The premise and the storylines were like fingers plucking at some of Britain's most taut emotional strings: social aspirations and prejudices but also repressed insecurities, doubts and regrets. In *Only Fools* there was no need to be smart or sophisticated. You didn't need a 2.1 degree or a proper career, or even any taste. A little bit of cash here and there was enough for a good night down The Nag's Head and a Ruby Murray. In other words, you didn't have to be a member of a middle-class that was so tense with competition and anxious for security. The Trotter existence was far more human, in its own sloppy kind of way. They were open about their emotions, even if that meant being obviously selfish or angry or petty. At least the emotions were genuine and on the surface; quite different from the cool restraint, the irony and manufactured enthusiasm that were becoming part of the expected modern way. Best of all, there was a community. In the markets, the pubs, waiting for the lift in the tower block, the Trotters had easy, natural friendships everywhere, among the same people they'd known from school days. Nobody going anywhere much. They'd take the piss and expect the piss to be taken out of them—without silent, account-taking resentment.

From the first to the last episode, the arc of the plot was similar to that of this book: it was about growing up, people moving on and struggling to find their place in the world. Underneath the flashy banter and dodgy schemes, the flat in Nelson Mandela House was a desolate setting, with its hooky gear and tat. The Trotters were a tragedy waiting to happen. They were members of an underclass trying to get by on bullshit and fry-ups. Del left to bring up his dopey younger brother, never able to get married, smoking and drinking his way to a heart attack. Grandad sitting in front of the telly all day then making something horrible for their tea. Living in an inner city wilderness, outside of the system, cut off from welfare benefits and living hand to mouth in a way that, until the final series, lacked the sanity and steadying influence of women.

Over time, *Only Fools* also acted as a record of social change, not least in the way Del Boy and Rodney switched their sheepskin coat and bomber jacket for suits and stripy shirts, the new uniform of business. The gentrification of British culture was something to laugh at. Like Del Boy asking for a bottle of Beaujolais Nouveau—"a '79"—in the trendy new wine bar. Mike, the landlord at the Nag's Head, handing a plate of "beef stew" to Denzil for a pound and then handing a plate of the same to a chinless yuppy for £2.50 with an ingratiating smile, "your boeuf bourguignon, sir". Uncle Albert tries to go back to the area where he was born in the busy East End docks, but finds a locked panorama of emptiness and exclusivity. The streets around Tobacco Road have been replaced by a new development of waterside apartments.[23] When the Trotters encounter the world of 'official' business, like the Top Buys Superstore, they meet with corruption and hypocrisy.[24] Even aspiring yuppy Del gets tired of business fads: "This 'ands-on management lark really gives me the 'ump." Rodney's marriage falls apart because Cassandra is relentlessly ambitious when it comes to her career at the bank, hosting dinner parties and spending her evenings at bank networking events. The impressive modern flat they try to share together, so different from the scuzz and flotsam of Nelson Mandela House, is a hollow shell.

---

[23] The scene from 'He Ain't Heavy, He's My Uncle' (1991) was filmed at Shadwell basin where a small two-bedroom flat now costs around £600,000. Coincidentally, the basin was the backdrop for an interview with Cathal Coughlan for the BBC4 Microdisney documentary in 2023 (he was living in nearby Limehouse at the time. Check out Cathal's lyrics to 'The Ghost of Limehouse Cut' on *Black River Falls* about the new breed of East End schemers: "To the east side of the city you can bring all life's mistakes... I'm a ghost, I don't exist, I wandered off and I was not missed.")

[24] The episode 'The Longest Night' (1986), where the store manager arranges for a young small-time criminal to stage a robbery (to pay off the debts stacked up from his wife's spending habits), was based on a true story.

The point here is that ordinary, unfiltered voices have become scarce. We've been worlded-over. By messaging and commercial demands for attention; and maybe there's a need to listen harder for what's authentic.

The making of *I've Seen Everything* itself raised questions about authenticity. Beginning with the enforced choice of recording studio: The Mill, a converted watermill on a backwater of the Thames that was once considered to be one of the finest studios in the world. The house had been converted in the late 1970s to create the state-of-the-art mixing lab needed to turn Elton's John's bestsellers into quadraphonic vinyl.[25] Rather than boarded and plastered for a crisp modern look, the studio desks and equipment stayed alongside the original wooden beams, exposed brickwork, chandeliers and panels of stained glass. A bridge over a weir in the gardens connected the house to a private island with residential bedrooms. Then the choice of producer: Steve Lillywhite. A big post-punk name famous for developing the sound of Peter Gabriel, U2 and Simple Minds. "We really liked the work he'd done with XTC and The Smiths, he had a good attitude to drums and guitar and vocals—making them warm and present, there was space and a big sound," said John. Steve had just come from another Go! job with

---

[25] The studio, also known as The Sol, was the work of Gus Dudgeon, a producer whose credits included Elton John's 'Your Song', David Bowie's 'Space Oddity' and Chris Rea's 'Fool If You Think It's Over'. The Mill was sold to Jimmy Page in 1980 and eventually became Chris Rea's home until it was sold again in 2006. The Mill was never named explicitly in studio credits—on LPs by Elton John, Chris Rea, Wishbone Ash, Bill Wyman, Ellie Brooks, Lindisfarne etc—because of local planning regulations.

the La's.[26] And finally, the choice of location: the English rural idyll of Cookham. An out-of-the-way, out-of-time village, known mostly as the home of artist Stanley Spencer and the setting for his curious Biblical fantasy paintings. Spencer had described it as "a village in Heaven". There was certainly something uncanny about the place when the Trashcans arrived in Cookham in the summer of 1991 to start recording their 'difficult' second album. Sleepy cottages in hot sunshine, the willow tree seeds drifting through the country scene like summer snow. Unpacking their bags and looking about the place they would have remembered that the Mill had been the home of Jimmy Page, the man with a collection of memorabilia relating to the arch-Satanist Aleister Crowley. Who could say what dark rites had been practised in that creepy old house in the middle of deepest rural England?

The Trashcans never really believed Steve Lillywhite would want to work with them—they suspected he must owe Go Discs! a favour—and they were right. Lillywhite was looking to move into A&R and producing a young Ayrshire band wasn't his priority. He hadn't wanted to travel up to Kilmarnock either. "He was really expensive 'cos he was a name producer and then he says, 'I stopped producing bands ages ago.' He was just like an engineer!" complained drummer Stephen. "I just don't remember him being that interested in what we were trying to do," added Frank. There weren't enough complete songs for an album anyhow, they

---

[26] Todd Rundgren had been the band's first choice. Go Discs! were willing to pay the $75,000 fee, but the band knew that amount of money was going to put huge pressure on record sales, and also weren't keen on Rundgren's demand that he should have control over the final tracks used.

knew that. So they mucked about. Took drugs. Did some paddling in the river. Fell into a state of giggly fatalism. Tried things out as a distraction from the dead-end they knew they were heading for: like Frank running on the spot while singing, or being attached to a long, straggling tail of home-made mic so he could sing while cycling up and down a country lane; or getting the band to do some early morning recording in the garden with tambourines. "There was a lot of silliness. A LOT of silliness," Frank admitted. But no great feeling of inspiration. The Mill sessions led to five re-corded songs, three of which were eventually re-worked for the album.[27] But when it came to mixing the tracks in Lon-don, Lillywhite stopped turning up. He'd done his bit. And then bass player George McDaid decided it was time to go (it felt like he'd already seen everything), and left to start his de-gree at the University of Aberdeen.

As it turned out, the answer to the sudden lack of dir-ection was back up the M8, in Kilmarnock and Shabby Road. "Shabby Road was our anchor. It's hard to imagine what we'd have done without it, we were so entranced by music it took over lives, we would have needed to be hiring space all the time," according to John. So the Trashcans didn't benefit from the industry's attempt at a leg-up, the in-vestment strategy, but needed the authenticity and feelings of confidence that came from being at home. Lads doing their stuff together rather than being fed into the premium-meat sausage-maker. "When a record label says go to some coun-try house and have free food and drink and record music it's

---

[27] 'I've Seen Everything', 'Killing the Cabinet' and 'Orange Fell'. 'Say' and 'Kangaroo Court' became B-sides.

hard to say no," explained John. "Especially when our levels of confidence weren't great, we knew we weren't ready to make another record. Steve had been very complimentary about songs like 'Orange Fell' and that was good for us, but the place was just too opulent—and we knew that the bill was going to end up on our tab. It's great to think that wee guys from council estates did that: we walked away and said fuck it. To us, Steve Lillywhite was just another dude in the room."

In their own way, each of the five albums was an attempt to sidestep or transcend the mainstream consensus and the agendas that had shaped it. As Cathal put it:

> The middle class have always been seen as patrons of the arts… Their 'likes' create the standards that we're supposed to live up to—that you can put a very small amount of money into a record and get a hit automatically because the figurehead they employ to deliver it will be perfect right down the line, with no kinks, no particular wants of its own and everyone is laughing all the way to the bank. If that's what the standard is, then pretty soon the human race won't be up to much.

There are varieties of old working-class non-conformism going on. Both defiance and perversity in how The Sundays refused to have a music career and preferred their back bedroom to the studio; Cathal's sulphurous music hall theatre; the old-fashioned values of the Sprouts; Peter's dogged attachment to the romance of evenings in spite of it all. The Trashcans themselves are a good example of the importance of community over outright individualism, as a co-operative with a common interest and a common good in mind. As they've always said, they have been a group, not a band. Early on, Eddi described them as being "dudes, all very much in cahoots, a wee gang… The five of them would come and stay with me whenever they were in London. They'd turn up in their van, drink and smoke me out of house and home and then leave again." They stayed together through hard times because they were "a collective of people… [whose] priority has always been to make music that they find interesting," according to David Scott of BBC Radio Scotland's *Classic Scottish Albums*. And that included everyone involved with Shabby Road, like Iain Wilson, the driver of the "wee red van", the occasional mix tape controller and manager of the merch stall, an all-round stalwart of operations. In the press release for *I've Seen Everything*, Paul said: "I think we're always going to be doing this. Even if everybody started hating us and our record company chucked us off, we'd still write songs and make records for ourselves." So it was only natural that when George left the band, the Trashcans would turn to a friend, Davy Hughes, one of Frank's earliest collaborators (strumming guitars together back in the Youth Training Scheme days) with the black glossy hair, the chin and the grin of a canny centre-forward—and who was much more than just a bass player. "He was an amazing songwriter and we'd always loved his shtick. We assumed he'd never want to join our band again," said Frank. Having been the lead signer with the Irvine legend that was the Galloping Gunshot Boys, Davy had kept his aura as the mystery man who could deliver the X factor, the one who always knew what new bands to listen to next, what films to see and books to read. "To have Davy involved felt like a stamp of approval from some effortlessly cool icon," recalled John.

The making of the album—take two—began with Frank, Davy, Paul and John living in adjacent first-floor flats in Fullarton Street in Kilmarnock.[28] "The rent was cheap and as we were nighthawks making noise we thought it'd be a good idea." It's now summer 1992. "John and Paul's flat was the more social place," said Davy. "Playing John's board games, watching and re-watching John's videos—the punk classic *D.O.A* and The Only Ones documentary were well worn." They'd argue over whose turn it was fetch the rolls from the shop in the morning or the sandwiches, and have to play a game of cards to settle it. They'd spend the morning sitting in their flat windows, letting in the sunlight and watching the world go by on the street, a terrace of red sandstone Victorian villas, milk bottles on doorsteps, mums pushing prams. When they weren't at Shabby Road (a mile's walk away) or tinkering with bits of tunes and lyrics, there were poker nights and TV. *Inspector Morse* was a favourite. Along with *Boys from the Blackstuff*, even a bit of *Brookside* now and again. Or they'd trying to catch old episodes of Frank's favourite, *Columbo*.[29] The flats would swap VHS tapes and

---

[28] Mostly. John moved around, and shared for a while with his girlfriend Allison Thomson, who played trumpet on the album.

[29] Like on 'The Hairy Years' where the "detective is descending". Classic Seventies TV could be a thing. The A-side of the 1993 vinyl release of *I've Seen* was inscribed with "Hail Mary, Mungo and Midge".

books between them. John was into the poetry of Yeats and Dylan Thomas at the time, and with the recommendations from Davy there'd be an exchange of copies of Kurt Vonnegut, James Kelman and Alasdair Gray. They would play *Sensible Soccer* on the Amiga. One of the highlights of the summer was jumping around at the sight of Graham Taylor's dismal England side getting knocked out of Euro '92 by Sweden. Regular trips were made to the Hunting Lodge, mostly on Mondays, Tuesdays and Wednesdays, when they could get a seat and concentrate on their drinking. "Fridays and Saturdays in there were too rowdy. We were proper drinkers—after hours they'd fill jugs with beer for you rather than having to buy cans." The Lodge also had a pop quiz machine that would fund the drinks and crisps (they'd often win the £20 jackpot because the final round was always the Beatles and the Rolling Stones, and Frank and Paul were the masters). Sometimes they'd stay in town at the Paris Match "where there was a whole different crowd".[30]

There was a special feeling about that summer, homely but other-worldly, like the dusty blue over familiar rooftops after a day of Mediterranean heat. They didn't just have to deliver an album for their label anymore, they were on a mission to dig into a vein of reality and the poignancy there: "searching for whatever gave it the 'hing," explained John. "You know... the 'hing.. the shiver up the spine, the nail on the head... the magic." They wrote the songs and lyrics as a collective, with no single member claiming ownership of any

[30] Not what you'd expect to find in the upstairs space of an old warehouse building in Kilmarnock: a recreation of a Paris café with candles in wine bottles, a black and white chequered floor, a red Citroen 2CV (with a mannequin at the wheel) and a tandem bicycle on the ceiling.

372

one song.[31] "The songs were made from being in the same room as each other, sitting round and someone plays something, someone sings, and the rest of us say that's good, we like that bit but maybe change that." And as Pete Paphides has written, it shows.

> *ISE* was the record where you could no longer discern the stitchwork that joined one band member's material to another. Trashcan Sinatras songs seemed to grow in a shared safe space where Romantic young men honour the unspoken pact they made to live a life of poetry rather than profit, but would nonetheless rather they didn't have to choose.

There were practical reasons too. "We didn't have serious girlfriends or girlfriend commitments, no big responsibilities, so we could focus our whole lives on these things. We were at gigs or writing music or recording—reaching for something," John explained.[32] "There's no-one in this band that has confidence in themselves," Frank had said in 1993. "We need each others' support. That way, even if one of us is happy, it doesn't mean that the rest of us are happy too. There's no-

---

[31] For a full account of how each track on the album came together, there's Craig McAllister's excellent book, *The Perfect Reminder: The Story of Trashcan Sinatras' I've Seen Everything*.

[32] For part of the writing and recording period of the album, John was living in another flat on the same street with Allison Thomson, a nurse: "She played trumpet with bands and understood the life of a musician." Allison contributed the trumpet on 'I've Seen Everything'.

Magic combo: Paul and John. Courtesy of Ross Mackenzie.

one who has exactly the same ideas or opinions as you, so you can't predict how the songs will turn out." It was what they called the "pigs trough" approach. Pour out a bag of ideas and then everyone gets to stick their snout in. Songs would be at different stages, from almost there and needing some tweaks to just being scraps, a single lyric or chord pattern. The new producer for the Shabby Road sessions, Ray Shulman, would encourage them to sit together in a circle on the floor (once the carpets had been hoovered) to play their acoustic guitars as a way of bringing songs together, or try out different kinds of percussion, like the pots of water on 'Worked a Miracle'. With Paul on lead guitar and John on rhythm, the pair had jammed enough to reach a new phase in their interplay, and the often glistening, wind and wave textures are a feature of subsequent recordings.

Wordplay was part of the fun, especially among Frank and John, both fans of the Herald newspaper's Wee Stinker cryptic crosswords.[33] When they got writer's block it was Ray who suggested the William Burroughs' cut and paste approach: everybody would find a magazine, brochure or book, open a random page and see what came up. The line "Hello, I'm Harry" at the start of 'Hayfever' was from a headline torn out of the *Herald* newspaper. "It's not as arbitrary as it sounds, you're guided all the way along by your choices, what interests you and catches your eye. We had this hat with scraps of paper in and we'd pull something out—someone might sing a melody to the words, pick out what had six or eight syllables, whatever fitted. One time we suddenly had a song about a guy we knew."

The bits and pieces came together. "The song writing is a many faced affair; arguments ensue, huffs are taken, it all blows over," was John's description. "Among the debris lie songs—songs strong enough, to our ears, to make the whole debacle worthwhile." Importantly, they shared a common sense of what they liked: "a good feel, unusual chord changes, something a bit off-kilter, impressionistic." 'Hayfever', the first new song after the Cookham period, started out with just Paul's piano line and became known as 'The Madness One'.[34] Before the Burroughs lyrics were used, they would sing the line "I'm not a Pandora" from a Kate Bush

---

[33] The Wee Stinker inspired the working title for 'I'm Immortal', which had been known as 'Nil-Nil Firhill'; itself a joke about the number of goalless draws at Partick Thistle FC's home ground. One of Billy Connolly's routines included the line that for years people thought the real name of the team he supported was actually 'Partick Thistle Nil'.

[34] Mike Barson of Madness was lined up to play the piano on 'Hayfever' but missed his flight.

song over the top.[35] Paul also had a guitar-driven song known as 'Peter Frampton' that turned into 'Bloodrush' via Frank's idea for lyrics. 'The Hairy Years' was bolted together from a Frank song and a John song. Both the title track 'I've Seen Everything' and 'Worked a Miracle' had been hanging around in the trough for a while, but needed more work.[36] As the lead singer (and someone who confessed to being "bossy") it was accepted that Frank should have the final tick of approval. "I always over-focused… but I like to think my obsessing over the small bits helped to make it that bit more interesting."

The result is lavish. There are so many musical layers and notions working on each track that Frank is only just able to interject with his vocals to make sure the full story's being told. "*I've Seen Everything* is a very cerebral album," says David Scott. "It's very ideas-based. It drips in music." The details, contrary to the cliché, contain much of what's angelic about the album. There's the guitar line behind the second verse of 'Orange Fell' that's been put through a Leslie speaker (with a rotor blade that produces tremolo) and then played backwards for a dreamily wonky effect. Faintly, in the background can be heard the haunting sounds of a music box, sampled and then freshly recreated. Davy's bubbly piece of bassline in 'I'm Immortal'. The nursery-rhyme round at the end of 'The Hairy Years'; the chime of nostalgia for lost

---

[35] From 'Suspended in Gaffa' on *The Dreaming* (1982): "I won't open boxes / That I am told not to / I'm not a Pandora / I'm much more like / That girl in the mirror between you and me."

[36] 'I've Seen Everything' was written when the band was first experimenting with the mixing desk they'd bought at Shabby Road, and was due to be on the B-side to the 'Circling the Circumference' single.

times that comes from the handmade guitar effects (some matchsticks stuck onto the strings). Using an Eventide Harmonizer gadget and its 'Crystal Echoes' effect on 'Iceberg' to produce the brooding arctic atmosphere, set alongside Frank's "weird" backing track vocals that were made from learning how to sing his backwards versions forwards.[37] Knocking over a guitar to add some extra lumber to the opening crash of 'One at a Time'.

Throughout there are the vocal combinations between Frank and John that make for unexpected harmonies, appearing from somewhere outside the lines of melody. And different kinds of voices. Like the duet between Davy and Frank on 'One at a Time' that recreates the pished-up macho of Irvine street-corners. "None of it was planned. Me and Frank serenaded each other for a few takes; random shouts, barks, a spontaneous yelping rap at one point, and Ray compiled everything together."

There was such a comfortable working routine in place —helped by the summer of felicity in Fullarton Street—that one of the finest songs on the album was written in a single evening. Davy's lyrics for 'Send for Henny' were already there, but the exquisite melodies came together after the day's recording work was over. The extraordinary feel of the track was augmented by Frank's edgy, mood-cranking synth sounds, and sweetened by the backing vocals of his sister.[38]

There were even extras planned for the album that didn't happen. Frank had written to the Scots poet and mu-

---

[37] As used by the Edge of U2, Johnny Marr and Brian Eno.

[38] Eddi was heavily pregnant at the time. "My heart was broken as my marriage had just ended and although I knew I still wanted to make records, I didn't know where I was going or what I was doing."

sician Ivor Cutler, c/o BBC, to see if he'd play harmonium on 'I've Seen Everything'. Ivor made the effort to write back personally and explain why he wasn't able to do it. "For maybe a year, we had the A5 glossy black and white promo pic of Ivor, his reply to Frank, stuck on the top of the dashboard facing the windscreen on the red van," said the Trashcan's driver Iain Wilson. The ending to 'Orange Fell' was due to be a fragment of 'Somewhere over the Rainbow' taken from a recording Davy and Paul had made after the pub one night on the piano (following the sheet music, using one hand each), but the rights were going to be prohibitively expensive.

I've Seen Everything is the band's only album where they worked with the same producer all the way through. It was curated by Ray—the same man who'd known when to keep in the background with The Sundays, quietly keeping a hand on the tiller of Harriet and Dave's personal journey and its grey wake; but then also willing and able to jump on deck and take charge. He was a calm and jovial presence who'd fix deadlines and give the Trashcans the advice and inspiration in order to meet them. "Working with Ray was one of the best things about the album," said John. "He'd keep finding ways to finish songs in a magical kind of way. A song like 'Hayfever' was a lot of jigsaw pieces for a long time, we knew there was something, but just couldn't get the right start or a finish. 'Killing the Cabinet' was the same. Ray would say: do this, do that, go and finish it."

Ray's family came from Glasgow but he and his two older brothers were brought up in Portsmouth. There was a musical lineage. His father was a musician in an army band who went on to play jazz trumpet professionally, and all three sons were multi-instrumentalists, comfortable playing anything rigged with strings. The plan was for Ray to join the National Youth Orchestra of Great Britain, but instead he stuck with his brothers as a member of the R&B band Simon Dupree & the Big Sound,[39] and then, from 1970, the prog-rockers Gentle Giant. Compared with peers like Yes and Genesis, Gentle Giant were at the obsessive-intellectual end of the prog spectrum, weaving freeform jazz and medieval choral music into their soul and blues. Never the easiest way to build a fan base. The sleeve notes to their album *Acquiring the Taste* (1971) set out their uncompromising mantra: "It is our goal to expand the frontiers of contemporary music at the risk of being very unpopular. We have recorded each composition with the one thought—that it should be unique, adventurous and fascinating." In spite of this (or maybe because of it), Gentle Giant had a large cult following by the time they split in 1980. Ray went on to write music for TV and advertising (including ads for Nike Air Jordan trainers and Budweiser in the US) before making a detour into production. "I met a guy who was working at a studio I used for my commercials [Derek Birkett of One Little Indian]. He wanted to start his own label, and I already had an interest in alternative music. I became house producer for the bands he signed [such as the Sugarcubes and A.R. Kane]."

The Trashcans hadn't heard of Gentle Giant but they knew Ray had worked on "grand-sounding records we were really into" [like Ian McCulloch's *Candleland* (1992)]. That

---

[39] For a few months, during a tour of Scotland, the Big Sound's keyboard player was Reg Dwight. Dudley Moore also played piano on a couple of Dupree sessions.

combination of sophisticated musical brain and indie experience—backed up by his wing-man and in-house engineer,
the joint-rolling Larry Primrose—made Ray the master.[40]
He had the authority to give direction and make fun of anyone taking themselves too seriously. "He just changed
everything," said Paul. "He'd say, 'That song just doesn't
work, get the acoustic guitars in there, don't do that bit,
that's pish.'" Summer days with a raspberry ripple feel. "It
was the experience we wanted—a producer comes in who
you love and you really want to make happy, so everybody's
smiling and the sun's shining and the ice-cream flows. It was
just great, a joy to make," sighed Frank. "I remember walking in the rain down Old Kent Road in London where we
were mixing it, and feeling really light on my feet. It was a
great time in my life. The harmony in the band was lovely to
experience." One of the first suggested names for the album
was *Chemistry*.[41]

*

*Cramming a prawn sandwich into his mouth with one hand, checking
his watch with the other, Adrian has things to do. He's equipped with
briefcase, suit and, for once, has a clear and urgent sense of purpose.*

---

[40] "Larry the engineer smoked hash 24/7," according to Davy. "Consequently so did
everyone else. Except me of course." Ray worked Mondays to Fridays at Shabby, driving in from the more sedate surroundings of Troon, and went home to London for the
weekends.

[41] Nirvana had started a trend with first single 'Smells Like Teen Spirit' where the last
word of the track was used to name "Nevermind". "Chemistry" was the last word of
the first single 'Hayfever'. Another suggestion was *Spooktime*, to reflect the vespertine feel
of much of the album. But, as the label pointed out, the term 'spook' would have had
negative connotations in the US.

The empty days had gone. Even his hair's combed and standing to attention.

He's waiting, poised, at Euston station and staring at the information board with the other workers. But was he like the others? Manual workers and secretaries mostly. The bloke in front of him with the Evening Standard *looks like he needs a nap. This was what the graduate fast-track felt like: the snap, pop and crackle of monthly performance targets and an individual personal development plan. And Oliver, the regional manager, had mentioned that an executive MBA was included in the firm's development strategy. How'd that sound?*

Adrian keeps his eyes on the board so he can move quickly, secure a seat and get on with preparing his report for the meeting. Duncan would be there, the other fast-tracker. Duncan the boffin with his hairy fingers. An Oxford graduate (a fact that was mentioned at every client meeting they attended, every bloody time).

Again, the signs roll and flutter and flick over: Cancelled. No-one moves. The staring continues. Cancelled. The casual check of watches. A shuffle of feet. The man with the Evening Standard *makes a noise like Eeyore.*

Adrian moves towards the row of phone booths. All he can think of is the look of the meeting room back at the office without him in it. Duncan would be there, schmoozing like a pro. What was it really like at Oxford? the admin assistant would ask him again. Nicola. The one who's always crawling to Duncan as part of her mission to get a consultant's job. Not like Adrian, says Nicola (who should really be answering the phone or opening post rather than chatting)—he went to an Institute of Higher Education. A what? says Oliver, grinning, eating biscuits. Oh, him. Couldn't even make it back for the account meeting.

Last quid in the slot.

"AP Consulting, how can I help you?"

It's Nicola.

"Hello—it's Adrian."

"I'm sorry, it's who?"

"It's ADRIAN."

She put 'Adrain' on memos.

"Oh. Hello."

"My train's cancelled. Can you tell Oliver —"

"Sorry, you're what?"

Sweat prickles around his shirt collar.

"I won't BE BACK, LET OLIVER—"

"Hmm. Can't hear him."

A click and a dialling tone.

He'd stay late, then go in early the next morning.

Looking through the station doors to the outside, he could see people sitting on the grass in the late autumn sunshine. There were little groups of them lying on jumpers and coats, sharing cans of drink and chocolate.

*

On *Cake,* the band had suddenly felt their youth was behind them. "I'm old—not wise, just worried." There they were, bachelor lads still living at home when their old pals were getting serious about work, about getting married, and more interested in a new satellite dish and saving for a holiday to Crete than going to gigs. They'd succumbed to a sense that the best years of simple excitements had already gone—the pain that twenty-somethings can feel at the passing of a very recent history. The songs of *I've Seen Everything* deal with the sticks and stones of how it feels to try and cling to Romance in an unromantic world. Was it even possible in the disenchanted Nineties? especially given the urgency of success and security as the only 'normal'. As we've seen, the message was inescapable and imperative.

But we do our own thing. We're still wild. Oddly singular. In a letter, the German Romantic philosopher Goethe wrote: "My dear friend, all theory is grey. Life's golden tree alone is green." In other words, direct experience always beats what's mediated, the noise of a media that tells us what's real (material success and failure), and consequently, what we should be (good consumers). We tend to think there's only one kind of language we share, describing the obvious, when there are lots of different kinds of languages just in terms of what we see and feel for ourselves; in the music of moments: the early morning bus station, a friend wanting to talk, roads shining wet after rain, an evening twilight descending over town, the sound of children playing. Which is why, in spite of the bombardment, we reject conformity and grey theory and recognise other sympathies. A further honesty. And, because of that, it's still possible to breathe and live in the confined spaces in-between the grinding cogs and spinning wheels of a world ruled by business and commerce. Under that light of common day, to the sound of ticking clocks and the pressure of mortality, Romantics continue to see a wider vista, an untouched innocence. They're starting fresh every day because nothing stays the same anyway.

It's what we've found again and again in the five albums and their street-level view of the early Nineties. And nowhere more distinctly than in the Trashcans' *I've Seen Everything* and its stories of a faltering progress into adulthood. "I know for a fact that the climate we're writing about is not unique to Irvine," argued John in 1990. "People all over the world go through that life. They go to school, it's crap and they get fucked off with it, they go and do shit jobs and get fucked off with that, then they go and sit on the dole for a few years." The end of familiar routines and not seeing friends anymore. Leaving home. Knowing nothing's going to be easy again, that freedom comes loaded with limitations and loneliness. Sadness and ennui. It's all there in the album's sleeve art: the bare room, the single bed, the candle.[42] Not so much a home as a temporary lock-up. "We had an idea of the album having a kind of darkness to it. It was almost like having a duvet thrown over it and we were underneath." And inside the album cover, a room with a single armchair, an ashtray and a burning cigarette. A portable electric fire, a bottle of booze perched on the TV.[43] But there's also a view to Irvine Bay and the stars—because the Romance is always there for those willing to see it—and sometimes there was nothing more needed than that in itself.

The artwork was taken from John's oil paintings of his rooms in Fullarton Street, which had been painted on the back of a Cornflakes packet. When he was in London he began to draw a picture of each of the bedsits he lived in, and the habit continued on his return to Irvine. "I had these lovely oil paints and the cover was the first painting I'd done.

---

[42] The candle isn't as innocent as it looks. John had left the bedroom candle burning one night when he'd come back to his room drunk, and woke up to find the bedside table on fire and the place full of smoke.

[43] In the original CD version the room's ceiling was a flap with postcards of the artwork inside. The image on the CD and the vinyl record label of the moon was taken from a picture on a lamp bought at Camden Market (which belonged to John's girlfriend at the time, Allison).

When the guys were stuck about what to do with the cover I showed it to them, and they thought it suited the mood of the songs." The occupant of those lonely-looking rooms is there with us—in that human shadow, the fag still lit—looking at where they've come to, the time in their life and all they haven't got. Thinking they're old. But at the same time sharply aware, for that moment at least, of the beauty of things.

There's a distinctly Romantic—and Scottish—masculinity about the album.[44] But it's still a mystery as to exactly what it is, and how it's come about. John has pointed to some of the potential ingredients: an empathy and warmth towards people, "there was a real community in Glasgow in the Fifties and Sixties, the place where social housing began. There was a saying in Govan, 'we are the people people', because there was no-one above you and no-one below, you'll sit down with a king and with a tramp, and that goes down the generations and into the books and TV and songs —being socially-minded." And this open-handedness was mixed with a feeling for the landscapes of Scotland. "There's a romance in the look of places. The sunsets on the west coast in Irvine are glorious, you're looking over the water to Arran, and after that it's America. In Scotland there's a sense of being at the end of the world. And that means a mixture of hope and sadness and beauty." That brand of Scots mas-

---

[44] Not that well-suited to a critical review by *Beavis and Butthead*. The US label hoped the single 'Hayfever' would be another 'Obscurity Knocks' and were happy for any kind of publicity. One of the *Beavis* show's researchers had been a college student when *Cake* was popular and arranged the slot. "This is just another bunch of British mamas' boys [concluded *B&B*]. Everybody talks like a wuss." "Yeh yeh, where is Britain?" "I think it's somewhere near England, somewhere everybody talks like a wuss." "Yeh, yeh, [with an attempt at an English accent] '*I believe I will go spank my monkey*'."

culinity is there in Frank's vocals and its note of vulnerability. Anything firmer, any drawling or macho rock-ness, would have destroyed the sound—Frank's voice is just right, because it also avoids a resemblance to the sound of so many C86 bands and what could be anonymous, lightweight vocals. And that certain variety of masculinity is also in the lyrics, which are glimpses of the personal, their own lives and those of people they knew and "their little ways": "we were attempting to be literate, poetic, impressionistic, evocative, intelligent… all the qualities we liked in other songs."

There are scenes of displacement. Like on 'Easy Read', inspired by Paul being turned away from the indie disco at the Attic for being too drunk: "Nobody wants me here at all"; the feeling of being like lost property, because the "biggest trade on earth is lost and found"; and in the football player who knows they're never going to be picked again on 'I'm Immortal'. They keep trying new roles and identities that might give them a sense of purpose—they've "read the script", "donned the uniform", "seen the rehearsing"—but nothing's working: "my understudy's eye grew tired". So you have to turn to whoever's left there for you, which might only be a voice on the end of a telephone ("Sometimes at night he'll phone me, he's lonely"; "Want to stop you feeling this way… Want to stop you feeling a waste of time"; because there was always the danger of someone losing the plot, running off the road by "putting [their] foot down and closing [their] eyes").

When it comes to relationships the boys take a defensive stance, there's a jokey self-deprecation because they don't want the rejection: "I'm happy alone". They're not trying to be the romantic leads, they're "sniffing, romancing and scaring the crows", turning up on the bus with their "homemade present" and "cheapskating over buying the ring". For a moment they become Kilmarnock's own Bacharach and David when Frank sings "I've had women, I've had germs… [they're] seductive in small doses".[45] But pain, they know, is a part of the disease and you could only treat the symptoms: "Why can't we take a couple of tablets?" Love is a confusing thing that comes with misunderstandings and mistakes. "I forget the conversation we had / I don't remember what you said or did / That made you so attractive… / The perfect reminder." If love was ever going to feel straightforward or pure, then it was only going to happen when they were on their own, as an emotion "recollected in tranquility". 'Orange Fell' was a product of John's walks home across Irvine on summer nights. "Going out at nine or ten pm, then coming home at four am and the look of the orange streetlights, the constant colour in the air."[46] The colour of first love.

The album ends up being like a dog-eared scrapbook, made from mementoes of ordinary days. One of the qualities the band liked about Shabby Road was its location in the thick of town life. "There was a buzz around of everyday lives, people going to work, doing their shopping over the road, and that focuses you as well. We soaked all of that up," John pointed out. But there was also a sense of nothing

---

[45] As per the song 'I'll Never Fall in Love Again' and the opening lines, "What do you get when you kiss a girl? You get enough germs to catch pneumonia / and when you do, she'll never phone-ya".

[46] Not an experience that can be recreated as the streetlights in Irvine are now all LED rather than sodium. There's also a connection to the blue waters of *Jordan* in there, via the town's River Garnock (the "stickleback waters") and the mention of Elvis's backing group the Jordanaires.

much happening at all. "Lyrically, we still had our lives of unemployment pretty fresh in our collective memories and, sadly, that is always relevant subject matter." Life could be like an iceberg: cold and austere. The "natural course" of every day was a kind of nothingness, with a "glacial pace", and could be populated by big bad wolf characters who were best avoided: "I'm gonna blow your house down, dynamite your cabbage town / Shit kicked derelict, no one at home." The scrapbook also includes a piece torn from a newspaper about the Brighton hotel bombing of 1984 in 'Killing the Cabinet'.

Underneath, it's sentimental, and sentimental in a way that maybe only lads approaching their thirties could make it. As Frank has suggested, many of the songs are "valedictory". A goodbye to youth, to the familiar streets and places, to the uncomplicated camaraderie: "we're leaving here". "Here's to all of us"—so cheers, and goodnight. Maybe catch you later, in another life. That nostalgia is nowhere more plangent than on 'The Hairy Years' and John's story of lost innocence. John was brought up in an Irish Catholic household, where mum would take them to Mass every Sunday as well as the occasional confession. Even if the dogma and stuffiness of the routine didn't appeal to the boy, there was something that did. "Before I started questioning things, life was very clear. There was God and forgiveness. You'd go to confession, say you'd been swearing or having thoughts that weren't for someone my age; do your penance and you felt cleansed. You were on the good side, feel all's okay." The hairy years began when John was on holiday with his family at Butlins in Ayr when he was around nine-years-old. He'd saved the usual 50p for spending money but when it came to the end of the holiday he had nothing left for buying a gift for his Gran. He ended up stealing her something from the site shop, a little bird with the holiday camp name on it. "It felt like a real life shift from everything I knew and had been taught, an independent action, secrecy, guilt, but also… success." A complicated taste of freedom. A complexity that would only grow with time, an angst that lingers in the background of the album: the importance of truth and goodness as principles, but how difficult they can be when it comes to choices in the immediate moment.

*

"The Trash Cans knocked out a skipload of songs of suicide, shoplifting and sex," announced the Go! Discs press release for *I've Seen Everything*. But you can never really trust the press release, especially when the alliteration has been more important than the truth, and there's such a desperate need to signal some Nineties cool. If *Cake* had managed to catch the tail-end of affection for jangle-pop, the follow-up had turned up too late to the party, the booze was all gone, there was crap all over the floor and a drunk couple were groping in the corner. In Britain, the baggies were out of fashion and bands like Suede, Blur and the Manic Street Preachers were now the flagship sound of mainstream indie. In the US, the college radio playlists had been taken over by Nirvana and Soundgarden. Worrying about melody and lyrics was for musos only. So *I've Seen Everything* was a "bit too old-fashioned for 1993," concluded *Melody Maker*, "awfully low on the sort of obvious excitement we regular indie-rock consumers are conditioned to expect… built from baroque acoustic guitar flourishes, hushed voices and downbeat, fragile sentiments… you need a hell of lot of patience to get through all the aggravating precious bits to the little glimmers of gold." The album's sensitivity, both to the mood of the times and to that particular phase in their twenty-something lives, was written off as "terribly world-weary and defeatist". The *NME* didn't even start to try and appreciate the album on its own terms, only as an echo from a past age.

> There have been worse bands in the mould of Trashcan Sinatras. The Bluebells for one, and look what happened to them. So go easy on this lot. Back, after two and a half years, and still, unsurprisingly, lagging at the back with Aztec Camera and Prefab Sprout. There's the same world weary crooning ('I've Seen Everything'? Gimme strength!), the same thesaurus robbery…even as you eagerly search for a reincarnation a la Deacon U2, something always tells you that behind such incendiary titles there'll always be some heart-string guitars and a winsome lyric about life's injustices… The single 'Hayfever' is an absolute peach, a sad afternoon love song halfway between Foreigner's 'Cold As Ice' (honest) and Madness' 'Embarrassment'… Having been away so long, the Trashcans have marginalised themselves without having built ups following to

sustain them… Not the final curtain, but the
end may well be near. 5/10.

The quality of the work resonated with music writers who
weren't so slavish when it came to the latest fads, who made
comparisons with The Beatles and XTC. As would be expected, *Q* magazine was one of them (awarding four out of five
stars): "It's possible they're going about this too quietly, but,
30 months on from their enticing debut, *Cake*, the Sinatras
are much the same band, just a bit better at everything.
Their most engaging songs ('Easy Read', 'Send for Henny'
and 'Earlies') follow the sweet-melancholy voice of Frank
Reader through thickets of *Smiley Smile*-ish whimsical harmony and a cyclic guitar jangling that's solemn and repetit-
ive but right." Pete Paphides was willing to swim against the
tide in a *Melody Maker* piece. "[The song 'I've Seen
Everything] is 36 radiant things all at once; a heartbreak-
ingly world-weary exclamation of despair, a pang-of-wonder
at the seemingly unnecessary emotional shit we put ourselves
through all because, at the end of the day, we love being with
people, 32 pangs of forlorn hope that tomorrow might be a
bit better, Norm from *Cheers*, every Bill Forsyth film ever and
all the things I thought acoustic guitars were no longer capable of doing."[47] And the greater the remove from the machinations of the British indie press, the more clear-sighted the
response of critics seemed to be. Like the *Santa Cruz Sentinel*
in the US that heard "luscious, flowing pop"; the *Morning
Call* recognised the album had "greater depth than you'd

---

[47] Pete did, however, finish his review of the single with the line: "Sadly the B-side's
shit." ('Houseproud' and 'I'm the One Who Fainted'.)

expect from just jangly guitars." While in Australia the *Sydney Morning Herald* concluded the album was "inspired".

In an age of in-yer-face, commercial indie rock, there was a general feeling, though, that the Trashcans weren't playing the game. Even among the polite Japanese. "After the interview I thought that, for better or for worse, they are an indie band. They are free and do whatever they like," wrote Shizuoka Wada after meeting them during the Japanese tour of late 1993. "They just want to be liked by the people who understand them, which I think is quite an indie stance. I think it's an ideal situation for the artist, but I think they are a little too deep inside their own little world. I found them to be friendly and likeable guys, but I just wanted to tell them to try harder and become something bigger and better. I'm sure people who understand them will get angry at me for writing this, but maybe that's the problem." Wistful British indie was too quaint to survive.[48]

Here began what would become known as the "indoor years". Short of money, the band camped out at Shabby Road together, sharing their resources and jamming. Relations with Go! Discs were becoming overwork and thin— although they would always be grateful to Andy Macdonald for giving them their chance. Worse, the label was bought up by PolyGram (what later became Universal) and that meant bringing in the accountants to take a long hard look at the books, closely followed by inspectors from the Inland Revenue. There were debts that needing paying to the label and

---

[48] *I've Seen Everything* didn't make the top 40 album charts in the UK, or the Billboard top 100 in the US, and Go! Discs decided not to go ahead with the planned schedule of single releases (which meant that collectors didn't ever get to complete the anchor symbol planned for the row of CD spines).

some massive unpaid tax bills. The band was bankrupt—and in an even more threatening development, each individual member was made personally liable for paying back the money owed. What had looked like a glittering showbiz career, was exposed for what it actually was (at least from the finance perspective) as a series of investments that had gone wrong. There had been risks involved, but almost entirely for the ones who'd put their talent and dedication into the venture. There were "unconfirmed reports of vulture sightings in the Ayrshire skies," wrote John. Shabby Road had to be sold in 1999. They stood and watched as the clearance gang dumped their hard-earned equipment and gear into a skip (although they did at least manage to save Angela).[49] "I just saw Paul's enthusiastic face, Frank laughing," said John of that moment, going on to make a link with the feelings of sadness and loss that had come with the closing of the Clydebank shipyards in the Eighties. "It was the place where we'd built big ships that were then sent out into the world." With no incentive to record or perform, the group disintegrated into individuals ("scattered to the winds, we wandered the wilderness alone"). John went to London and busked in the underpasses (there was "great reverb") near to Hyde Park Corner and Marble Arch, and took a secret pleasure from taking money from the suited passers-by, some of which would have come from the nearby Inland Revenue offices. Paul volunteered to be the one to represent the Trashcans when their case was heard at the Ayr Sheriff Court. Sense

---

[49] Sold to the "man at a local school who used to come in and repair it", "he treats it with great love".

393

prevailed: the judge decided they had been punished enough.

It wasn't until 2003 that the group began working together again, and they have continued to be a group (not a band) ever since; remarkably, as the only surviving group of all the ten of *Like Magic* and *Behind the Moon*. Bands fall out (musical differences), they want to try out new ventures, they're encouraged by managers to go solo, or get tired of the cycle of work and promotions. The Trashcans remain, and it's partly, it has to be said, because of technology. One positive consequence of Internet communications and social media has been the coming together of fans of cultish bands and forgotten heroes. The love for the Trashcans was rekindled and given a platform, a little community and outlet for expression. The mustering of support convinced the band to self-finance future releases and tours, as well as make use of crowdfunding, side-stepping the business processes that would have left them, again, at the mercy of finance departments.[50] They've stayed together because they've always had songs they wanted to hear played, another project to at least try to finish. And moments continue to resonate. The ideas and melodies keep coming. And while they're now geographically divided, with Frank and Paul living in the US,

---

[50] When the planned release of the *Wild Pendulum* album was announced in 2014, fans signed up to bid for guitar lessons and to be read a bedtime story, among other creative funding options.

and John and Stephen in Glasgow, they're friends.[51] "We were really special to each other without really admitting it to ourselves," said Frank (being about as heartfelt as a bloke could be in public about their friends). "Even if I didn't see them every day, I was happy that they were near me." The song 'Got Carried Away' on the first comeback Trashcans album *Weightlifting* (2004), seems to sum up the kind of patience and forgiveness that was needed for real, long-term friendship and collaboration ("You told me go easy, got carried away…told me everything would be all right… I love you and I know you'll do better—next time.")[52] And as a group they still haven't got over the thrill of creation. The special thrill of being working-class lads, self-taught in everything they do, and somehow able to make a connection with a wider world of listeners.

"There's always been a kind of motif in our music… that it's about the collective," said Frank. "We've retained that spark and slow-burning desire to be sophisticated even if we never quite achieve it. We're all old punks and we have that kind of clunkiness but we're still trying to make everything sparkle like a little Gold Star Studios diamond."[53]

---

[51] Frank has lived in Pasadena, California since 2008 with his wife, a schoolteacher. Paul has been living in Tacoma, a city south of Seattle in Washington state, still close to the sea and the views from Poverty Bay. Davy lives in Kilmarnock. John married Frank's sister Eddi in 2003. "With the missus, I get to be musical with her and share in her onstage world. She has an old-school jazz approach and is very improvisational, set lists are non existent and you never know what's coming next. That is such a joy to be part of. It keeps you on your toes and creates magical unplanned moments."

[52] Featuring the guest backing vocals of Norman Blake. Teenage Fanclub were in the studio at the same time.

[53] Gold Star was where Phil Spector developed his 'Wall of Sound' and parts of the Beach Boys' *Pet Sounds* were recorded, as well as material by Bob Dylan, The Righteous Brothers, Leonard Cohen, Ike and Tina Turner, Jimi Hendrix, Neil Young etc.

Click

*T*he end of the world was nigh, or looked as if it could well be. Every through route and by-road connected to the A1 in Hertfordshire was at a standstill, broiling with queues of traffic. Half the country seemed to have lost its mind, packed up and got on the road. The drivers shared a single obsession between them: how they were going to reach a Tudor manor house and its rolling green parklands in time for the biggest music event ever held in Britain, the hottest gig of that or any other summer.

Estimates suggest up to 15 per cent of the British population tried to get tickets to see Oasis at Knebworth House in August 1996.[54] Even with the limited Nineties telephone technology, 250,000 tickets were sold out in nine hours (today it would have taken less than five minutes). The Gallagher brothers had done the maths and realised they'd

---

[54] Makes sense, considering that by 1996 nearly half of British households had a copy of either *Definitely Maybe* (1994) or *What's the Story Morning Glory* (1995).

have to do dozens of shows at their usual venues to meet demand. So instead they concluded they'd do: "two fucking big gigs at Knebworth." Looking back twenty years later, Liam said: "Without sounding like an arrogant cunt, I wasn't surprised Knebworth happened that quickly. I knew we were going to be massive."

How did he know? Oasis were a pub rock band from Manchester; a traditional guitar, bass and drums combo who played likeable, sing-a-long anthems that tapped into the myth of the Sixties, when we had the Beatles and the Stones and Britain was swinging and prosperous; a sound they mixed with the fuzz of Seventies' glam. The Nineties version came with a new twist of attitude, a (fuck you) laddism. Oasis had the right image at the right time, the moment when the music industry was desperate for a new package that could disrupt the dynamic of slow decline. 1995 had been the year of drastic price cuts in singles and an expansion in the range of available formats, CD, cassette and vinyl—to make the sales figures look better and add to the sense of a successful bandwagon. The marketing of Britpop and Cool Britannia (based around the idea that if a message is repeated often enough people will start believing it) coincided with a reaction against the years of cultural doldrums. There'd been signs of a deep-rooted longing for something to matter, for something to share in common, to belong to. We loved the big news, the big event.[55] So Oasis, suddenly, looked perfect. A great product because they went down like a cold pint of

---

[55] Like the death of Princess Diana in 1997. Three million people decided to travel to London's royal parks the day after Diana's funeral, with no other purpose than to make a public demonstration of their grief over the death of someone who'd lived in a very separate and highly privileged universe.

Stella, hardly touching the tastebuds: they were classless (everyone know they were the sort of geezers who'd stop and have a beer); they had no beliefs or politics (other than things to say about the cunts who intruded on their personal paradise); an unchallenging musical formula; and songs that repeated the value of being (fuck you) cool, full of emotionless emotion and unsentimental sentiment.[56] The masses at Knebworth waved their flags and sang along to every word, feeling more and more choked. Liam wandered to the front of the stage and looked about at the phenomenon he'd helped to create. "We've been away for three months picking our noses and scratching our bottoms, and it's good to see youse all 'avin it… youse is all bonkers, all youse is off yer fuckin tits!"

Not everyone could stomach what Cathal called the "hideous spectacles and pageants of Britpop". "I was nauseated by it, and I wasn't a fan of any of it at the time," agreed Frank. "It's just lazy to drape a flag around you and think that you're making a statement." Paddy wasn't much tempted by the branding either. "I couldn't… no. It wasn't me. I couldn't believe *that* was passing itself off as something grown from the roots of Lennon and McCartney. The Beatles weren't like that." Whatever the rights and wrongs of the fad—and most music fans would agree there was plenty that was good along with the hyped mediocrity—Britpop had proved, again, that marketing and awareness mattered more than substance or individuality. You could get mass

---

[56] The claims that Oasis could sometimes be sub-Beatles imitators turned out to have something in them. Beatles parodists the Rutles successfully sued Liam and Noel for copying one of their songs for 'Whatever'.

buy-in as long as the business and marketing operations were strong, there was a comfortable brand and an offering that suited an artless kind of age.

New Labour's election victory in 1997 was itself a demonstration of that model: the transformation of a political party that had shed inconvenient beliefs and adopted a business-like approach to improve awareness and achieve a result. Not a socialist alternative to the Tories anymore, according to writer Peter Baynham, but a "media-friendly, highly electable platoon of smiling thugs."[57] New Labour's action plan had been based around domination of mass media channels through 'story management'. Blair and a hand-picked team had flown to Australia to pitch to Rupert Murdoch in 1995 and got him on-side. A 'rebuttal unit' was set up around a database of media articles and speeches (known as 'Excalibur') that was used to respond instantly to Conservative party statements. It was the equivalent of a matey arm round the shoulder for hard-pressed journalists looking for facts and quotes (and who didn't want to be shouted at by Alistair Campbell).

Even an exercise in "good works", the National Lottery, was an example of how marketing noise could win over truth. In its first year of operation, 1994, ticket sales topped £4.3 billion. The majority of the adult population became regular players in the belief that their money would go towards funding local community projects around the country. The scale of the money pouring in attracted the attention of powerful groups, which led directly to "an elaborate exercise in misinformation". Only around 7% of National Lottery

---

[57] The co-creator and writer of *I'm Alan Partridge* (1997).

awards went to small projects, those looking for less than £100,000. Of the total raised in 1996, the poorest and most densely populated regions of the nation received just 15% of the National Lottery funds for improvement projects. The great bulk of the money went to schemes like Lord Rothschild's National Heritage Memorial Fund to support the repair of stately homes occupied by wealthy families, to the Royal Opera House and the Tate Gallery.

*

This book has tried to understand five remarkable musical creations in the context of history, and by thinking about the less considered chemistry that happens between people and their blooms of lived experience, memories and ideas. A constantly changing weather of influences and counter-influences. And how, in turn, we respond to that music and it becomes part of our experience of seeing and thinking. Whether that's at the time or decades later. It's only been a rough sketch, trying to suggest what might have been happening rather than a definitive account. Material to think with. An attempt to shift perspectives out of a rut.

Like Magic in the Streets was about one special moment in time and its teenage soundtrack. *Behind the Moon* has explored the next chapter: growing up while also trying to find a way to stay above the waters of expediency. The common thread is the argument that music could mean something. That it relates to our intuitive sense of what might lie beyond the mechanics of getting and spending; that there might be a poetry at the heart of the most ordinary of things. And those thoughts we used to have, maybe they weren't just an adolescent phase of pretension.[58] Not just a dross that slopped about inside us before rationality had time to build a hard crust and the glue to hold us together. Those romantic years included signals and intimations of something important. There were plenty of excesses—the *Smash Hits* posters on the wall, the crushes, the stickers on exercise books and evenings spent copying out lyrics—but we knew there was something meaningful, somewhere, just outside our range of comprehension. But when we were younger we could be more open-eyed and open-hearted, not simply more gullible. More human even.

In *The Matter with Things: Our Brains, Our Delusions and the Unmaking of the World* (2021), the polymath Iain McGilchrist, a neuroscientist, philosopher and literary scholar, has set out a monumental argument for why Western societies are struggling.[59]

> At the core of the contemporary world is the reductionist view that we are—nature is—the earth is—'nothing but' a bundle of senseless particles, pointlessly, helplessly, mindlessly, colliding in a predictable fashion, whose existence is purely material, and whose only

---

[58] And by 'adolescence' I would include the twenty-somethings who have been our focus. Anglo-US culture might insist on adolescence ending at 18—because that's when we can start working full-time etc—but in continental Europe there has been a more thoughtful and realistic attitude that has seen adolescence lasting until people are in their mid-twenties.

[59] In a more receptive age, McGilchrist's book would be lauded as 'important' in the same way that Sigmund Freud's *The Interpretation of Dreams*, Oswald Spengler's *The Decline of the West*, Mary Wollstonecraft's *The Vindication of the Rights of Woman* and *The Communist Manifesto* of Marx and Engels were.

value is utility… Not only is it mistaken, I
believe, but actively damaging—physically to
the natural world; and psychologically, mor-
ally and spiritually to ourselves as part of that
world. It endangers everything that we value.

McGilchrist has explained in extraordinary detail how we
have come to understand and build a civilisation around the
workings of the left hemisphere of the brain that deals only
in material facts and what can be fixed and enumerated; the
part of the brain that struggles with understanding the world
as a whole and how to relate to it—in other words, it doesn't
bother with what anything means or whether it has value,
anything that might be called beauty. Reality is only ever a
bunch of stuff and processes.

So being an independent thinker is crucial. Being a
bad poet is better than no poet at all. Because the only real
wealth we have has nothing to do with bank balances or
stock options, not even the number of friends we have on
social media, but the truth and the good we find in the world
for ourselves. So what you love matters. The rest is only con-
tingent dazzle, dust and noise.

*

Tony, head of digital at Patter Media plc, is ready for the
call.

Marcia, his hotline to the industry buzz in New York,
has some big news for him. But he's going to keep her waiting at least ten minutes so she doesn't think this is going to be

a regular thing, Zooming him in the evening just because it suits her schedule better.

Tony plays with his Nespresso selection and makes himself a San Marino Lungo. Dark roast. He's got the Mac-Book ready, checked his hair in the mirror (distinguished grey with silver fox highlights), and decides to shut the Venetian blinds with his remote control. It would be a nice part of town, next to the Thames footpath, if it wasn't for the social housing. The kids were a constant distraction when he was trying to work at home, circling round down there on their bikes, kicking footballs. And then there was the little twat in a denim jacket with a boombox, sitting on the wall outside Tesco Express playing his music in the evenings like he was living in the Eighties. Sometimes you could hear it squawk through the triple-glaze.

Tony drinks his coffee down to the end and replaces the little Italian cup into its saucer. He sighs and clicks the Zoom icon.

"Tony! Tony! Hey, I'm so excited I'm not even going to ask you about your sex life."

Marcia's grin, teeth like a horse, takes up most of the screen. He resists the urge to flinch at her sudden appearance.

"So what I've got to tell you must be exciting huh? But listen, Tony—like I said—we have guys in Beijing, and they're doing stuff with our guys in Cali you won't believe. You've got to move fast if you want it—I mean fast, with the branding, the marketing. It needs—"

"Hello Marcia. Yes, sure. It's kind of late here, and it's been a busy one. What can I do for you, digital queen?"

Marcia's looking more like a yoga teacher every time he sees her. Or the leader of a kombucha-drinking cult. Whatever happened to the make-up, the power suits and gin cocktails?

"Yeah, look," she says. "I'm not gonna talk, because I don't need to."

The window splits into two and a box of green blobs appears with the words ALGAE-RHYTHM.

"See it?"

Tony could hear the denim twat starting to play his tapes outside. Status Quo probably. Not right for a public place, this wasn't Kettering town centre after all.

"Er—yes."

"See this, it's bleeding-edge AI. The future of music. Finally, music is in the hands of the fans and not some losers with musical differences. And it's going to be a goldmine."

"Looks like blobs."

"Huh. Yeah. I've got something specially for you Tony, you're gonna love this. You remember *Indie Baby*, hell, you remember, that Nineties thing? Look at this."

An album-shaped cover appears. It's an expressionist painting of hellfire with a man in a white cloak and cap riding a pony, his long mouth shrieking. There's writing: The Fatima Mansions. *Put That in Your Pope and Smike It.*

"You've gotta be kidding Marcia. What is it?"

"The brand new Fatima Mansions LP, and it's called *Put That in Your Pope and Smike It.* See this? All new, original tracks. ALGAE-RHYTHM has created it all from scratch, yes, on its own. No input from any musicians, nothing. The songs, the lyrics, the titles, even the album cover—look there."

A list appears, one track name dropping in after another: 'Cemetery City'. 'Ceiling Mirror'. 'St Tima's Carnivale'. From the New York end of the call comes an explosion of guitars, followed by a Cork-infused grumble of vocals.

"Fans never have to wait for more of their favourite music again. Doesn't matter if the band are still together or they've run out of ideas. Doesn't matter if your all-time favourites were the Broken Bananas, this thing can make more of anything you want, whenever you want."

The screen changes and Tony's listening to a noodling spangle. The Sundays and their new album *Bicycles & Cigarettes*. Featuring: 'If You Turn Around Now', 'Happy', 'Drunk Song' and 'Definitely Not'.

"Get it Tony?"

More changes and a box appears with the design of an album cover like a ceramic tile. Prefab Sprout's *Marine/Blue*. 'Alpine Holiday', 'Some Ordinary Notions Don't Hide (Even in Me)', 'The Learning Yawns', 'Durham County Blues', 'Snowy Comes Back Alone'.

Marcia keeps going: "Because human creativity is unreliable, and so's the quality. Never been any good for planning and revenue cycles anyway. You take away the unpredictability and the business is sweet for investors."

"AI music. It's just AI music."

"The music sounds exactly like the original if you ask me Tony. Isn't that what matters?"

"Looks fun, but customers won't stand for it. It's not real. And all AI can do is just re-work old stuff."

"That's naive Tony. A misunderstanding of what music is. Don't people just do the exact same thing as AI? They learn from what's gone before, they imitate and play around with it. Musicians learn a code for playing a piano or the xylophone or whatever and then make up a new pattern from that old stuff. AI does that too."

More songs start to appear. The Apartments loads up with a picture of Peter Milton Walsh in a fedora: *Out of the Show, Into the Street*, including 'This is How to Forget Me', 'Hello for a While', and 'What Would You Rhyme with Over?'.

"Anything can be reduced to a code—like human conversations can, even human emotions—and then the AI will do its stuff. I've heard it do Taylor Swift with a sizzle you wouldn't believe. She couldn't do it better. Musicians learn codes, but they do it less well and a lot more slowly. AI can learn everything about songwriting, every combination, every instrument, in milli-seconds. And they can match the personality at the same time."

"The user interface needs a lot of work."

"Think big Tony, it's evolution. The Mechanisation of Labour in the industrial revolution meant we didn't have to rely on people for labour anymore, and think what that did for economies and standards of living everywhere. Beautiful. This is about Mechanisation of Creativity for the same reasons. You get so many efficiencies it's unreal. Cheaper and easier for everyone."

The blobs disappear and are replaced by a new Trashcan Sinatras album cover for *The Highwaymen*. 'Last Man

Standing', 'Red Red Rose', 'Night Burns', 'Who Missed a Round?', 'Snowblind'.

"So you're saying I can generate as many new Elvis albums as I want to?"

"You could. But that would be stupid. We don't saturate the market, we sell subscriptions to fans. We say, look, pick five favourite bands and sign up for one new album from each of them every year. Three hundred dollars a year, something like that. Super low overheads for exponential global subscription potential. Imagine."

"Crazy."

"It's insane Tony. And it's so much better than you think. This thing does blends. Okay, look at this—we want some Sundays, yeah, and then—I know, I want a bit more Smiths, there wasn't enough Johnny Marr in the original."

A blink and a fizzle. The blobs dance on the screen.

"Here it is. How long did that take ALGAE-RHYTHM? Three seconds and we have a new album by a Sundays and Smiths supergroup called—yeah, called *This Better Be About Me*. Hear that? That's a little number called 'Keep Your Clothes On, Please'. Or you could stick some Fatima thingy in there too. Wait—and yeah: another song, this one's 'Blush Like Stalin Would Never'."

Bump-bump-bump-bump. Some tickly guitar.

"Okay. Quite like that one. Kind of a croony disco thing. *Would never, ever, ever.*"

"Wooh! yeah—*would you ever, ever, ever.*"

"How do we sell this to artists though? This is going to be micro-money, like Spotify. Maybe worse."

"Definitely worse. They're not doing anything, right? They're making money off their brand. We'll get labels on-board no problem, and the artists will have to follow. Sell the paradigm."

"Won't be easy."

"The paradigm will sell. Think of all the cycles of publicity it will create for them when they're promoting other things."

"Tours."

"Yeah, and they don't even have to do that if they don't want to, not anymore. The AI guys will get holograms to play all the new and old stuff too. That ABBA Voyage shtick is only getting cheaper. Might be wobbly but who's going to notice? No more moaning fans asking when's the new album coming, 'hey crap, we've been waiting five years'. 'When are they going on tour in my country?', all that crap. The bands will be touring for eternity. Everyone will get to see Oasis play live at Knebworth or the pub car park if they want. Then you get the sustainability angle, think about the carbon footprint saved from not recording or touring anymore. They'll think they're saving the planet."

"Okay, okay. I'll set up some meetings. We'll need you here to go through the figures and present to the board though."

"Just gimme a date Tony."

After the call, Tony can't settle. He fusses over emails and then decides not to bother with any replies tonight. There's a fug of coffee and spicy pulled pork about the place. Times like these he wished he could open the windows. He paces round the kitchen and clicks the control to open the blinds and let in the evening sun.

It had never been his plan to become a manufacturer of computer music, an IT man. Were they really going to use a machine that thought it was as horny as Prince? But why sweat over the whys and how. It was just the law of business. If he didn't do it, someone else would.

If only they could manufacture customers for the stuff at the same time. Shit. He shouldn't mention that, he shouldn't even be thinking it. Marcia would know someone in Moscow or Guangzhou who could do that already.

*

Outside, the lights of the bars are coming on by the river, where the scene is as slow and solemn as a waltz. A breeze picks up, moving the smell of river-mud and chips and falafel through the evening air.

On the horizon there's a train of clouds over Canary Wharf, a mysterious message written into a pale blue sky. A quiet expectancy everywhere.

The river goes on sliding to the sea, loaded with the reflected ripples and streaks of our places, of our evening in the city.

Acknowledgments

Thanks to the people who contributed their time so generously: Aindrías Ó'Grúama, Hugh Bunker, John Douglas, John Willsteed, Keith Armstrong, Kevin Jamieson, Lindsay Jamieson, Neil Conti, Nick Allum, Paul McKercher, Peter Milton Walsh, Ralph Jezzard, Sean O'Hagan and Victor Van Vugt. Also to the gurus: John Birch (on the Sprouts—as well as being someone who survived the Mansions' mosh pit at Wigan Rugby Club) and Craig McAllister (the Trashcans), for sharing their knowledge and insights. And Ian Howe for his support and first-class editing skills (in other words, any mistakes will be mine).

Further listening

The Fatima Mansions, *Against Nature* (1989)
Cocteau Twins, *Heaven or Las Vegas* (1990)
Lloyd Cole, *Lloyd Cole* (X) (1990)
The Fatima Mansions, *Bertie's Brochures* (1991)
Lloyd Cole, *Don't Get Weird on Me Babe* (1991)
American Music Club, *Everclear* (1991)
The Fatima Mansions, *Valhalla Avenue* (1992)
Tom Waits, *Bone Machine* (1992)
The Sundays, *Blind* (1992)
Red House Painters, *Red House Painters* (Rollercoaster) (1993)
The Fatima Mansions, *Lost in the Former West* (1993)
American Music Club, *Mercury* (1993)
Shack, *Waterpistol* (1995)
The Apartments, *A Life Full of Farewells* (1995)
Trashcan Sinatras, *A Happy Pocket* (1996)
Prefab Sprout, *Andromeda Heights* (1997)
The Sundays, *Static & Silence* (1997)
Stephen Duffy, *I Love My Friends* (1998)
Shack, *HMS Fable* (1999)

Sources

Whirr and hiss

Alwyn W. Turner, *A Classless Society: Britain in the 1990s*, Aurum, 2013.

John Robb, *The Nineties*, Ebury, 1999.

Keith Armstrong, Telephone interview, 21 November 2023.

"I can't be sure what I want anymore, it will come to me later."

Andy Strickland, 'Songs of Praise', *Record Mirror*, 7 January 1989.

Bradley Bambarger, 'The Modern Age', *Billboard*, 27 September 1997.

Caitlin Moran, 'Season of Sundays worth the wait', *The Times*, 19 September 1997.

Chris Roberts, 'The Sundays, The Falcon, London', *Melody Maker*, 3 September 1988.

Chris Roberts, 'Throwing Muses/The Sundays', *Melody Maker*, 18 February 1989.

Craig McAllister, *The Perfect Reminder: The Story of Trashcan Sinatras'* I've Seen Everything, Last Night from Glasgow, 2021.

Dave Simpson, 'The Sundays, The Warehouse, Leeds', *Melody Maker*, 27 May 1989.

David Obuchowski, 'Searching for The Sundays', *Longreads*, 30 July 2019.

David Sinclair, Review: The Sundays, *The Times*, 12 January 1990.

Don McLeese, *Chicago Sun-Times*, 11 May 1990.

Everett True, 'Schools out! The Sundays', *Melody Maker*, 20 January 1990.

Ira Robbins, *Rolling Stone*, 14 June 1990.

Jeff Lippold, 'The Sundays', *Vox* magazine (University of Calgary, Canada), May 1990.

Jill Pearlman, 'Ordinary People', *Spin* (US), August 1990.

Kevin Jamieson, Email interview, 2 February 2024.

Kurt Loder, The Sundays interview, MTV, 1990.

Lindsay Jamieson, Zoom interview, 24 January 2024.

Martin Aston, 'The Sundays Interview', *The Catalogue*, 1989.

Neil Crossley, 'Making The Sundays': *Reading, Writing and Arithmetic'*, *Classic Pop*, 14 February 2022.

Neil Taylor, *Document and Eyewitness: An Intimate History of Rough Trade*, Orion, 2010.

Patrick Carroll, 'They're nice, okay. So what's wrong with that?', *Discorder* (University of British Columbia magazine), September 1990.

Patrick Hannan interview, *The C86 Show*, 18 August 2020.

Penelope Layland, *Canberra Times*, 29 March 1990.

Peter Stanford, 'The comedy gang: the Jewish youth group that made Sacha Baron Cohen', *The Independent*, 7 May 2011.

Randee Dawn, 'The Sundays', *Lime Lizard*, April 1991.

Randee Dawn, 'Heaven Knows They're Comfortable Now', *Alternative Press*, 1997.

Raymond Rogers, 'The Sundays, The Marquee NYC', *Melody Maker*, 21 July 1990.

RepHERtoire, 'Paddy McAloon as you've never heard him before', 13 December 2013.

Rob Young, *Rough Trade*, Black Dog, 2006.

Simon Williams, 'Teachers' Pets', *New Musical Express*, 13 January 1990.

'Sundays, Bloody Sundays', *New Musical Express*, 6 January 1990.

Ted Mico, 'Eat/The Sundays, The Boston Arms, London', *Melody Maker*, 24 September 1988.

The Morning Call, 21 February 1993.

'The Sundays' High-Calorie Guitarscapes', *Guitar Player*, May 1993.

"Got a trampoline: your fucking head."

Aindrías Ó'Grúama, Email, 11 March 2024.

Andrew Mueller, 'Hysterical Miracles', *Melody Maker*, 15 June 1991.

Anne Marie Hourihane, *She Moves Through the Boom*, Sitric Books, 2001.

Anthony Sampson, *The Essential Anatomy of Britain*, Hodder & Stoughton, 1992.

Barry Egan, 'Obituary: Cathal Coughlan Maverick, Cork-born singer for Microdisney and The Fatima Mansions', *The Independent*, 29 May 2022.

Bill Graham, Review of *Viva Dead Ponies*, *Hot Press*, 1993.

Bill Prince, 'Disney Time', *New Musical Express*, November 1985.

BEHIND THE MOON

Bleddyn Butcher, 'England Under the Microscope', *New Musical Express*, January 1987.

Brad Conroy, 'Paul Livingston and John Douglas: The Trashcan Sinatras', *Guitar International*, 2010.

Dave Fanning, Interview with Cathal Coughlan, 19 February 1990.

Dave Simpson, 'The Sundays, The Warehouse, Leeds', *Melody Maker*, 27 May 1989.

David Giles, 'Blowing in the wind', *New Musical Express*, March 1988.

David McKenna, 'An Improbable History: Microdisney Interviewed', 20 February 2014.

David Quantick, 'Cathal-ic Guilt', *New Musical Express*, 1990.

David Wild, 'Paddy McAloon: The Last Pop Genius', *Rolling Stone*, 7 March 1991.

Edwina Currie, *Diaries 1987 1992*, Little Brown, 2002.

Ed Power, 'B-side the Leeside: The Fatima Mansions and the story of *Viva Dead Ponies*', *Irish Examiner*, 27 May 2020.

Eleanor Levy, 'What do I hate most today?', *Record Mirror*, October 1987.

Emmanuel Tellier, 'Sunset Hotel', *Les Inrockuptibles*, July 1993.

Everett True, 'Schools out! The Sundays', *Melody Maker*, 20 January 1990.

'Fifteen Questions Interview with Cathal Coughlan of Microdisney and The Fatima Mansions', *Fifteen Questions*, 2019.

Helen FitzGerald, 'Disney Times?', *Melody Maker*, December 1985.

Hugh Bunker, Video interview, 2 November 2023.

Ian Dickson, 'Home is where the art is', Record Mirror, 1987.

Julie Perkins, 'The Story of Microdisney: the Clock Comes Down the Stairs', BBC4, 15 March 2024.

Juliet Schor, *The Overworked American*, Basic Books, 1993.

Keith Armstrong, Telephone interview, 21 November 2023.

Ken Sweeney, Facebook post, 13 January 2024.

Liam Fay, 'How the West was Won', *Hot Press*, 1994.

Martin Aston, 'Microwaves', *Melody Maker*, January 1985.

Martin Gray, 'The Fatima Mansions: Valhalla Avenue, 1992-2022, 30 Years On', *Louder Than War*, 29 May 2022.

Mick Heaney, 'Do not adjust your Telefís: A very Irish musical duo', *Irish Times*, 5 February 2022.

Nick Allum, Telephone interview, 31 October 2023.

Paul Mathur, 'Everybody is, well um, relatively ok', *New Musical Express*, 1984.

Paul McDermott, 'Iron Fist in Velvet Glove—the story of Microdisney', radio documentary, 2017.

Paul McDermott, 'The Story of Microdisney' (Oral History), *Medium*, May 2018.

Paul McDermott, 'To Here Knows When—Great Irish Albums Revisited, Episode 3, *Viva Dead Ponies* by The Fatima Mansions', 25 September 2021.

Ralph Jezzard, Telephone Conversation, 19 October 2023.

Roy Wilkinson, 'Malice in Disneyland?', *Sounds*, February 1988.

Siobhán Kane, 'A Troubadour Looks Back', *Winter Papers*, October 2022.

'The Material World of Cathal Coughlan', *New Musical Express*, October 1987.

'The Stars that Time Forgot: Cathal Coughlan', *Uncut*, January 2008.

Tim Burgess's Listening Party, *Viva Dead Ponies*, 28 November 2021.

Tony Clayton-Lea, 'Bossing himself back to business from the brink', *The Irish Times*, 29 June 2002.

Tony Clayton-Lea, 'Cathal Coughlan: "Microdisney ran its course. Let's just leave it"', *The Irish Times*, 16 February 2019.

Victor Van Vugt, Zoom interview, 25 January 2024.

Will Russell, 'Jacknife Lee: "Cathal Coughlan was a giant. His perspective was unique - he was intellectually so far ahead of everybody else"', *Hot Press*, 14 October 2022.

"Is there one spell can bring, the once and future king?"

Adrian Thrills, 'Young, Gifted and…White?', *New Musical Express*, 27 August 27 1983.

Alex Luke, Excerpts from an interview with Paddy McAloon, 30 June 1988.

Alwyn W. Turner, *A Classless Society: Britain in the 1990s*, Aurum, 2013.

Andreas Hub, *Fachblatt*, June 1988.

Andrew Smith and Bob Henrit, *International Musician and Recording World*, 1988.

Andy Strike, 'The only band I like is Prefab Sprout', *Record Mirror*, 27 April 1985.

BEHIND THE MOON

'Banana Yoshimoto v. Paddy McAloon', *GQ*, April 2000.

Billy Smith, 'From Genius to Revelation', *Cut*, March 1988.

Bruce Clark, 'Don't be fooled by the name', *Brisbane Courier*, 29 July 1985.

Caitlin Moran, 'In God's Prefab are Many Mansions', *The Times*, 25 April 1997.

Chris Heath, *Jamming!*, July 1985.

Christophe Conte, *Les Inrockuptibles*, May 1997.

Christopher Gurk, 'A Work of Love', *Spex*, May 1997.

Clive Aslet, *Anyone for England? The Search for British Identity*, Little Brown Co, 1997.

Daniel Beauvallet and Renaud Monfourny, 'L'homme de l'Atlantide', *Les Inrockuptibles*, November 1990.

Danny Kelly, 'Songs Worshipped Out of Necessity', *New Musical Express*, 3 August 1985.

David Wild, 'Paddy McAloon: The Last Pop Genius', *Rolling Stone*, 7 March 1991.

Enrico Sisti, *Rockstar*, April 1988.

Falling and Laughing fanzine, June/July 1984.

Francis Dordor, 'But who do they hope to seduce with a name like that?', *Best*, December 1985.

Gardner, 'Ten Passions', *Record Mirror*, 14 December 1985.

Gareth O'Callaghan, *Video File*, RTE, September 1990.

Giles Smith, *The Independent*, 3 August 1990.

Graham K. Smith, *Record Mirror*, 3 March 1984.

Hanspeter Kuenzler interview (unpublished), August 1990.

Ian Pye, 'Run Silent Run Deep', *Melody Maker*, 1 June 1985.

Jean-Daniel Beauvallet, *Les Inrockuptibles*, July 1988.

Joe Breen, 'Style of a Sprout', *Irish Times*, 25 May 1984.

John Birch, *Myths, Melodies, Metaphysics and more: A Prefab Sprout Compendium*, Paper Portal, 1993/2017.

John Birch, Paul Gomersall interview, 10 June 2011.

John Birch, *Prefab Sprout: The Early Years*, Paper Portal, 2017.

John Birch [editor], *The Missing Interviews* [a collection of interviews with Paddy McAloon following the release of *Crimson/Red*, including pieces by Arnd Ziegler, David James, Florian Toussaint and Mark Goodall], 2024.

John Birch, Thomas Dolby interview, 22 August 2011.

John Earls, 'Prefab Sprout: Paddy McAloon interview', *Classic Pop*, 22 July 2021.

John Morrish, Interview intended for *One, Two, Testing*, 12 June 1985.

Jim Reid, *Record Mirror*, 31 August 1985.

Karen Swayne, 'From Brussels with love', *No. 1*, 21 January 1984.

Karin Aderhold, *Musik Szene*, June 1985.

Keith Armstrong, Telephone interview, 21 November 2023.

Killian Laher, 'A year in music—2020—Peter Milton Walsh (The Apartments), *No More Workhorse*, 15 December 2020.

Koju Wake, 'Prefab Sprout', *Record Collector*, June 2000.

Len Brown, *Interviews with Morrissey*, Omnibus, 2009.

Linda Ryan, 'The Sundays: Here's Where the Story Begins', *The Gavin Report*, 25 May 1990.

Luca Dondoni, *Tutti*, January 1986.

Mark Cooper, 'No Sweat', *Q* magazine, December 1988.

Mark Ellen, *Smash Hits*, 5 December 1984.

Mark Linsenmayer, *Nakedly Examined Music Podcast*, November 13 2020.

Martin Aston, 'The Sundays Interview', *The Catalogue*, 1989.

Michael Leonard, 'The King and I', *Guitarist*, September 1990.

Midori Tsukagoshi, *Music Life*, October 1990.

Neil Conti, Email, 19 December 2023.

'Paddy McAloon and Thomas Dolby: how we made Prefab Sprout's *Steve McQueen*', *The Guardian*, 30 June 2020.

Paul Gorman, *Totally Wired—The Rise and Fall of the Music Press*, Thames & Hudson, 2022.

Paul Lester, 'McAloony Tunes', *Melody Maker*, 5 January 1991.

Peter Van Brummelen, *Vinyl* magazine, December 1984.

Piergiorgio Brunelli, *Ciao 2001*, January 1986.

Rob O'Connor, Review of *Jordan*, *Spin*, January 1991.

Serena Nono, *Rockerilla*, November 1985.

Simon Potter, TV feature on Kitchenware Records, *Music Box*, 1985.

Sorrel Downer, 'The Prefab Four', *Sky*, April 1988.

www.sproutology.co.uk (the brilliant website resource for Prefab Sprout fans).

Stuart Maconie, 'A White Sport Coat and a Reincarnation', *New Musical Express*, 11 August 1990.

BEHIND THE MOON

Thomas Dolby's 80:10 podcast.

Thomas Dolby email to Scott McPherson, 6 March 2015.

Tom Doyle, *International Musician and Recording World*, October 1990.

Tom Nolan, 'The Beach Boys: A California Saga', *Rolling Stone*, 28 October 1971.

Wendy Varley, 'Gasp! Singer with Prefab Sprout has Wham! on bedroom wall', *Just Seventeen*, 11 December 1985.

Willy Heynen, *Backstage* magazine, August 1984.

"You will go from place to place, leave, then leaving never ends."

Alwyn W. Turner, *A Classless Society: Britain in the 1990s*, Aurum, 2013.

Andrew Stafford, 'I Thought it Put a Stop to Songs Forever', *Mess + Noise*, August 21 2012.

Andrew Stafford, *Pig City: From the Saints to Savage Garden*, University of Queensland Press, 2006.

Benjamin Howarth, 'The Apartments—Interview', *Penny Black Music*, 29 October 2020.

Benjamin Locoge, 'The Apartments—Peter Milton Walsh, a case apart', *Paris Match*, 25 March 2022.

Chuck Klosterman, *the nineties*, Penguin Press, 2022.

Dave Graney, *Workshy*, ReadHowYouWant, 2022.

Dave Steinfeld, 'Trashcan Sinatras reflect on *Cake*, 'I've Seen Everything' and More', *Glide* magazine, 17 May 2018.

Emmanuel Tellier, 'In truth, I never ran out of songs', *La Blogotheque*, 4 November 2009.

Emmanuel Tellier, 'Sunset Hotel', *Les Inrockuptibles*, July 1993.

Francois and Jean-Marie Pottier, 'The Saga of The Apartments, a hidden treasure of Australian rock', *Slate*, 15 July 2015.

Gilles Tordjman, 'The Apartments, *Drift*', *Les Inrockuptibles*, Summer 1993.

Jérôme Florio, *No Song, No Spell, No Madrigal* review, Sefronia, 2 May 2015.

John Robb, *The Nineties*, Ebury, 1999.

John Willsteed, Video interview, 23 April 2024.

Killian Laher, 'A year in music, 2020, Peter Milton Walsh (The Apartments)', *No More Workhorse*, 15 December 2020.

Laurent Berger, 'Entrevista a Peter Milton Walsh', *Rock The Best Music*, 7 October 2023.

Laurent Coudol, 'The Apartments Interview', *Froggy Delight*, 4 December 2012.

Les Frères Poussiere, 'No Fixed Abode', *Magic — Revue Pop Moderne*, 5 April 1995.

Mark Linsenmayer, Nakedly Examined Music Podcast, 13 November 2020.

Matthieu Dufour, *No Song, No Spell, No Madrigal* review, *Pop, Cultures & CIE*, 12 April 2015.

Matthieu Grunfeld, 'Peter Milton Walsh (The Apartments) confides in his years of silence and renewal', *Magic — Revue Pop Moderne*, 25 September 2015.

Nick Allum, Telephone interview, 9 November 2023.

Paul McKercher, Email conversation, 11 December 2023.

Peter Milton Walsh, 'A Saturday Afternoon in Paris', December 2012.

Peter Milton Walsh, *drift* — sleeve notes, Talitres, 2013.

Peter Milton Walsh, Email, 28 June 2024.

Peter Milton Walsh, *G stands for Go-Betweens Volume 1* — sleeve notes, 2015.

Peter Milton Walsh, 'Man with a Blue Cornflower, a refuge in Paris for the music of The Apartments', *Neighbourhood*, 2018.

'Peter Milton Walsh — My Favourite Things', *A découvrir absolument*, 5 January 2014.

Peter Milton Walsh, Riley Records blog, May 2010.

Philippe Mathé, 'The Apartments, pop goldsmiths, on tour in the West', *Ouest-France*, 17 April 2015.

Pierre Lemarchand, Interview with Peter Milton Walsh, *Equilibre Fragile*, November 2015.

Robert Edelstein, Paddy McAloon interview, *Rockbill*, January 1986.

Robert Forster, *the evening visits… and stays for years* — sleeve notes, 2015.

Stephane Gobbo, 'Peter Milton Walsh: "In Europe, the public is more receptive"', *Le Temps*, 11 October 2018.

Tyler Jenke, 'The Apartments: Back in to the Light', *Rolling Stone Australia*, 18 September 2020.

Tyler Jenke, 'Song You Need to Know: The Apartments, 'She Sings to Forget You"', *Rolling Stone Australia*, 14 April 2021.

BEHIND THE MOON
Victor Van Vugt, Zoom interview, 25 January 2024.

"Here's to all of us. I know you are worried."

Andrew Clayman, 'Frank Reader of Trashcan Sinatras: Legends of Obscurity', *The Big Takeover*, 20 March 2011.

Andy Goldenberg, 'Ray Shulman and Gentle Giant's Funny, Progressive Ways', *Goldmine*, 26 February 1999.

Anna Battista, 'Zebras of the Family: Interview with Trash Can Sinatras', *Erasing Clouds*, August 2003.

Billy Sloan, 'Nil-Nill Firhill touched on the romantic side of the Scottish male', *The Herald*, 5 September 2021.

Brad Conroy, 'Paul Livingston and John Douglas: The Trashcan Sinatras', *Guitar International*, 2010.

Brian Farrelly, 'An Interview with The Trashcan Sinatras', CLUAS, 2005.

Craig McAllister, plainorpan.com blog, 2022.

Craig McAllister, *The Perfect Reminder: The Story of Trashcan Sinatras'* I've Seen Everything, Last Night from Glasgow, 2021.

Craig McLean, 'Whatever you say, say nothing', *The List*, April 1993.

Dave Jennings, 'Rock of Garbages', *Melody Maker*, 14 July 1990.

Dave Steinfeld, 'Trashcan Sinatras reflect on *Cake*, *I've Seen Everything* and More', *glide* magazine, 17 May 2018.

Davie Scott, 'Classic Scottish Albums: Trashcan Sinatras', BBC Radio Scotland, 21 November 2020.

Dougie Smith, 'Made in Scotland: The Trashcan Sinatras' Life Story', August 2022.

Jane Rockwood, Trashcan Sinatras interviewed at Aron Records, Hollywood, 10 October 2004.

John Douglas, Zoom interview, 11 June 2024.

Ken Sweeney, 'The Trashcan Sinatras Documentary', Radio Nova, 26 May 2024.

Nick Fuller, 'Old punks, still sparkling', *RnR* magazine, 2022.

Paul English, 'Scots indie favourites The Trashcan Sinatras return with new album Wild Pendulum and Glasgow gig', *Daily Record*, 10 November 2016.

Paul Kingsnorth, *Real England: the Battle Against the Bland*, Portobello Books, 2008.

Paul Moody, *I've Seen Everything* review, *New Musical Express*, May 1993.

Pete Paphides, 'I've Seen Everything' single review, *Melody Maker*, June 1993.

Pete Paphides, *I've Seen Everything* sleeve notes, Last Night from Glasgow, 2021 re-issue.

Phil Sutcliffe, *I've Seen Everything* review, *Q* magazine, May 1993.

Rachel Basela, 'Trashcan Sinatras visit Ferndale's Magic Bag', 30 October 2019.

Roy Wilkinson, 'Malice in Disneyland?', *Sounds*, February 1988.

Shizuka Wada, 'The Trash Can Sinatras', *Music Life*, December 1993.

Stephanie McNicholas, Trashcan Sinatras at the Powerhaus — London, *Record Mirror*, 25 November 1989.

Steve Hochman, 'Trash Can Sinatras Do It Their Way', *Los Angeles Times*, 22 December 1990.

Steve Lamacq, 'Bin Liners', *New Musical Express*, March 1990.

Surprise Cast, John Douglas podcast interview, 8 February 2024.

Tim Ingham, 'Essentially, music is an emotional language that connects people', *Music Business Worldwide*, 27 February 2020.

Will Harris, 'Hooks 'N You: The Trashcan Sinatras, Interview with Frank Reader', *Popdose*, 20 July 2009.

Click

Andrew Adonis, *A Class Act: the myth of a classless Britain*, Hamish Hamilton, 1997.

Chris Roberts, Interview with Paddy McAloon, *Record Collector*, November 2018.

'Fifteen Questions Interview with Cathal Coughlan of Microdisney and The Fatima Mansions', *Fifteen Questions*, 2019.

Iain McGilchrist, *The Matter with Things: Our Brains, Our Delusions and the Unmaking of the World*, Perspective Press, 2021.

Jill Furmanovsky and Daniel Rachel, *Oasis: Knebworth: Two Nights that Will Live Forever*, Cassell, 2021.

Printed in Great Britain
by Amazon